"The essays translated here are a treasure trove of theological reflection linking liturgy to ecclesiology. They are as fresh today as they were when Congar first wrote them. We are in Paul Philibert's debt."

—*John F. Baldovin, SJ*
Professor of Historical and Liturgical Theology
Boston College School of Theology and Ministry

"What a gift to the Church by translator and editor, Paul Philibert, as he makes these essays of Yves Congar available in English! The essays gathered here, although written decades ago, are totally applicable today as the Church continues to grapple with a key principle of the Second Vatican Council's teaching that the whole local community of faith is the subject or agent of worship. Philibert gives us both accurate and readable translations of Congar's French while also providing us with sound hermeneutical principles of interpretation in his brilliant Introduction and Conclusion sections. We owe him a great debt of thanks!"

—*Gerard Austin, OP*
Rice School for Pastoral Ministry
Arcadia, Florida

"These essays combine immense erudition with arguments that are accessible to the non-specialist. They offer a rare combination of passion and precision, and they are at least as relevant today as when they were first published."

—*Timothy Radcliffe, OP*
Author of *What Is the Point of Being a Christian?*
and *Why Go to Church?: The Drama of the Eucharist*

"Congar may have written these chapters decades ago (even before the Council), but they read like they were written for us today. They are relevant, timely, and challenging for us now because they call us to be church, to exercise our common priesthood, to live what we celebrate."

—*Joyce Ann Zimmerman, CPPS, PhD, STD*
Director of the Institute for Liturgical Ministry
Dayton, Ohio

AT THE HEART
OF CHRISTIAN WORSHIP

Liturgical Essays of Yves Congar

Translated and edited
by Paul Philibert

A PUEBLO BOOK

Liturgical Press   Collegeville, Minnesota
www.litpress.org

A Pueblo Book published by Liturgical Press

Cover design by David Manahan, O.S.B. Illustration by Frank Kacmarcik, Obl.S.B. Photo courtesy of photos.com.

This volume is a collection of essays first published in French: *L'Ecclesia ou communauté chrétienne, sujet intégral de l'action liturgique*, collection *Unam Sanctam*, n° 66; *Structure et sacerdoce chrétien*, collection *Unam Sanctam*, n° 41; *Situation du « sacré » en régime chrétien*, collection *Unam Sanctam*, n° 66; « Pour une liturgie et une prédication réelles », in *La Maison Dieu*, n° 16; « Présentation simple de l'idée essentielle du Dimanche », in *La Maison Dieu*, n° 13. © Les Éditions du Cerf.

Library of Congress Cataloging-in-Publication Data

Congar, Yves, 1904–1995.
    [Selections. English. 2010]
    At the heart of Christian worship : liturgical essays of Yves Congar ; translated and edited by Paul Philibert.
        p. cm.
    "A Pueblo book."
    Includes index.
    ISBN 978-0-8146-6229-8 — ISBN 978-0-8146-6235-9 (e-book)
    1. Liturgics.   2. Catholic Church—Liturgy.   I. Philibert, Paul J.   II. Title.
BX1970.C668   2010
264'.02—dc22   2009053884

Contents

Introduction

The title of this book, *At the Heart of Christian Worship*, refers above all to the corporate life of the Christian faithful, who offer their lives to God as a living sacrifice at the same time as they bind themselves more deeply to their Lord and Savior. This movement of self-offering and identification with Christ is precisely what is at the heart of worship, as expressed both in ritual acts and in the daily living of the Christian faith. Summarizing the theological developments of the Second Vatican Council with reference to the participation of the faithful in the Eucharist, the *Catechism of the Catholic Church* explains:

> *The Eucharist is also the sacrifice of the Church.* The Church which is the Body of Christ participates in the offering of her Head. With him, she herself is offered whole and entire. She unites herself to his intercession with the Father for all men. In the Eucharist the sacrifice of Christ becomes also the sacrifice of the members of his Body. The lives of the faithful, their praise, sufferings, prayer, and work, are united with those of Christ and with his total offering, and so acquire a new value. Christ's sacrifice present on the altar makes it possible for all generations of Christians to be united with his offering. (CCC 1368)

This summary paragraph reflects in capsule form the fundamental argument of the essays in this book as well as the penetrating theological intuition that lies behind it. In the "age of the church," as Yves Congar puts it, the risen Christ can never be thought of apart from his body; the head cannot be thought of apart from the members.

Like the Fathers of the Church centuries ago, Yves Congar appreciated the twofold consequence of this revealed truth. First, as baptized faithful, our real, our most authentic life is a life shrouded in mystery, yet nonetheless it affects and conditions the entirety of our human experience. To live in Christ, as St. Paul so often puts it, means to replicate in our spontaneous daily experience the patience of Christ in the face of undeserved suffering, on the one hand, and his confidence in the will and the power of his divine Father, on the other hand. His paschal journey of suffering, death, and resurrection is an anthropological paradigm, a pattern for authentic living that both explains the point of life and offers the faithful the grace of moving from dying to rising.

Second, the solidarity of the Christian faithful with their divine head already draws them into the divine Son's singular relation with his Father. If the risen Christ is the unique priest of the new covenant, then the members of his body share in that priesthood. If the risen Christ presents as his priestly sacrifice the one perfect gift of his own self-offering, then the members of his body have the vocation to make this same self-oblation of themselves.

The biblical and conciliar theme of the People of God is, at root, the expression of this mystery which fulfills all the promises of the old covenant and inaugurates a new age, a new covenant of grace. The vocation of all those rooted in Christ by baptism and by the anointing of the Holy Spirit is to become a great, living sacrament—a holy sign that achieves what it signifies. They are meant to become the presence of God inserted into the midst of human life and culture by means of their graced actions as members of Christ's body.

In Congar's writings, as in the council's dogmatic constitution *Lumen Gentium* (On the Church), the link between the theology of the People of God and the mystery of the Mystical Body is inseparable. As we shall see in the pages that follow, for Congar, this theme about the People of God could never imaginably be considered a claim to some sort of secularized social autonomy. It is precisely the expression of a spiritual rootedness so profound that its influence finds expression in the totality of the relationships and activities of the faithful.

I remember some forty years ago discussing with Father Congar the theme of incarnation and its pastoral expression in the years immediately after the council. As an inexperienced graduate student, I was suggesting that the church needed to stress "incarnationalism" as opposed to eschatology, so as to draw the faithful into a deeper involvement with their religious life. Congar became quite animated, insisting that Catholic theology can never lose its balance between the incarnational and the eschatological—that in sacramental and pastoral terms, "incarnation" means making visible, accessible, and palpable a mystery that is itself fully eschatological. Put more simply, in attending to the concerns of communicating with the present day, we can never lose focus on the mystery of Christ's heavenly priesthood. Contemporary human involvement in the liturgy and pastoral service must find its source and its energy in divine gifts bestowed by the Holy Spirit.

At the Heart of Christian Worship

These pages provide plenty of evidence for the assured, authoritative theological balance that is so characteristic of Congar. He never lacked pastoral focus in his theological writing, but that never led him to compromise his exhaustive quest to articulate the most sure, the most ancient, and the most authentic biblical and theological tradition of the church. Like his Jesuit colleague Henri de Lubac, Congar was a skilled master of the theological method of *ressourcement*—reaching back into the most important sources of the Christian theological tradition to discover the genesis of ideas, the reasons for their development, and their present meaning within a continuous trajectory of faith and experience.

Although he is not characteristically classified as a liturgical theologian, in fact, Congar made a signal contribution to the development of the liturgical movement, especially in France. The essays collected here provide examples of his theological instincts. For him, liturgy is ecclesiology in action, or more simply, Christian worship is the visible manifestation of the church's spiritual reality.

Some of his essays, for example, the first given here, constitute a kind of working agenda for liturgical theology in the years leading up to the council. Other essays, especially chapters 2 and 3, provide the historical and theological background needed to appreciate the full significance of the constitutions and decrees of the council. Even as Congar shows himself to be patient and dispassionate in sifting through an astonishing mass of documentary evidence, he remains nonetheless passionate in pressing for an appreciation of the pastoral significance of the church's living tradition.

He even uses Tradition with a capital *T* when he wants to signify the continuous authoritative voice that arises in the Scriptures, that is celebrated in the church's liturgy, that is refracted through the wisdom of the Fathers of the Church and the theologians of the High Middle Ages, leading to such contemporary church teaching as Pius XII's *Mediator Dei* and the documents of the council.

Throughout his career as a theologian (he died in 1995) Congar was aware of the dangers of limiting a liturgical point of view to baroque Catholicism or to nostalgia for the customs and protocols of the nineteenth century. The true glory of Congar's vision is its profound biblical rooting and its erudite grasp of the coherence of the church's twenty centuries of life and witness. This is why his voice is so important for the present moment, when not a few Catholics are concerned to drink from the purest wells of tradition and to be in touch with the most authentic teaching of an ancient church.

The Essays Gathered Here

Congar's essays, presented here in translation, provide a solid ground for understanding the liturgical theology of the Second Vatican Council. In the essay "'Real' Liturgy, 'Real' Preaching," Congar develops an interpretation of the word "real" that is linked to the Latin word *res*. In this way he is able to show how, in the view of both Augustine and Aquinas, what is most *real* about the Eucharist, namely, its transformation of the faithful by deepening their insertion in the Body of Christ through Holy Communion and self-offering, is also what is most *real* about contemporary Christian life. This notion of the *real* weaves its way through all the essays in this book. For this reason I placed this clear and compelling essay first, so that it could provide the groundwork for later developments.

In chapter 2, in order to explain how the Christian community as a whole celebrates the Eucharist, Congar retrieves in a remarkable way the continuity within the church of the New Testament perspective on the spiritual sacrifices of all the faithful, united in the Eucharist to the Lord's own redeeming self-sacrifice. While doing so Congar points out the significant shifts brought about by key moments in history, including the movement from ancient to medieval ideas of authority and jurisdiction, the impact of the Reformation, and the church's alienation from secular society in the modern period.

Despite all these social and cultural transformations, the guiding principle for understanding the role of the faithful in liturgy has remained the affirmation in the rite of the Eucharist itself of the self-offering of the baptized as members sacramentally linked to their divine Victim and Priest. This second chapter has immense practical importance for today's church. The faithful's profound involvement in the central action of the Eucharist could be surprising news for many of them.

In chapter 3, discussing the structure of Christian priesthood, Congar sheds light on a topic of the greatest importance for which, in recent years, many pastors have almost never provided an adequate catechesis. Here, the stepping stones to a proper understanding of the church's theological tradition are the radical distinction between Hebrew and Christian priesthood (so radical as to be the basis for the shift from an *old* covenant to a *new* covenant), the theology of the Letter to the Hebrews that affirms Christ himself as the unique priest

At the Heart of Christian Worship

of the new covenant, and the revelation (especially in 1 Peter) of the character of the faithful as members of a royal priesthood. Completely lucid about the necessity and importance of ordained ministry within the great tradition, Congar proceeds to illuminate the pastoral significance of the priestly quality of the baptized, who offer themselves and the world as a living sacrifice to God, along with the sacrifice of Christ.

At first glance, chapter 4, about the role of the sacred in a Christian worldview, may not immediately seem to fit into the same trajectory as the essays that go before it. However, it soon becomes apparent that this essay too is an exploration of the genuine meaning of what is *real* (in the sense of *res*, as we have explained). Drawing upon the contrast between old and new covenants traced in the previous chapter, Congar demonstrates that a facile or inappropriate contrast between sacred and profane ultimately saps the Christian life of its capacity to be a transforming agent in the very heart of society. This is a fascinating essay, counterintuitive to the sentimental piety of some nineteenth-century writers or to Jansenist spirituality but definitely challenging in terms of the demands that it makes upon Christian spirituality today.

The final essay is very brief and, I think, very timely. It was written in 1945 for the French liturgical review *La Maison-Dieu* as an outline of possible points to emphasize in developing a catechesis of the meaning of Sunday. Here, perhaps more than elsewhere, Congar's own deep piety shows itself. Likewise, we discover here his impatience to find ways to communicate to the faithful—and their families and neighborhoods—the beauty and value of their Catholic identity.

These lines challenge us (as Congar himself intended) to discover our own agenda or points of development for a catechesis of Sunday. Sixty years have passed since these lines were first written. So in *our* world and circumstances, how can *we* speak of the meaning of Sunday today? I think that his somewhat dated contribution can definitely still help us to rise to the occasion.

Congar's Extraordinary Life

Born in April 1904 in the northeastern French city of Sedan, Yves Congar was the youngest of four children. His young life was deeply marked by the First World War (1914–1918). Encouraged by his mother to write of his experiences, he kept the first of his many journals in order to record his account of the war. By the end of the war Congar was already thinking about a priestly vocation.

After three years in a diocesan seminary (Les Carmes in Paris) he entered the novitiate for the Dominican Province of France in the fall of 1925. He was ordained a priest in July 1930. This was a defining moment for him because during his ordination retreat, while reflecting on the words of Christ in John's Gospel, "May all be one, as you, Father, are in me and I am in you" (John 17:21), he received what he called his ecumenical vocation. As he put it, "I clearly recognized my vocation to work for the unity of all who believe in Christ."

In the 1930s Congar taught theology in the Dominican seminary Le Saulchoir, which was at that point in exile in Belgium. Two important influences marked his life there: the harmonious blend of hard work, liturgical prayer, and community life in a large and creative Dominican priory; and the ethos of a school of theology where biblical studies and history were the context within which dogmatic theology (including St. Thomas Aquinas) was read and interpreted.

The declaration of war in September 1939 uprooted Congar from his scholarly life. Lieutenant Congar was mobilized for the war, then captured and imprisoned in 1940. He then spent five years (until 1945) behind barbed wire in the German camps of Colditz and Lübeck. For the rest of his life Congar lamented this break in the momentum of his scholarly work. However, he returned to Le Saulchoir in 1945 and remained there until 1954, when he was exiled in disgrace for having been judged by Vatican officials as a troublemaker. (Although he sought for the rest of his life to discover the exact accusations which had been lodged against him, he never succeeded in doing so.)

Two of his decisive books, *True and False Reform in the Church* (1950) and *Lay People in the Church* (1953), came from this period.[1] Both of them include immense dossiers of references to Scripture, the Fathers of the Church, and the teachings of the magisterium. Congar's ideas in these writings in large part would be vindicated by the teaching of the Second Vatican Council but were "premature" in 1954. Consequently, he was exiled from Paris and spent a number of years in official disfavor, forbidden even to reside in Paris.

In 1959, however, a new pope, John XXIII, announced the preparation of an ecumenical council. Congar was pleasantly and joyously surprised by this initiative, but nothing less than astounded

---

[1] Yves Congar, *Vraie et Fausse Réforme dans l'Eglise* (Paris: Editions du Cerf, 1950); idem, *Jalons pour une théologie du laïcat* (Paris: Editions du Cerf, 1953), revised edition with addenda by author published in 1964. English translation: *Lay People in the Church*, trans. Donald Attwater (Westminster, MD: Newman Press, 1959), revised edition with addenda by the author published in 1965.

At the Heart of Christian Worship

to discover that the new pope had appointed him a member of the preparatory theological commission for the council. Only later, with the opening of the council in the fall of 1962, did Congar begin to appreciate the significant role he would play as a theological expert in this largest and most diverse ecumenical council in the history of the church.

Yves Congar performed backbreaking work in helping to create the conciliar documents. It is generally agreed that Congar seems to have been the one who contributed most to the formation of the council's texts. Often, as he acknowledged in his voluminous journals of the council, he was led to accept solutions that he considered the least disagreeable or perhaps the most productive among those possible at a given moment. For him, the texts of the council represented the best of what was available, given the context and conditions of the time. He would say later, "The entire work of the council is a way station toward a better future."[2]

Already in the 1960s Congar's health began to decline seriously because of a chronic neurological disease—a form of muscular sclerosis. His captivity during the war certainly had not helped things, but his exhausting efforts during the council and his equally draining attempts to disseminate the council's teaching through talks and conferences later on only added to his physical burden. By the 1970s he was most frequently confined to a wheelchair, and by the 1980s he was forced to take refuge in a rest home where, however, he never stopped working. His huge, three-volume work, *I Believe in the Holy Spirit*, was produced during years of serious illness.[3]

With respect to the present work translated here, perhaps the most cogent observation about Congar is that he was a man of destiny, shaped by his heritage and background, his formation and his constant study, his ecumenical relationships and his telling presence at the Second Vatican Council. This council, fashioned by Pope John XXIII who convoked it, chose as its path to be a council not of condemnations but of affirmations and clarifications, a council not with a metaphysical or defensive agenda but one seeking a new voice for biblical and pastoral catechesis. Congar, with his extraordinary knowledge of history and

[2] *Une vie pour la vérité, Jean Puyo interroge le Père Congar* (Paris: Centurion, 1975), 149.

[3] Yves Congar, *I Believe in the Holy Spirit*, trans. David Smith (New York: Crossroad-Herder, 1983)

tradition and his passion for unity, often became the most sought-after adviser in the theological commissions preparing the council's documents, precisely because he became known as someone with a sure grasp of both Catholic tradition and contemporary pastoral sensitivities. These essays are excellent examples of the fruitfulness of his gifts.

The Context for the Present Essays

The chapters presented in this collection come mostly from an earlier period of Congar's work. Even chapters 3 and 4, although published in their present form in the 1960s, are a reworking of materials originally produced in the 1950s, before the council. In several places we meet theological anachronisms because Congar wrote these pieces for the most part before the introduction of the vernacular in Roman Catholic liturgies and before the postconciliar reforms of the liturgy simplified and clarified the rites.

We might say that these essays allow us to dip into the theological imagination of the author such as it was before his long and grueling labors over the council documents. That being so, it is worth observing here some of his pastoral preoccupations during that preconciliar period.

Congar was aware of the alienation of the working class from the life of the church, especially in the postwar period. He recognized that new patterns of urban crowding, industrialization, mechanized labor, and economic hardship had a role to play in casting a pall of seeming unreality over the ritual life of the church. In successful parishes community life could be an oasis of social refreshment. But in the crowded inner city, priests were scarce and overworked and largely out of touch with the working-class culture. He was more than aware of the challenge.

Congar had met the pastoral movements of Father Joseph Cardijn in the 1930s in Belgium, where Cardijn had founded the organizations known as Young Christian Workers and Young Christian Students. Congar recognized the pastoral fruitfulness of the small-group methodology (observe, judge, and act) of YCW and YCS. These phenomena nourished his optimism that with effective catechesis the masses of Christian faithful might find a genuinely theological spiritual life within the context of everything that was ordinary in their world. Further, as a result of these movements, he saw even more clearly the critical role of the lay faithful themselves in evangelizing society. A byword of the French catechetical movement, after all, was "like to like"—evangelization within the context of neighborhood, workplace, society, and culture by those who live there.

At the Heart of Christian Worship

Congar's French Dominican colleagues were, like himself, frequently called upon to serve as advisers or even chaplains of small gatherings of committed Catholics. Like these colleagues of his, Congar was profoundly interested in developments in biblical studies, the liturgical movement, and adult catechesis. He had many opportunities to work pastorally in the laboratory of extended catechesis and conversation inside such groups. There was a spirit of vitality and optimism in the post–World War II French church, and Congar's writings reflect this.

In the 1940s Congar responded with enthusiasm to the theological possibilities opened up by the two great encyclicals of Pius XII, *Mystici Corporis* (1943) and *Mediator Dei* (1947). In chapter 3, especially, we can observe his meticulous study of these texts and their pastoral significance for a preconciliar Catholic Church. Congar's own theology, as will be clear to readers of this volume, is consumed with the significance of the theological mystery of the Body of Christ. The author's exacting study and exegesis of these encyclicals of Pius XII demonstrate, as nothing else, his loyalty and deference to the teaching authority of the church's ordinary magisterium. Here, as elsewhere, Congar—despite all the struggles in his life and all the obstacles placed in his way—shows himself (almost inexplicably) a determined optimist.

These observations make it clear that the conciliar theology of Vatican II did not just drop from the heavens as a complete surprise. The pastoral vision of the council was, at least in part, a testimony to the experience of pastors in European countries where the traditional, rural context for parish life was no longer dominant. Many of the most influential theological experts at the Second Vatican Council were scholars who, like Congar, were concerned to address the growing distance between ecclesiastical culture and an increasingly technological and morally autonomous society.

Parish religious life could no longer afford to be a mere parenthesis in the life of busy working people but had to become relevant to the increasingly hectic, urban hustle where most of the faithful lived and made their professional contributions. Therefore, as we read Congar's extensive reviews of the historical trajectory of Catholic theology through the centuries, we should keep in mind that this is the work of someone who is not at home in an ivory tower but continually in dialogue with the most creative pastoral movements of his day.

A Few Notes about Methodology and Terminology

Chapters 2, 3, and 4 are important pieces of research, densely interspersed with footnotes. These texts are clear and understandable, accessible to readers without a high scholarly formation. Their message touches upon very real questions in contemporary pastoral life and contains information about matters terribly relevant for understanding church practices in this period of transition and renewal following the Second Vatican Council.

The heavy scholarly apparatus in these three articles illustrates Congar's methodology of reviewing an immense breadth of materials demonstrating the biblical, patristic, and theological tradition of the church. Congar's bibliography shows us his use of Latin and Greek sources, his familiarity with all the great scholarly theological dictionaries and encyclopedias, and his study of penetrating books and periodicals in French, English, German, Italian, Spanish, and even Latin. The credibility of his argument is founded upon this immense erudition; it shows his broad but also penetrating reading of sources.

One of the great influences on Congar's work was the library at Le Saulchoir, the Dominican seminary near Paris. Books and periodicals from all the European languages arrived at this library, where Congar was able to consult them and remain aware of both the latest editions of ancient sources and the most notable new contributions to Christian history and theology. (His exile from Paris in 1954 was so dramatic and painful for him in no small part because it separated him from this tremendous resource for his theological research and his personal scholarly growth.)

I am perfectly aware that for many readers of this book, the majority of these footnotes, many with arcane abbreviations, will appear to be as incomprehensible as hieroglyphics. Some readers, I am sure, will be able to (and will want to) profit from the information provided there. But, in any case, it would be unthinkable to produce an edition of these works lacking this scholarly apparatus.

For the non-scholarly reader: do not be intimidated, please, by the presence of all this highly technical information. You may look upon it as a testimony to the laborious effort of the author to produce as dependable an account as possible of a Catholic understanding of the theology in question. It is one of the reasons why Congar was later so highly esteemed by the council's two popes, its bishops, and his theological colleagues.

I will mention here as well a few theological terms used by Congar in these essays that are not common currency in North American

At the Heart of Christian Worship

theological writing. Congar was greatly influenced by ecumenical discussions and, in particular, by Orthodox ecclesiology. But most of his more unusual expressions are due principally to a continental and French vocabulary which is a bit different from our own. At this point I will explain four terms he uses that require a bit of commentary.

economy: a term used especially in Orthodox theology, taken from the Greek word oikonomia, meaning "management" or "dispensation." The Fathers of the Church distinguished "economy" from "theology," economy having to do with the external manifestation of God's purposes, while theology refers to the inner life of the Blessed Trinity. Congar uses the term more loosely to express the interface of divine interaction with human persons and the resulting dialogue of grace and obedience. For readers of these texts, I suggest that they translate "economy" roughly as the graced context of God's initiatives in the lives of the faithful.[4]

messianic, messianism: a term denoting Christ as Messiah and evoking these two important themes linked to the Messiah: (1) the fulfillment of the promises of the Old Testament and (2) the one anointed by God. The literal meaning of the term—Christos in Greek, Masiah in Hebrew—is "anointed one." Jesus proclaimed the imminent coming of God's kingdom, and so messianism always has a note of prophetic urgency. Here, for Congar, messianism or messianic indicates above all the role of Christ as the one who fulfills the ancient promises of the Old Testament and who, once returned to the right hand of the Father, pours out his Spirit upon his people. The term evokes fulfillment, urgency, and spiritual generativity.

sacrament: Congar explains that the Latin word sacramentum is the translation of the Greek word mysterion; both refer to a palpable material sign of an invisible spiritual reality. In a manner that is consistent with the biblical evidence and with the theology of the Fathers of the Church, he broadens considerably the meaning of sacrament beyond its use for the seven sacramental rites in Roman Catholic liturgy. As the Second Vatican Council itself did in its documents, Congar, going beyond the sacramental rites, applies the category of sacrament to the physical body of Christ, then to the church as the social visibility of Christ in his members, and finally to the faithful themselves insofar as they bear a living witness to this solidarity as members of the Body of Christ.

[4] See "Economy," in The Westminster Dictionary of Christian Theology, ed. Alan Richardson and John Bowden (Philadelphia: Westminster Press, 1983), 171f.

prophet, prophetic principle: For Congar, the prophetic principle in the life of the church is essentially the ministry of the word, including the incarnation of the Divine Word in the manifestation of Christ in his words and actions. Just as there are two tables of the Eucharist—the table of the word and the table of the sacrificial meal—so there are always two dynamics at work in the pastoral ministry of the church, the prophetic and the priestly. As will be clear, especially in chapter 3, Congar sees the prophetic principle as applicable to the life of all the faithful in the exercise of their baptismal priesthood.

There are also a few other places where I have placed a translator's note in the text to explain Congar's use of language. In most cases, if readers are patient, they will find that the author explains himself as he goes along.*

Congar's Legacy

A great many of Congar's writings have been translated into English already. However, at present, I consider the absence of a translation for especially chapters 2, 3, and 4 a real lacuna or lack in our pastoral literature. These essays represent a rich legacy of theological reflection, the more important because de facto they reflect the development of the resources from which the theology of Vatican II was harvested.

These essays do help us reach into the heart of Christian worship, allowing us to see both the radical transformation of believers through Christian sacramental life and the evangelizing resonance of a people who live in solidarity with their divine head. Like the breathing in and breathing out of a living being, these two dynamics were always present to the mind of Congar, who held his mystical and his pastoral instincts in the closest communication.

As we saw, Congar's historical destiny, despite bitter previous disappointments, was to bring his exhaustive and exacting ecclesiological research to fruition in the midst of a council whose great mission was to redefine the church from the bottom up. In 1994 his role as one of the principal theologians of Vatican II was acknowledged by

---

* In addition to Congar's scholarly apparatus and continental and French vocabulary, he frequently uses ellipsis points at the end of a phrase, perhaps to indicate that more could be said on a particular point. Though this may be unconventional in English usage, the ellipses have been retained in this translation.

At the Heart of Christian Worship

Pope John Paul II, who brought Congar into the College of Cardinals. By that time, he was in the last year of his life and very ill. The same patience that had sustained his years of indefatigable work also sustained him in his suffering.

I will conclude this introduction with some lines of Congar, written in the last decade of his life, that reveal his charism of love of the church and love of truth:

> Withdrawn from active life, I am united to the mystical body of the Lord Jesus of which I have often spoken. I am united to it, day and night, by the prayer of one who has known his share of suffering.
>
> I have a keen awareness of the vast dimensions of the mystical body. By and in the Holy Spirit I am present to its members, known and unknown. Ecumenism obviously plays a part in this. It is intercession, consolation, thanksgiving, as the Lord wills.[5]

In order to allow readers to reach more deeply into Congar's thought—and thereby into the heart of Christian worship—questions for individual reflection and group discussion have been added at the end of each chapter.

[5] *Fifty Years of Catholic Theology: Conversations with Yves Congar*, ed. and introduced by Bernard Lauret (Philadelphia: Fortress Press, 1988), 86–87.

Chapter 1

"Real" Liturgy, "Real" Preaching

Translator's observations: *This article was first published in 1948. In his introductory note to the article, however, Congar revealed that he had first formulated these ideas in 1943, when he was still a prisoner of war in the German camp at Colditz. His article was offered to* La Maison-Dieu *(16 [1948]: 75–87) as a contribution to the task of articulating the mission of the Centre de Pastorale Liturgique in Paris. Patrick Prétot, O.S.B., director of the Institut Supérieur de Liturgie, brought these pages to my attention recently. They are as fresh today as they were sixty years ago.*

The central point in this piece is the retrieval of the idea of the "real" as it was understood in the theology of St. Augustine and St. Thomas Aquinas. Congar was aware of the powerful rhetorical impact of the almost exclusive use of the phrase "real presence" for the eucharistic species, the consecrated bread and wine. By explaining how the eucharistic Body of Christ has the function of a means *toward the creation of the mystical body (or toward the intensification of the mystical body's identification with its Head), the author provides an avenue that allows the faithful to repossess the traditional teaching about the* end *of the eucharistic celebration, namely, a People of God sanctified and on mission.*

There are a number of anachronisms in this text, written some fifteen years before the Second Vatican Council. Some of Congar's complaints about the remoteness and inaccessibility of liturgical rites can be attributed to the fact that Latin was the only language for liturgical celebration in the Roman rite at that time. He would surely have changed his assessment, I think, based upon the intelligibility of the rites as they have been reformed in the years following the council. I have to wonder, however, whether the proposed new translation of the Missal in English will not end up reinstating in our present-day context many of the problems Congar raised here.

As to preaching, Congar complains of preachers in his day giving dry, technical, dogmatic homilies that did not connect with the life experience of the faithful. I would say that our situation today is almost

What is the meaning of "real" liturgy and "real" preaching? To plead for the "real" is not to discount the "intellectual." There are real ideas, even abstract expressions that are real. Neither am I creating an opposition to the word "notional." Notions or intuitions can be interpretations of personal knowing and of human experience. Nor do I mean "real" in the sense of literary realism or realistic painting. In calling for preaching that is real, I am not asking for slices of life representing the fads of the moment, even less for a coarse or vulgar style of speaking. The realism I have in mind, which I want to apply to both liturgy and preaching, can't be restricted to a question of literary form. Compared to the "real" that I want to describe, all these other meanings of the word, interesting though they may be, remain rather superficial.

When theology talks about the *res* of the sacraments, that gives us a clue to a meaning of the word "real" that has great amplitude and great precision, and one that is attuned exactly to the point of my present remarks. This is a way of discussing what is "real" in terms of doctrines that are both central and profoundly important in classical Catholic theology. I trust that my explanations here will justify my understanding of "real" liturgy and "real" preaching as that which is genuinely able to bear fruit in the understanding and the lives of our contemporaries. Since it won't be a waste of time to explain this idea, which at first might seem both vague and maybe even enigmatic, I intend to explore how this question of "real" liturgy and "real" preaching is linked to the deepest vein of God's revelation and to the meaning of the church itself.

God's plan, as the Bible reveals it to us, can be considered as a process that moves from outside to inside, from symbols accessible to the senses toward another reality that becomes rooted in the very person. The Fathers of the Church adopted a theological structure which is the

At the Heart of Christian Worship

same for both Christian iconography and for the liturgy, and (before either of these) for the structure of the New Testament as well. According to this structure, what is to be found in the Old Testament has the character of figure, promise, or sketch of what is to come. The real meaning of the Old Testament is to be found beyond its pages. *Sacramenta Veteris Testamenti* (the sacraments of the Old Testament) was the Fathers' expression of this idea.[1]

More precisely, the idea is this: what is found by way of preparation and prophecy in the Old Testament is still an *extrinsic* reality which, under the new and definitive covenant, must be internalized within believers to become spiritual and interior to the person. The Epistle to the Hebrews gives us the perfect example when it confronts the law, priesthood, sacrifice, the temple, or even the presence of God as they are found in the Old Testament with their status in the New. For the present, let's pursue further the idea of sacrifice.

From one end of the Bible to the other, God requires rituals and sacrifices. In the Old Covenant, worship and sacrifice were prescribed by law and were executed according to precisely defined rituals. In particular, the Old Testament prescribed animal sacrifice. However, we find that the prophets bitterly railed against these sacrifices and even claimed that God detested them. Some historians have been so carried away with this idea that they have imagined that this meant a condemnation of all rituals as such.[2] Yet the fact is that the same prophets who condemned sacrifice went on to call people to a perfect sacrifice that the old law was impotent to achieve. As Hebrews 7:19 tells us, the old law was unable to lead religion to its perfection.

Louis Bouyer's *Le Mystère pascal* and even the Anglican theologian Gabriel Hebert[3] describe clearly how, under the old covenant, God

---

[1] To get at the meaning of this idea of sacrament in the larger sense, nothing is more helpful than Henri de Lubac, *Corpus mysticum* (Paris: Aubier, 1944). English translation: Corpus Mysticum: *The Eucharist and the Church in the Middle Ages—an Historical Survey,* tr. Gemma Simmonds et al. (Notre Dame, IN: University of Notre Dame Press, 2007).

[2] For example, see Adolphe Lods, *Les Prophètes d'Israël et les débuts du judaïsme* (Paris, 1935), 74ff. (for Amos, 95; for Hosea, 106).

[3] Louis Bouyer, *Le Mystère pascal* (Paris: Cerf, 1945), 273f., 456f. (his translation of a text of Augustine is cited below); Gabriel Hebert, *The Throne of David* (London, 1941), 111–122 (this is a rich contribution—a French translation is needed).

"Real" Liturgy, "Real" Preaching

simultaneously demanded sacrifices and yet proclaimed that he does not want them. This is a typical example of the prophetic function in the divine economy. The prophets, charged both with developing and maintaining religious institutions and also with realizing God's plan, ended up saying at one and the same time: That's what must be done; but no, perhaps not. God wants it; no, God doesn't want it. God wants sacrifice but not as you imagine it and practice it. God wants it, but in another form, of another sort, going beyond what you are presently used to . . .

So, God wanted a sacrifice, but not the one that the old law with its imperfections prescribed, that is, the sacrifice of the blood of bulls and goats. God wanted a sacrifice, but he wanted none other than the sacrifice of the very person. What God seeks in worship is neither ceremonies nor the offering of gifts—nothing extrinsic to the person who offers, nothing other than the opening up, the conversion and the gift of the hearts of believers themselves.

Here as elsewhere, Jesus' fulfillment of the law did not consist in adding to the law of Moses some new demand, some legal improvement, some new (perhaps rigorous) obligation. Rather Jesus fulfilled the law by identifying and reaffirming the original and pure meaning of the law according to God's intention, namely, the perfection of love. Jesus fulfilled the law by bringing about the full development of God's plan that gradually manifested itself in the twists and turns of the history of salvation.[4] Sacrifice is fulfilled not in the offering of anything external but rather in believers' offering their very selves. That is what was inaugurated in the sacrifice of Jesus Christ, and following him and thanks to him, that is what we are able to do in union with him.

This idea is at the heart of a text of St. Augustine whose depth and beauty would be hard to surpass. (Louis Bouyer has translated this text in his *Mystère pascal*.[5]) There St. Augustine develops the theme that I have just evoked. He develops the idea to the point that it will become central to his theological program: conversion to the deepest Reality is a movement of conversion from the outside to the inside, from sense experience to spiritual reality, from signs to the Truth itself. This schema, already equivalently present in the writings of Irenaeus, Tertullian, and Cyprian, is the source of Augustine's famous analysis

---

[4] To understand this meaning of the fulfillment of the law, see (Protestant) Wilhelm Vischer (Zürich: Zollikon, 1943), *Das Christuszeugniss des Alten Testamentes*, t. I (6th edition), 309ff.

[5] Cf. pp. 456f. (the text comes from *De Civitate Dei*, bk. X, chs. v and vi).

At the Heart of Christian Worship

of the sacraments that Scholasticism will systematize in the categories of *sacramentum* (the ritual of the sacraments, the exterior sign), *res et sacramentum* (the effect produced that is *not*, however, the complete fruition, *not* the ultimate reality which the sacred action of the sacramental rite intends), and finally the *res tantum* (that which is the complete fruition of the sacrament, the spiritual reality signified by the sacred ritual and brought about in mystery by the rite).

The analysis was not formulated by Augustine with this degree of definition. He was content to analyze the *sacramentum* as belonging to the category of *sign*, as a reality within the order of signification, and thus to claim that every sacred sign has reference to a *res* (a spiritual reality) that will be its fulfillment. The *res* [complete fulfillment] of all *sacramenta* [sacred signs] is Christ himself. Augustine does not himself apply this analysis to the question of the efficacy of the ritual of the sacraments.[6] But later, when the scholastics proceed to analyze the rites, they quite naturally identify the *res* of the sacraments with the reality of grace produced by them in the souls of the faithful.

This analysis allows us to grasp the deep meaning of God's plan revealed in the Scriptures. It becomes systematized for the scholastics in the following formula: every "sacrament" exists for the sake of its *res*, which is a spiritual reality *in the believer*. Therefore liturgy, rituals, and the church, which is itself the Great Sacrament, have to find their fulfillment and their verification *in the persons who live out their meaning*. So to be "real," then, means to arrive at this reality, to become one's true self—a reality and a truth which have become a spiritual fruition in believers themselves. Put another way, for sacraments to be "real" means for them to achieve their *res*, the fulfillment of their spiritual reality, which is light and grace in the consciousness of a spiritual person.

Application to the Liturgy

The liturgy is not a *thing*. The worship of God doesn't just happen because there is a celebration, even a good one, using the rites of the sacraments. It doesn't happen until the *res* (the spiritual reality) of the liturgy is achieved in the believers who celebrate. This is the deeper meaning of the axiom, *sacramenta propter homines*. Sacraments are for people not only with respect to their *purpose*, which governs and guides

---

[6] See the article of Henri-Marie Feret, "*Sacramentum-res*, dans la langue théologique de saint Augustin," *Revue de sciences philosophiques et théologiques* (1940): 218–243.

the logic of their "administration," but also with respect to their *reality*, with respect to the true efficacy of the spiritual action which they are intended to bring about. Once this is understood it becomes clear that no liturgy is worth the effort it takes unless it achieves its spiritual impact in the understanding and the hearts of believers. St. Paul said that he would prefer to speak five words with understanding than ten thousand words in tongues (1 Cor 14:19). He also spoke of "spiritual" worship, which means precisely the offering of oneself (Rom 12:1).

A living liturgy does not consist in the impeccable performance of ceremonies or in a restoration of all the external niceties of the rites, but rather in their spiritual perfection. All of that might contribute, by way of its pedagogical value, to restoring to liturgical action its full truthfulness or "reality." Neither does a living liturgy consist in the spiritual initiation of a handful of people in the midst of a general (and intractable) disinterest on the part of the majority. A liturgy that can only succeed in becoming "real" for a chapel of "oblates," that is, for those who have undertaken a long and sophisticated special education in liturgical expression, is not what we are after. A "real" liturgy is one adapted to being internalized, to producing its *res*—its spiritual effect—in the souls of the faithful, to being received and personalized in people's awareness. As long as what occurs is merely *something special happening* that remains exterior to the hearts of the faithful, what we still have are sacrifices of the kind criticized by the prophets, worship that continues the rites of the synagogue.

The essential objective here, quite distinct from liturgical antiquarianism or ritualism, is to discover a liturgy that can readily be received directly into the hearts of the faithful. By *faithful* here, I mean those who live normal lives in our own time and culture, and not just people living in a fixed, closed agricultural economy as did our ancestors at the time that our liturgical forms were being created. The type of humanity structured and conditioned by the life of those times possessed characteristics which are not at all like those of a humanity shaped and conditioned by industrial labor, mechanical standardization, urban crowding, intense and rapid commercial exchanges, and the harshness and competition of struggling for a livelihood. Neither can today's liturgy be received and internalized under the conditions that prevailed at the end of the Roman Empire or during the feudal system of the Carolingian period. The psychological and moral characteristics of that kind of humanity could only continue to exist exclusively in some kind of specialized environment that would have to be both protected and closed.

At the Heart of Christian Worship

6

The difficulty for a liturgical movement that hopes to be both popular and fully pastoral will always be a temptation toward ritualism. Its job, after all, is to give new meaning to texts and to gestures whose essential sense is symbolic. These texts and rites were created at a fixed moment in the past, drawing from a system of ideas and symbols that were reasonable then—even understood by the great majority of people at that time. Now, however, that system of ideas and symbols is today either forgotten or at least terribly remote.

Admittedly, the most important of these symbols are still valid, but they are sometimes difficult to understand. They now require a special preparation that the faithful no longer have. Some of them are simple and linked to the most common human experiences. A great number of ritual actions or of key texts taken from the Bible are like this. In themselves, they are infinitely rich; they arise from a providential divine pedagogy. But now they need to be explained. And even when they are grasped and internalized, they require an intellectual effort to keep them in mind and to apply them to experience.

Other gestures or formulas are excessively subtle. They do not make sense without a historical explanation that requires a lot of erudition. For example, we may do this or that because in the past the pope or the emperor on certain days performed this ritual whose historical antecedent is such and such . . . It should be clear that certain subtle symbols and almost all those ritual gestures that require a complicated historical explanation in order to make sense are not adapted to the spiritual needs of our contemporaries. These are symbols that can be meaningful and nourishing only for those who have the special education or the necessary leisure to understand them and to apply them to their own experience.

Interpreting symbols is fascinating and even entrancing. Discovering relationships, correspondences, and the logic that links words, symbols, and texts is both engaging and enriching. I have thrown myself into this work and gained enough from it to be able to understand how much it can mean. However, the pastoral problem is not that of specialists placed in conditions that offer the historical culture necessary for understanding liturgical symbols and for finding profit in them. There will always be people who withdraw from the mainstream because their social condition or their personal tastes allow them to abstract themselves from the spirit of the age, which is technological and non-contemplative.

Indeed, one might even wonder if the formation which priests receive for their apostolic ministry, formation immersed in a world of pretechnological ideas, doesn't contribute to cutting them off inevitably from those for whom they are supposed to be a spiritual leaven. Maybe

"Real" Liturgy, "Real" Preaching

the concrete conditions of the church require such seclusion so as to assure the continuity of the tradition, which we cannot afford to neglect. Maybe adaptations to the changing conditions of the world are the business of the laity . . . Who knows? But the key question here is the fate of the masses—the majority of the faithful to whom our ceremonies mean less and less. On the whole, they don't understand what's going on in the liturgy, and they can't get beyond that.

Take as an example the liturgy of Palm Sunday. (I began writing these pages after presiding on Palm Sunday in a parish church jammed with people.) This is one of the days of the year (and in some places this is *the* day) when the largest number of people come to church. The prayers for the blessing of the palms are beautiful. However, nobody in the assembly understands them and almost nobody wants to be bothered to try to follow them.[7] So what are we doing then? What is our objective here; who are we doing this for? *Whose* worship, *whose* prayer is this? Is it even *somebody's* prayer?

It's the church's prayer, you might say; and that's true. You could never get me to say otherwise. But can't we admit also that the church that prays is in fact this very community of faithful gathered here today? Often when I take part in liturgical functions in the parishes, or when I reflect on problems like these, I think spontaneously of an anecdote told me by a Dominican confrere. In a little town in eastern France, about 1927 or 1928, Father B. was preaching for Lent, giving one after the other the parish retreat for men, followed by the one for women. Finally there was the retreat for the domestic servants of the parish's families. The old pastor told the preacher, "Your sermons will be at 5:00 p.m. But I can tell you now, you won't have much of a crowd. That's an hour when these people just can't get away . . ."

It seems to me at times that in commissioning priests to minister the word and the sacraments of Jesus Christ for the people of God, we might just as well tell them, "You can perform these rites according to the rubrics, even chant the epistle and gospel in Latin, if you like. But I can tell you now, you won't have much of anyone there. These are things that these people just don't understand . . ."

As a faithful minister of Christ in the holy Roman Catholic Church, when I celebrate the sacred mysteries (not just the Mass) according to the prescribed rubrics, I can't get out of my mind the Lord's phrase in

---

[7] Translator's note: keep in mind that Congar wrote this article when the Roman Catholic liturgy was still celebrated exclusively in Latin.

the gospel: "You have taken away the key of knowledge. You yourselves did not enter and you stopped others trying to enter" (Luke 11:52). In many of our ceremonies, isn't there in fact an element of the unreal—an obstacle that impedes their bearing spiritual fruit in the lives of the faithful for whom they were created?

Whatever the case may be, we need to strive for a liturgical "realism" that can emerge within the existing norms imposed by the church. Nothing said previously is meant to underestimate the immense value and priceless heritage of this treasure. Liturgical "realism" is the internalization of worship by the faithful, the development in their hearts of the fruitfulness of their prayer and their love. Therefore we have to enrich and make telling for them the liturgical action itself, not only by providing a good explanation of the symbols, but also by explaining the meaning that worship can have for their lives in the context of the problems and circumstances that they must live with.

Generally, liturgists hardly ever develop this kind of catechesis. Sometimes I get the impression that liturgists are working for the liturgy itself, rather than for the people. That's why they may fail to have a pastoral impact. By contrast, it is essential that the liturgical renewal get beyond focusing on the liturgy for its own sake and that it become absorbed (obsessed, I might even say) by the concern of being in touch with ordinary people and leading them to a "spiritual" worship lived out in their daily lives.

This won't happen, however, unless the *prophetic* element—the word—is incessantly at play to help internalize and personalize the sacramental celebration. The rite will have to be explained not just in historical and biblical terms or in terms of symbols from the past; it must also be presented in a way that integrates human attitudes and life options, touching the concrete realities of the faithful as real, contemporary persons. To take another example, how could the exorcisms of the rite of baptism represent something "real" for the people today with whom they are used, unless they are explained and, further, explained in terms of their actual experiences, their problems and their needs? Only by such an effort can they achieve the kind of internalization of meaning that is essential.

This discussion shows us how "real" liturgy is linked to preaching and, more precisely, to a sort of preaching that is equally "real."

Application to Preaching

Almost everywhere, the more demanding members of the faithful are somewhat critical of our preaching. They complain that our sermons sound prefabricated. It's not a question of their rejecting the Christian doctrine which is the revealed deposit of the faith, the dogma of the church which comes to us from the apostles. That is not being called into question—which makes this critique quite different from the complaints of modernism at the turn of the twentieth century.

The Christian people of our time genuinely want to be put into meaningful contact with the apostolic and patristic sources of Catholic teaching. However, they complain that preachers are too bookish in their expressions, that they are overly concerned to use canonical formulas or to pass on passages of official documents (where they often betray a merely superficial reading). Therefore they find the doctrine offered them from the pulpit out of touch with their personal needs and their own spontaneous questions.

They complain that preachers too seldom speak like persons with a genuine spiritual life of their own who are living the things that they preach. This is a question not so much of moral witness but of the way they think. Preachers propose a kind of teaching whose doctrine is orthodox enough; the complaint is not there. But they talk like licensed dealers of orthodox formulas that sound impersonal and fixed. In fact, as fathers of souls who need the example and the nourishment of their pastors for living their Christian lives, preachers should be showing them what it looks like to live this Christian teaching.

Pastors are ordained to be the head of the local community and supposedly in communion with their people. Yet, from the pulpit, in the sacristy, or at the altar, pastors "administer" more than they "live" their ministry of God's word. That word should be both a life-giving response to the questions of the people as well as nourishment for their hearts. Behaving this way, preachers continue to represent a religious system *that exists in and for itself* but which in fact is not really in touch with the religious realities of human life. Religion has to be transcendent, of course; but should it be transcendent *in that kind of way*? Can it afford to manifest transcendence as something extrinsic, as a completely distinct order of things which is less the vertical dimension of human life than a world apart, a world juxtaposed to the world of ordinary human experience?

In the end, the complaint about our preaching boils down to this: too often it is itself little more than a ritual. It is more or less impressive talk about what we are expected to say in this special setting of the parish church, typical of things uttered from a pulpit in the course of a ceremony that is artificial and uses language that is uncommon. One day, during a confirmation, I heard the preacher talk about the "Sevenfold

At the Heart of Christian Worship

Spirit." What is that supposed to say to the lay faithful? As a priest and a theologian, of course, this expression means a lot. But for the laity who have never undergone a specialized initiation into the clerical world, it means strictly nothing. It's part of the ritual, that's all.

As Abbé Georges Michonneau pointed out from experience, when something has become nothing more than a ritual, it adds nothing and changes nothing even in the lives of those who still practice it.[8] In our preaching, the things we say are generally correct—that's not the problem. They are *sacramenta* where everything is just fine from the perspective of the validity of the *sacramentum*. But they don't succeed at producing their *res*, and can hardly hope to do so. The *res* is the spiritual fruit in the awareness and consciences of the faithful which I have described earlier in these pages. The words of the preaching remain too much on the order of *ritual* and don't arrive at the spiritual fulfillment that the ritual was created for, without which it no longer has any point. Reflect on this: if the sacraments were made for the benefit of the people, what must we say about the purpose of the word?

What I understand as "real" preaching is never going to be non-intellectual, nor should it always necessarily be expressed without some complicated ideas. But "real" preaching does have to have these characteristics:

1. It deals with real problems and gives real nourishment to the souls of the faithful.

2. It is directed to an audience of people who earn a living, who are married and have a family, who have real responsibilities and live in a society of initiative and cooperation. It is preaching addressed in such a way as to be understood by just such people, talking about what is true in such a way as to say it, eye to eye, to an ordinary person—and not just to a church full of almost exclusively women, or to a group of children, or to a community of nuns.

3. It is preaching that is likely to produce its effect, its *res*, in the mind, the conscience, and the heart of just such people.

This topic is endless. I could go on and on. But I think that I have explained my idea. I need to add this, however. The normal condition for producing "real" preaching is "real" study. At present, many

---

[8] It is worth rereading pages 257ff. in Georges Michonneau, *Paroisse, communauté missionnaire: Conclusions de cinq ans d'expérience en milieu populaire* (Paris: Cerf, 1946).

priests who want to preach in the way I have described are more or less obliged to repeat the parts of their theological studies that provide a foundation for their preaching. That shouldn't be necessary.

I don't imagine that seminary education is able or ought to prepare students immediately to go out and preach after each course. To impose that, to put into place a purely practical or pragmatic orientation for clerical studies, would be to frustrate something essential and irreplaceable for the pastoral objectives at hand. Pastoral theology still has need for a thoughtful distancing, a disinterested reflectiveness. These are the foundation for any true culture, and for a scientific seriousness and a judicious approach to the truth.

So I don't think that clerical studies, in order to be better adapted for pastoral success, ought to become less intellectual. But in the criticism often made of Scholasticism, there is, I believe, a genuine and a profound problem—sensed rather than articulated by many (and sometimes trivialized by those who don't get the point). What we need is not less intellectual or less scientific, less rigorous or less traditional academic formation. What we need, however, are studies that focus on thinking about reality, that respond to the real needs of real persons and don't just focus on manipulating a conventional vocabulary with flair or brilliance. That kind of scholastic theology gives us only mere *sacramenta* and so only mere ritual.

Pay attention to reality, then, to real questions, without losing touch with the centuries-long heritage of great Christian thought. Real questions deserve real answers of a kind that real people struggling to live in today's world can take to heart and live. This can't mean concentrating only on modern philosophy, politics, economics, or literature. The responses needed from the pulpit are God's answers, the Gospel's—the answers of the apostolic tradition that lives on in the church. We are ministers of the word of God, not agents of contemporary civilization. However, the word of God and the doctrine of the church in which this word is applied and developed ought to be studied in order to be handed on to the faithful, so as to give them spiritual nourishment capable of changing their lives.

Linked with the celebration of the liturgy, the ministry of the word has to focus on producing its *res*—its spiritual fruit in the consciousness of the faithful. This is the meaning, both precise and rich, of "real" liturgy and "real" preaching.

⳼

At the Heart of Christian Worship

Agenda for Personal and Group Reflections

Questions for the Individual Reader

1. On the basis of his retrieval of the classic theological tradition, Congar's use of the word "real" points to a transformation in the believer. Do you personally recognize in your own life what he means by the "realized mystery" (the *res*) of the Eucharist as a present-day overflow of sacramental grace? What examples might you give of what you have experienced?

2. Can you think of things in the pastoral preaching and in the liturgical celebrations of your parish that would help you to arrive at a deeper appreciation of the transformation that sacramental life offers to you?

3. Congar speaks of a movement in Catholic spirituality that goes from externals to interiorization, we might say from rites and things to experience. For him the *interior* is always *corporate*, rooted in the Body of Christ. How does this help you to refocus your understanding of the Eucharist and what it asks of you?

4. If you were to share some key ideas that you have taken away from reading this chapter, what two or three points would you emphasize? What struck you the most?

Questions for Group Discussion

1. Congar sees the church and its ritual life as the fulfillment of an ages-long preparation in the Old Testament. Does this insight help you look at the Lectionary readings from the Old Testament with new understanding? How, for example, does the church interiorize and deepen the great Old Testament theme of the People of God through the celebration of the Eucharist?

2. Can you explain how understanding the eucharistic bread and wine as a *means* ("Take and eat," says the Lord) deepens and makes even more urgent the eucharistic reality of the church that has as its vocation to become itself a great sacrament of God's presence?

3. Congar insists that in the new covenant there is only one sacrifice, the self-offering of Christ (and, with him, of the members of his body). Do we have to *unlearn* old habits of seeing liturgical actions as supernatural substitution sacrifices of which we are unworthy to be a part? How do you bring yourself to understand the awesome truth that you give yourself along with your Lord in solidarity as a self-offering accepted with delight by God the Father?

"Real" Liturgy, "Real" Preaching

4. Congar fears that sometimes the complicated nature of liturgical rituals turns people off. Have you had experiences like that? What are they? How do they get in the way of your fully understanding the church's liturgical action?

Chapter 2

The *Ecclesia* or Christian Community as a Whole Celebrates the Liturgy

Translator's observations: *This essay on the role of the worshiping assembly as the acting subject of the liturgy appeared in a volume entitled* The Liturgy after Vatican II, *itself edited by Congar.* Published in 1967, the purpose of this volume was to provide expert commentary on the text of* Sacrosanctum Concilium *(SC), the council's Constitution on the Sacred Liturgy, and then to illuminate certain theological themes of central importance to understanding the theology of the document.*

In the light of Congar's previous work, it is not surprising that he turned to this particular theme. In his Lay People in the Church, *he had explained in detail how laypersons, even without holding any ecclesiastical office, enjoy the gifts of the Holy Spirit and participate in the prophetic, priestly, and royal ministries of Christ. He rightly considered SC 26 to be a crucial text because of the following affirmation: "Liturgical services are not private functions but are celebrations of the Church which is 'the sacrament of unity,' namely, the holy people united and organized under the bishops. Therefore, liturgical services have to do with the whole body . . ."*

Reacting against what some have since labeled clericalism and centralization during the previous few centuries, Congar revived the church's ancient understanding of the priestly people offering the Eucharist in solidarity with their Divine Head. This essay is a sublime work of ressourcement, *demonstrating an incredible mastery of patristic and medieval sources. As we see here, Congar could always find reputable sources to support his proposals.*

This is a work of synthesis of the highest order. Nothing quite like it exists, and it has never been surpassed. The message is still pastorally practical—the faithful need to know their role as a priestly people offering the saving sacrifice of their Savior-Head.

---

* *Vatican II: La Liturgie après Vatican II—Unam Sanctam* 66 (Paris: Editions du Cerf, 1967), 241–282.

The primary concern of Vatican II's Constitution on the Sacred Liturgy, *Sacrosanctum Concilium*, was to promote the active participation of the faithful. The council states this as follows: "Liturgical services are not private functions, but are celebrations of the church, which is the 'sacrament of unity,' namely, the holy people united and organized under the bishops. For liturgical services have to do with the whole Body. [The rites] make [the Body] visible and have effects on it. But they also touch individual members of the church in different ways, depending on ranks, roles and levels of participation" (SC 26).

This same teaching can be found in the Dogmatic Constitution on the Church, *Lumen Gentium*, in a form more fully integrated into its ecclesiology, especially in LG 11. Clearly, Vatican II teaches that the *ecclesia*, or this organically structured body that is the church, is the subject of liturgical acts. We might even wonder if this is not a tautology, since liturgical acts are precisely public acts of Christian worship. Nonetheless, it is worth taking the time to clarify what this idea means and what it implies.

In any case, there is no doubt that this teaching is rooted in the church's most ancient and most certain continuing Tradition. It will be wise and helpful, therefore, to verify this fact by reviewing some of the most significant testimony from history.

I. THE ANCIENT TRADITION: THE CHURCH AS SUBJECT OF LITURGICAL ACTIONS AND, NOTABLY, OF THE OFFERING OF THE EUCHARIST

This topic needs to be addressed first of all from the revealed witness of the Scriptures. It deserves a more thorough study than what can be done here. We will have to make do with only some general indications.

In the Old Testament everything was dominated by the relationship between the people of Israel, whose identity consisted in being the People of God, and their service of this covenant God. The twelve tribes were gathered into a single people by God's free choice and so consecrated, a consecration which he asked them to accept in order to serve him according to his word and his law: "Now therefore, if you obey my voice and keep my covenant, you shall be my treasured possession out of all the peoples. Indeed, the whole earth is mine, but you shall be for me a priestly kingdom and a holy nation" (Exod 19:5-6; cf. Isa 61:6; 2 Macc 2:17).

During the Exile Israel was represented as the servant of Yahweh in Isaiah 40–55, in which texts the *collective* meaning of this singular servant (without being the only meaning) is clearly dominant. This is why the offerings made in temple worship were not the action of a single individual but the action of a people considered in their totality.[1] This temple worship was carried out, however, by priests.

This theme of a consecrated people is carried over in the term "People of God" in its New Testament context in 1 Peter 2:5, 9-10, where the expression of Exodus 19:6 is understood in a collective sense, as a corporate priesthood; and in Revelation 1:6; 5:10; 20:6; 22:3-5, where the meaning is extended in a distributive-individual sense to the faithful as priests.[2] Second Isaiah had clearly hinted at an extraordinary extension of priestly dignity to all those who would know Yahweh.[3] First Peter then applies to every Christian what the Old Testament applied to the Levites (cf. Selwyn in n. 2). Christians are called "saints" because they make up the new community of divine worship. There is a profound difference between the new and the old dispensations of worship.

If in the New Israel there are still ministers who preside, teach, and direct the communities, and who have the obligation to celebrate worship in their midst, nonetheless the New Testament clearly insists on the uniqueness of the one mediator, Jesus Christ, and on the fact that in him and through him (δια Ιησου χριστου: 1 Pet 2:5) everyone has access to God, everyone can approach God (cf. Heb 4:14-16; 7:19; 8:1; 10:19-22). With the exception of this last text (cf. also Heb 13:10), none of these passages that we have just referred to, touching the priesthood of all Christians, refers directly to the Eucharist.[4] Rather,

---

[1] See E. Lohmeyer, *Kultus und Evangelium* (Göttingen, 1942), 12.

[2] For the theme "People of God," see my article and also the review article by R. Schnackenburg and J. Dupont in *Concilium* 1 (January 1965): 15–32 and 91–100. On the priesthood of all believers from a New Testament perspective, see Lucien Cerfaux, "Regale sacerdotium," in *RSPT* 28 (1939): 5–39 (reprinted in *Recueil Lucien Cerfaux* [Gembloux, 1954], vol. II, 283–315); J. Blinzler, *Ierateuma. Zur Exegese von 1 Petr. 2,5 u. 9, in Episcopus, Studien über das Bischofsamt*, ed. Michael Kardinal Faulhaber (Ratisbonne, 1947), 49–65; Edward G. Selwyn, *The First Epistle of St. Peter* (London, 1958); E. J. Hall, "The Elect and the Holy: An Exegetical Examination of 1 Peter 2:4-10 and the Phrase 'Basileion hierateuma,'" *Novum Testamentum* Suppl. XII (Leyde, 1966). For the patristic and theological point of view, cf. Blinzler, op. cit., p. 49 n. 1 and infra n. 67.

[3] Cf. 56:6–7; and in the context of Israel, cf. 61:6; cf. 60:7 and 11f.

[4] Cf. L. Cerfaux, op. cit.; E. G. Selwyn (op. cit., pp. 294–298), following E. Lohmeyer (*Theologishe Rundschau* [1937]: 296), thinks, however, that 1 Pet 2:4f. contains an implicit reference to the Eucharist.

The *Ecclesia* or Christian Community

this priesthood proposes spiritual offerings drawn from personal life. These offerings are not referenced in these texts as having a liturgical character. On the other hand, to separate the two domains would be to misunderstand the authentic nature of Christian worship. The Eucharist is supremely the "sacrifice of praise" of which each believer is the priestly celebrant throughout his or her entire life and witness.[5] However, note this difference: while the spiritual sacrifice of life is personal, the Eucharist is communitarian. Its celebration is *corporate* in the strongest sense of the word.[6]

The new People of God have become the Body of Christ (cf. n. 2 above) by the action of the Holy Spirit: Romans 12:4-6; 1 Corinthians 12:4-13, 27. Christ is always still alive, and he is our high priest (cf. Hebrews), but the church, which is his Body, is as such the very place where he continues his life and manifests it here below, where he operates through his Spirit, and where he makes the Christian mystery actual; this is achieved especially in the celebration of baptism and Eucharist (1 Cor 10:16-17).[7] There is a profound unity between the physical body of the Lord, crucified and risen, his sacramental body offered in the Eucharist, and his ecclesial Body which offers itself up and, by this very fact, becomes the spiritual temple of God.[8] According to the New Testament, then, it follows that the whole church, as People of God and Body of Christ, celebrates the spiritual worship, both personal and communal, inaugurated by Jesus Christ, of which he himself remains the chief celebrant.

---

[5] See J. Juglar, *Le sacrifice de louange—Lex orandi*, 15 (Paris: Cerf, 1953); and my *Jalons pour une théologie du laïcat—Unam Sanctam* 23 (Paris: Cerf, 1953), ch. iv, 159–188, 196f.

[6] Cf. 1 Cor 11:17-34; Acts 2:42, 46-47; 20:7: the ομοθυναδον of v. 46 (cf. 1:14) expresses the idea of a corporate totality; cf. B. Reicke, *Glaube und Leben der Urgemeinde* (Zurich, 1957), 21 and 60; also Cerfaux, op. cit., 129; and ibid., vol. I, 143, 151–152 on επι το αυτο.

[7] For this (semitic) value of *sôma*, without forgetting other aspects or other studies, see especially J. A. T. Robinson, *The Body: A Study in Pauline Theology* (London: SCM Press, 1952); W. Hillmann, "Die Kirche in der neutestamentliche Glaubensverkündigung," in *Die Kirche und der heutiche Mensch—Liturgie und Mönchtum*, 3, Folge, H. 17 (Maria-Laach, 1955): 18–33; P. A. Harlé, "Le Saint-Esprit et l'Eglise chez Saint Paul," *Verbum Caro* 74 (1965): 13–29; B. M. Ahern, "The Christian's Union with the Body of Christ in Corinthians, Galatians, and Romans," *Catholic Biblical Quarterly* 23(1961): 199–209.

[8] Cf. C. F. D. Moule, "Sanctuary and Sacrifice in the Church of the N.T.," *Journal of Theological Studies* (London) (1950): 29–41.

At the Heart of Christian Worship

We find exactly this understanding in the life and the consciousness of the early church.[9] According to St. Justin,[10] in the oldest description that we have of the Eucharist, after the community has reaffirmed its unity through the kiss of peace, the presider gives thanks over the bread and wine and "all the people present show their approval by acclaiming together: Amen!" St. Irenaeus writes that the *ecclesia* "offers throughout the whole world" the new oblation of the New Testament which it received from the apostles.[11] I don't want to exaggerate the importance of this text, because the use of the word *ecclesia* here does not point to a liturgical or ecclesiological affirmation. Rather, what is in question here is the opposition between church and synagogue (cf. Mal 1:10-11). We shall find this to be the case also in quite a number of medieval texts.

The *Apostolic Tradition* of St. Hippolytus is even more explicit. There, in the prayer for the ordination of a bishop, we read: "May [God] grant you the gifts of your Holy Church"[12]; and in the eucharistic *epiclesis*: "We ask you to send your Holy Spirit on the offering of the Holy Church."[13] Gregory Dix (see n. 9) believed that there existed, beginning with this period, a ritual presentation made by the faithful of gifts to be offered in eucharistic thanksgiving. Bernard Botte disagrees (op. cit., pp. 30 and 53), noting that this is not found anywhere in Hippolytus, who attributes this offering to the deacons.

Justin simply says: "Someone brings to the presider from the brothers [and sisters] some bread and a cup of water and wine mixed together." On the other hand, the offering of the faithful is attested to in the West, probably from the middle of the third century (St. Cyprian)[14] and certainly by the fourth century.[15] For St. Cyprian, the plural form used in the prayers of the liturgy is telling: "When *we* gather together

---

[9] This point is particularly addressed by Gregory Dix, "The Idea of 'the Church' in the Primitive Liturgies," in *The Parish Communion*, ed. A. G. Hebert (London, 1937), 97–143.

[10] *I Apol.*, 65 and 67 (PG 6:427f.).

[11] *Adversus Haereses*, IV, 17, 5 (PG 7:1023; Harvey, II, p. 197).

[12] Ch. 3: trans. B. Botte, *Sources Chrétiennes* 11 (Paris, 1946), 29.

[13] Ch. 4. Gregory Dix thinks that these words are interpolated—see *Theology*, vol. 28: 127f., and his edition of the *Apost. Trad.* (London, 1937), 75–79. But Bernard Botte (op. cit., 22–23) maintains their authenticy.

[14] Cf. *De opere et eleemoysinis*, 15 (PG 4:636; Hartel, III/1, 384); H. Leclercq, art. "Messe," in *Dictionnaire d'archéologie chrétienne et de liturgie* [DACL], XI: 592.

[15] Cf. F. Cabrol, art. "Offertoire," *DACL*, XII: 1950–1951. St. Augustine says, for example: "The priest takes from you that which he is going to offer for you, when you desire to appease God by your prayers," *Ennar. in Psalmis* 129,

with the brothers [and sisters] and *we* celebrate the divine sacrifices with the bishop . . ."[16] In the *Acta Saturnini, Dativi et sociorum*, an account of martyrdom in 304 (the later reworking of this text by the Donatists does not affect these passages), the expression that the faithful employed, *"egi dominicum, dominicum celebravi*—I have taken part in the Sunday celebration," repeatedly has a formally eucharistic meaning: the entire assembly has celebrated the mystery of the Lord.[17]

St. Augustine was the teacher par excellence about *ecclesia* taken as the unity of the Body of Christ. (We will return to this idea.) He thought that it was legitimate to baptize infants who had been presented by their parents for reasons unconnected with the faith, because in his view it is not really the parents who offer children at baptism but rather the *ecclesia*, taken as the society of saints and believers united in charity.[18] Augustine says something similar with respect to the forgiveness of sins: it is the *ecclesia*, or rather the corporate unity of the *ecclesia*, that has received the keys and that exercises them.[19] Augustine doesn't misunderstand the role of the ministries nor the

---

7 (PL 37:1701; cf. J. Juglar, op. cit. n. 5, 186); see also *Sermon* 82, 5 (PL 32:508). The faithful are said to *"sacrificare . . . ferre oblationem ad altare Dei*—to sacrifice [and] to make an oblation at God's altar" (*Epist.*, 111, 8; 33:426). In the East, see the account of St. Gregory Nanzianzen, *Orat.*, 43, 52 (PG 36:564).

[16] *"Quando in unum cum fratribus convenimus et sacrificia divina cum sacerdote celebremus": De oratione dominica* (PL 4:538; Hartel, p. 269).

[17] See the texts cited in my *Jalons pour une théologie du laïcat* (Paris: Cerf, 1953), 277 n. 314. English translation: *Lay People in the Church*, trans. Donald Attwater (Westminster, MD: Newman Press, 1967), ch. 4, 121f.

[18] Epist., 98, 5: "Offeruntur quippe parvuli ad percipiendam spiritalem gratiam non tam ab eis, quorum gestantur manibus, quamvis et ab ipsis, si et ipsi boni fideles sunt, quam ab universa societate sanctorum atque fidelium. Ab omnibus namque offerri recte intelliguntur, quibus placet, quod offeruntur, et quorum sancta atque individua caritate ad communicationem Sancti Spiritus adiuvantur. Tota hoc ergo mater ecclesia, quae in sanctis est, facit, quia tota omnes, tota singulos parit" (PL 33:362). I gladly adopt this text of the Louvain edition for this passage of Augustine *In Ioan.*, tr. LXXX, 3 (PL 35:1840) : "Hoc verbum fidei tantum valet in ecclesia Dei, ut per *ipsam* credentem, offerentem, benedicentem, tingentem, etiam tantillum mundet infantem."

[19] It would be too long to reproduce here even the principal texts: *De baptismo*, III, 18, 23 (PL 43:150), reproduced almost word for word in *In Ioan.*, tr. CXXI, 4 (35, 1928); *Sermo* 195, 2 (38:1349); *In Ioan.*, tr. CXXIV, 5 (35:1973); *Tractatus sive Sermones ined. ex Cod. Guelf.* 4096. Ed. G. Morin, 1917, *Tract. XVI*, 2, 62. See Karl Adam, cited below in n. 76.

At the Heart of Christian Worship

efficacy that follows upon their action when Christ acts through them, but he refuses to isolate ministry from the community of believers.

Is it the same for the Eucharist? Augustine speaks about this with great discretion. However, we are aware of some unforgettable texts from *The City of God* on the subject of true sacrifice—that of Christ—which Augustine likes to call "*sacrificium christianorum*—the sacrifice of Christians"[20]: "The Church never ceases to reproduce this sacrifice in the sacrifice of the altar well known to the faithful, where it is clear that along with what it offers, the Church offers itself"[21]; "[Christ] wanted a daily sacrament of this reality, the sacrifice of the Church which, being the Body of which he is the head, learns to offer itself through him."[22] Augustine seems to tie the idea of the *ecclesia* offering the Eucharist to the fact that, in offering Christ sacramentally, the church is obliged to offer itself. Both the church's priestly role of offering and its role as victim of the sacrifice are rooted in the unity that Christ has established between himself and us. Augustine loves to link the priestly quality of Christians to the fact that they are the members of the same Priest, their head, Jesus Christ.[23] Following St. Augustine, St. Leo,[24] Gelasius I,[25] St. Gregory the Great,[26] St. Isidore,[27] and others do the same.

[20] Here are some texts from Augustine on this point (in chronological order): *De div. quaest.*, 83, q.61, 2 (PL 40:50); *Ennar. In Ps.*, 33, *Sermo I*, 5 (36:303); *De cons. Evang.*, I, 3, 5 (34:1044); *Sermo 307*, 2,3 (38:1407); *Ennar. In Ps.*, 106, 13 and 109, 17 (37:1427 and 1459–1460); *De peccato orig.*, 23, 33 (44:401–402); *De Civ. Dei*, XVI, 22; XVII, 5 and 17 (41:500, 533 and 536, 550–551); *Contra adv. leg. et proph.*, I, 20, 39 (42:626–627); *De Civ. Dei*, XVIII, 35, 3 and XIX, 23 (41:594; 650–655); *Tract. adv. Iud.*, 9, 12–13 (42:60–62). Cf. *C. Faustum*, I, 20, 18 (42:282–283).

[21] *De Civ. Dei*, X, 6 . . . : "Quod etiam sacramento altaris fidelibus noto frequantat Ecclesia, ubi ei demonstratur, quod in ea re quam offert, ipsa offeratur" (PL 41:284).

[22] *De Civ. Dei*, X, 20 . . . : "Cuius rei sacramentum quotidianum esse voluit Ecclesiae sacrificium: quae cum ipsius capitis corpus sit, seipsam per ipsum discit offerre" (41:298).

[23] *Quaest. Evangel.*, II, 40 (PL 35:1355); *De Civ. Dei*, XX, 10 (41:676): "sic omnes sacerdotes quoniam membra sunt unius sacerdotis."

[24] *Sermo 3*, 1; 24, 6 (PL 54:145 and 207). St. Leo proposed eventually multiplying the number of Masses available to the faithful "si unius missae more servato sacrificium offerre non possint" (*Epist. 9 ad Dioscorum Alex.*, 2: PL 54:626–627).

[25] *Adv. Andromachum*, 4: "Numquid quia in ministerio sacro non es, in plebe sacra non es? An nescis et te membrum esse summi Pontificis? An ignoras totam Ecclesiam sacerdotium vocitatam?" (PL 59:112; Thiel, *Epist. RR. Pontif.*, I, 600).

[26] *Moralia*, XXV, 7, 15 (PL 76:328); *Hom. In Ev.*, II, 31, 8 (1231).

[27] *De. eccl. offic.*, 2, 26, 2 (PL 83:823B). Other references can be found in Schulte (cited in the following note, and in n. 40f. below).

The *Ecclesia* or Christian Community

Fr. Raphael Schulte published a book that treats historically, for the period of the High Middle Ages in the West, the question of the Eucharist as the offering of the church.[28] His documentation is abundant. Not all the witnesses whom he invokes are equally convincing. Some remain a bit vague. Sometimes in the passage where we find *"ecclesia offert*—the church offers," the point is less that "the church offers" than "this is the (new) sacrifice offered by the *church*," in contrast with the *synagogue*.[29] Ultimately, what we find here finally are ideas whose exact content escapes us because Schulte does not give us their precise context.

To know what is really going on it is necessary to have recourse to the history of the Offertory and of the offerings made by the faithful.[30] This liturgical gesture is attested to from the third century in Africa, from the fourth century in Milan and Rome, and from the fifth century in the East, with abundant examples also from Gaul and Spain. The *Ordo I* describes its usage in eighth-century Rome, where it is practiced down to the period of Innocent III (but the word *oblationes* has a broader content by that time).

The offering took two forms: in Rome, Milan, Africa, and Spain the faithful came in procession toward the altar; whereas in the East, following the development of the rite of the *prothesis*, and also in Gaul,

---

[28] *Die Messe als Opfer der Kirche: Die Lehre frühmittelalterlichen Autoren über das eucharistische Opfer—Liturgiewiss. Quellen und Forschungen*, 35 (Munster, 1959). For the 9th to the 12th centuries, see A. Kolping, "Der active Anteil der Gläubigen an der Darbringung des eucharistischen Opfers," *Divus Thomas* (1949): 369–380; (1950): 79–110 and 147–170.

[29] Such is the case, for example, of the text of St. Fulgentius (*De fide ad Petrum* 19, 60: PL 65:699), which Ratramnus uses (*De corpore et sanguine Domini*, ch. 90: PL 121:165–166 [in Schulte, 183]). This is also the case for several passages where St. Isidore places the sacrifice of the Christians in parallel with the worship of the Old Testament (Schulte, pp. 31–34), or where St. Bede does the same (*Hexaemeron* III: PL 91:151 B-D; *Expos. in Lucam*: PL 92:596B-C, cited by Schulte on 97–98); and finally Florus of Lyons (*De actione missarum*: PL 119:16A [Schulte, p. 164]).

[30] Cf. Franciscus de Berlendis, *De oblationibus ad altare communibus et peculiaribus* (Venice, 1743), which gives the original documentation. He concludes, "*offerentes vocati etiam celebrantes*—those offering are also called the celebrants" (489); F. Cabrol, "Offertoire," *DACL* XII (1946–1962) (bibliographies up to 1935); J. Juglar, op. cit. n. 5, 186; N. M. Denis-Boulet in *L'Eglise en prière* (Paris, 1961), 292 and 362–372 (bibliography); G. Nickl, *Der Anteil des Volkes an der Messliturgie im Frankreich von Chlodwig bis auf Karl dem Grossen* (Innsbruck, 1930).

the faithful left their offerings in the sacristy before the liturgy began, and their holy gifts were brought solemnly by the ministers during the celebration. Sinners and the notoriously unjust were not permitted to take part in the offering.[31] The expression *vota sua,* employed in the Memento of the Living of the Roman Mass, indicated these offerings were made by the faithful, down to the period when a different explanation of the meaning of the Mass came about as a result of "private Masses."

Such is the case, in the twelfth century, of Odo of Cambrai or of Stephen of Autun, who reduced the meaning of this expression to a merely moral sense, an involvement by way of desire and prayer. But if the fact of bringing the bread and wine was not sufficient to make the assembly of the faithful celebrants of the Mass, given that the decisive gesture of the consecration carried out by the priest was outside their scope, nonetheless the gesture of offering is true worship in the ritual context of the consecration and communion, and it has its place in the celebration and in the active role that the faithful take in it.

Even if not all the texts cited by Schulte are equally significant, it is nonetheless certain that St. Isidore makes the *ecclesia* (or "we," "Christians," "believers") the subject of the act of offering the Eucharist.[32] Schulte shows clearly (pp. 37–45, 50–52) that this is tied to Isidore's whole ecclesiology of the church as the organic unity or priestly Body of Christ, our high priest, "*corpus Christi sacerdotis.*" Therefore whether it be in its ministerial form or in its common form, the priesthood is first of all the priesthood of the *ecclesia* by the very fact that it is the priesthood of Christ. It is this priesthood that is operative in all Christian celebrations; the ecclesial-corporate dimension is primary.

Felix of Urgel (+ 818), who has the same ecclesiology as Isidore, uses the formula (before the Council of Trent) "*Ecclesia per sacerdotes Domino offert*—the church makes its offering to the Lord through the priests."[33] It is the church that offers [the Eucharist], and this is so exactly because the church is the Body of Christ. Beatus of Liébana and Etherius of Osma based these same ideas on the fact that the church, born from the sacrifice of Christ, is the body of the Priest who, having offered

---

[31] You can find references in *Eglise et Pauvreté—Unam Sanctam* 57 (Paris: Cerf, 1965), 249f.; for sanctions for penitents, see A. Kolping, art. cit. in n. 29, 86 n. 3.

[32] Schulte, op. cit., 36; 51 n. 276; and for the Spanish-Visigothic Liturgy, pp. 61f., 74f.

[33] *Liber de variis quaest. adv. Iudaeos,* ch. 29, 8, ed. P. A. C. Vega and A. E. Anspach, under the name of Isidore (Escurial, 1940), 85; cf. Schulte, op. cit., 85–86.

The *Ecclesia* or Christian Community

himself once for all in sacrifice, now offers himself again, unceasingly, in and through us.[34]

The viewpoint of the church—we might say the primacy of the *ecclesia*—so dominates the thought of St. Bede that he attributes to the church, in a way similar to Augustine, the power of the keys that had been given to the apostles.[35] Bede has an organic notion of the church: he is able to see it as being the "we" of all Christians . . . and so as being anterior to its members, because he sees the church, from the perspective of Christ, as the Body of the sovereign Priest, born from his side on the cross. These ideas form the foundation of what Bede writes about the *ecclesia* concerning the way it offers the Eucharist.[36]

The pastoral explication of the Mass *Primum in ordine*, written around the year 800 in Frankish territory, speaks of "sacrifices that are offered by us and consecrated at the hands of the priests."[37] These catecheses of the Mass in the Carolingian period accentuate the role of the hierarchical priest. Yet they do not isolate the priest from the people or from the assembly whom he personifies.[38] Some forty years later, Walafrid Strabo explained the meaning of the Mass as the bread and the blood "*quem universalis offert ecclesia*—which the whole church offers together."[39]

However, the most interesting witness for the tradition of antiquity is without doubt Florus of Lyons. His sense of the liturgical mystery and of the eucharistic celebration is remarkable, and it is undergirded by a profound ecclesiology, still very little explored. Here is his commentary on the "*qui tibi offerunt*" of the Memento of the Living. (But how can you translate the full richness of such a Latin text?):

> These words [of the Mass] stimulate the following reflections: it is the whole church that offers to God this sacrifice of praise; the words "who offer to you" are applied to all the faithful (all the baptized) who stand about the altar. For that which is brought about by the ministry of priests is also produced communally by the faith and devotion of

[34] *Adv. Elipandum* (PL 96:893–1030); cf. Schulte, op. cit., 90–93.

[35] *Exp. Apoc.* (PL 93:163A); *Exp. supra Parab. Sal.* (91:1016B) Schulte, op. cit., 109 n. 614.

[36] See the interesting comments of Schulte, op. cit., 97–118.

[37] PL 138:1183A; Schulte, 126.

[38] See Schulte, op. cit., 131–138 for an explanation of *Quotiens contra se.*

[39] *De exordiis et incrementis* . . . , c. 23, ed. Knoepfler (Munich, 1899), 64 (Schulte, 142).

At the Heart of Christian Worship

all. It was about the whole church that the Apostle Peter said: "You are a chosen race, a royal priesthood" (1 Peter 2:9), "chosen to offer spiritual sacrifices acceptable to God through Jesus Christ" (2:5). The whole church is called a holy priesthood here, a title and a responsibility which under the Old Law was given only to the family of Aaron; because now all the faithful (the baptized) are members of their high Priest (. . .) Therefore the priests of the church make the offering, although the whole church offers, through them and in them, a sacrifice of praise to God—that which God commanded those adoring him to offer, when he said: "Immolate to God a sacrifice of praise, and pay your vows to the Most High " (Psalm 49 [50]:14).[40]

Commenting on the silence that follows the Preface and the *Sanctus*, Florus, the deacon of Lyons, writes: "United to the wishes and desires of all present, the priest begins the prayer of consecration of the mystery of the body and blood of the Savior. It is fitting at this moment of such a holy and divine action—the mind far from all earthly thoughts—that by the grace of God, the church with the priest and the priest with the church, filled with spiritual yearning, they enter the heavenly, eternal sanctuary of God."[41] In this whole chapter and in the following the word *ecclesia* designates first of all the assembly gathered to participate in the celebration. Later, commenting on the "*Hanc igitur oblationem servitutis nostrae*," Florus writes: "We see in these words the unity of the *ecclesia* in its act of offering . . . ,"[42] an idea which he

[40] "*Qui tibi offerunt hoc sacrificium laudis, tibique reddunt vota sua aeterno Deo vivo et vero. In quibus verbis considerandum est, quod tota Ecclesia offerat Deo illud sacrificium laudis; et quia de omni multitudine circumstantium fidelium dicitur: Qui tibi offerunt. Quod enim adimpletur proprie ministerio sacerdotium, hoc generaliter agitur fide et devotione cunctorum. Omni enim Ecclesiae dicitur per beatum Petrum apostolorum: Vos autem genus electum, regale sacerdotium (1 Pet 2: 9), offerre spirituales hostias et acceptabiles Deo per Iesum Christum (v. 5). Omnem ergo Ecclesiam sacerdotium sanctum appellat, quod sola domus Aaron in lege nomen et officium habuit, quia nimirum omnes fideles summi sacerdotis membra existunt (. . .) Offerunt ergo sacerdotes Ecclesiae, offert per ipsos et in ipsis tota Ecclesia Deo sacrificium laudis, quod a cultoribus suis sibi offerri ipse praecepit dicens: Immola Deo sacrificium laudis, et redde Altissimo vota tua (Ps. 49 [50], 14)." Opusc. de actione missarum, c. 52 (PL 119:47–48; ed. Duc (Belley, 1937), 126–127.*
[41] Ch. 42 (PL 119:43). In ch. 72 Florus writes: "Totius namque ecclesiae vox est, id est sacerdotum et plebium" (63B); and ch. 64: "Sacerdotes et populus, universa scilicet ecclesia" (55D). Cf. Schulte, op. cit., 162f.
[42] Ch. 58 (col. 50D).

The *Ecclesia* or Christian Community

repeats in his commentary on the "*Unde et memores*": thus "*tum sacerdotes quam plebs fidelis offerunt*—both priests and faithful people make the offering."[43]

The formula used by Florus, "*quod enim adimpletur proprie ministerio sacerdotum, hoc generaliter agitur fide et devotione cunctorum*—whatever is done properly by the priest's ministry is, in general, also done by all through their faith and devotion"—an expression worthy of a St. Leo—has become a classic phrase.[44] It says a lot in a certain way, but its real meaning depends upon the ecclesiology within which it is used. The ecclesiology of Florus is still very close to that of the Fathers.

So is the ecclesiology of Paschasius Radbertus (+ 865). You can't have Christ without the church, he said. The church exists through Christ; it is born from his sacrifice which the church continues to offer in offering itself. It is in this act that the church becomes Christ's Body.[45] The idea of the liturgy that we will find later in the encyclical *Mediator Dei* is already present here.

One of the classic expressions of the idea of the spiritual presence of the whole church in every celebration, even private or solitary ones, is surely that of St. Peter Damian, the rough but tender hermit of Fonte Avellana. In commenting on the text of the Memento of the Living, he wrote (around 1048–1055):

> These words show us that the sacrifice of praise is offered by all the faithful, not only by men but also by women, even though it might appear to be offered in a special way by the priest alone. For that which the priest takes in his hands to offer to God, the multitude of believers also offers by the attentive devotion of their souls. This is brought to light in the following words: "This oblation of us, your servants, but also of your whole family, we beg you, Lord, to receive with kindness."
>
> If then we are the one body of Christ and if, while appearing to be separate in physical appearance, we are unable to be separated from

[43] Ch. 64 (col. 56A).

[44] Repeated by St. Peter Damian, *Liber qui dicitur Dominus vobiscum*, 10 (PL 145:239B); also by Innocent III, *De sacro altaris mysterio* III, 6 (PL 217:845D); and even by Pius XII, encycl. *Mediator Dei* (AAS, 39 [1947], 554).

[45] "Quia per aquam populus ablutus unda baptismatis significatur, et per sanguinem Christus, qui ex eo nos redemit: ac per hoc intelligitur et formatur Christus et Ecclesia unum corpus. Itaque nec Christus sine Ecclesia pontifex in aeternum nec Ecclesia sine Christo Deo Patri offertur," *Epist. de corpore et sanguine Domini ad Frudegardum* (PL 120:1352–1353); Schulte, op. cit., 180.

At the Heart of Christian Worship

one another because of the Spirit (we who live one same life in him),
what is wrong (I myself see nothing wrong) in our being united as
the faithful in the church's communal action even when we are physi-
cally separated, we who, by the mystery of our unity, are undivided
and so can never really be separated from the church? Because when
I pronounce the words of the church's common unity in my solitude,
I prove that I am still one with the church and that by a spiritual presence, I truly remain within her; and since I am truly a member of the
church, there is nothing wrong in the fact that I perform this office in
the name of my universality.[46]

Witnesses of the Eleventh and Twelfth Centuries

The authors whom we are about to meet—particularly Odo of Cambrai (+ 1113), who wrote in the final years of the eleventh century, and
Stephen, bishop of Autun, who wrote around 1170–1189—translate
the traditional theological understandings for a new climate. The traditional was inspired by the theology of the Mystical Body, to which
there is a strong attachment here. (We will come back to this.) The
change of climate that Dom Wilmart clearly observed in expressions of
piety can be best illustrated with respect to the Eucharist by these two
facts. Between the explications of the Mass composed at the beginning
of the ninth century and those composed in the middle of the eleventh,
there was introduced into the text of the Memento of the Living the
words which I will italicize in the following citation: "Quorum fides
tibi cognita est et nota devotio, *pro quibus tibi offerimus vel* qui tibi offerunt . . .—whose faith is known to you and whose devotion is recognized, *for whom we offer to you*, or who themselves offer to you . . ."[47]

The early church only had the experience of eucharistic celebrations
performed with the community actually present. However, private
masses, which had already appeared in the West in the seventh and
eighth centuries, had multiplied among hermits and monks by the
twelfth century. The actual participation of the faithful at Mass had
diminished. The meaning of the *vota* [offerings] of the faithful had
been spiritualized, interiorized, and moralized.[48] It is especially note-
worthy, then, how common it is, even in this new context, to describe

---

[46] *Liber qui dicitur Dominus vobiscum* (opusc. XI), c. 8 (PL 145:237); transl. *La Maison-Dieu* 21 (1950): 180–181.

[47] See below, n. 101.

[48] For example, Odo of Cambrai, *Expos. in can. missae* (PL 160:1057D): "audientes qui votis et orationibus assistunt cooperantes, et osculo pacis tanquam

a spiritual unity of all the faithful, brought about by the Holy Spirit, whether they are present or absent.[49]

This shows us that, although there are ecclesiological conditions that create a fully authentic liturgy, there can also be, under less than satisfactory conditions, a liturgy that still maintains a certain ecclesiological fullness. Despite the changes in the climate, the corporate sense of *ecclesia* and a real feeling for the Mystical Body remain very much alive. This is still true in the theology of the sacrament of penance.[50] Likewise, it is true in the theology of the Mass.

Odo of Cambrai describes the faithful who assist at Mass as true "cooperators." The sacred mysteries imply in their celebration not only the grace of God but also the communion of all the faithful (cf. above, n. 49); the priest is able to enter into the sacred action only with the assistance of the prayer of the assembly.[51] Guerric of Igny (?) goes

---

communicant, confirmantes quod actum est." Cf. A. Kolping, art. cit., 152; and also Stephen of Autun, *De sacramento altaris*, ch. 13 (PL 172:1288D): "Offerimus re, ipsi offerunt fide et devotione. Offerimus sacramenta conficiendo, ipsi offerunt vota solvendo, immolant sacrificium laudis, et reddunt Altissimo vota sua. Aiuti virtute sacramenti comprimunt ipsi vitia et peccata, in aedificando et Deo vovendo virtutes et bona opera. Offerimus vinum et oblatam, ipsi offerunt mentem sanctam et devotam . . ." It is no longer the bread and the wine that the faithful are offering, but their own life of devotion . . .

[49] Odo, op. cit., col. 1057B, addressing the question of private Masses, where the priest still uses formulas phrased the plural: "virtute totius communionis in Ecclesia confici sancta mysteria per gratiam Dei . . . secundum quem sensum in hoc loco circumstantes accipiuntur omnes ubique fideles"; Stephen of Autun, op. cit., col. 1289: "Ita, uno presente, sacerdos plures alloquitur et salutat, quia praesens astat omnis Ecclesia. Singula enim membra sibi invicem et capiti et corpori cohaerent quandiu vegetantur Spiritu Dei. Inde est quod non solum sacerdotes et clerus . . . , etiam et audientes osculo pacis communicantes cooperantur, et omnes ubicunque sint fideles, nulli separantur, nisi a corpore Christi praeciduntur."

[50] See, for example, Hugh of Amiens, *Dial.*, V, 19 and 20 (PL 192:1213); Master Bandinus, *Sent.* (PL 192:1101); Isaac of Stella, *Sermones* 11 and 42 (PL 194:1728, 1832).

[51] Op. cit., col. 1056D: ". . . Neque enim tanta sufficio sacramenta conficere, nisi collectae multitudinis adiustus oratione, quam prius etiam sum adhortatus ad orationes, dicendo: Orate, fratres . . ."; Stephen of Autun: "quotquot enim sunt de corpore Christi, quod est Ecclesia, salutantur: et eorum suffragia postulantur, quorum fides per gratiam Dei adiuvat fieri tanta mysteria (. . .) Haec oblatio non tantum est sacerdotis, sed cunctae familiae, id est cleri et

At the Heart of Christian Worship

so far as to say: "The priest does not sacrifice alone, he does not consecrate alone; rather the whole assembly of the faithful who are present
consecrate with him and sacrifice with him."[52]

Texts from the twelfth century that speak of the sacrifice the church
offers are numerous, but we cannot always attribute a technical theological meaning to them.[53] Their awareness that the priest offers the
sacrifice of the church led some theologians to hold that, outside communion with this church, the priest might consecrate but not really
offer sacrifice,[54] or even hold that he would not have the power to consecrate.[55] Nonetheless, for most theologians of the twelfth century the
use of convenient distinctions allowed them to address the question in
a more satisfactory manner (see below, n.142).

Some well-known texts of Innocent III will complete this review
of medieval authors. This pope wrote: "Although only one offers the
sacrifice, we always express ourselves in the plural [in the eucharistic
prayer]: '*we* offer,' because the priest does not sacrifice in his name

---

populi, et non assistentis familiae, sed totius Ecclesiae" (op. et loc. cit., col.
1289–1290); cf. Giraud de Barry (or de Galles), *Gemma Eccl.*: "et eorum suffragia postulantur, quorum fides per gratiam Dei adiuvat fieri tanta mysteria"
(ed. Brewer, II, p. 140).

[52] *Sermo* 5, 16 (PL 185:87AB); cf. A. Kolping, art. cit., 156.

[53] Here are some texts (verified) taken from references in F. Holböck, *Der
eucharistische und der mystiche Leib Christi in ihren Bezeihungen zueinander nach
der Lehre der Frühscholastik* (Rome, 1941), 226: Bruno de Segni, *Com. In Exod.*,
ch. 29 (PL 164:356D); Alger de Liège, *De sacramentis*, bk. I, ch. 16 (PL 180:789D);
Rupert de Deutz, *De div. off.*, bk. II, ch. 2 (PL 170:34 and 35: one finds here "offert Ecclesia" several times); Honorius Augustodunensis, *Gemma animae*, bk.
I, ch. 106 (PL 172:570: "Super quod altare [coelesti] Ecclesia hostias spirituales
immolat et super quod Deus vota fidelium et sacrificium iustitiae acceptat");
ch. 134 (col. 586D: "altare [the material altar in our churches] super quod sac-
rificatur et Christus super quem sacrificium Ecclesiae acceptatur"); Peter the
Venerable: "offert Ecclesia" (*Contra Petrobrusianos* PL 189:789B-C); "Unus est
populus christianus qui illud offert . . . et una fides per quam offert" (798A);
Eckbert de Schönau, *Sermones contra Catharos*, sermo 10 (PL 195:70B): "Ipse
(Christus) quotidie invisibiliter offert per manus Ecclesiae Deo Patri."

[54] Hölbock, op. cit., 236, cites Hugh of Rouen (d'Amiens) in this sense, Ger-
hoh de Reichersberg, and even Duns Scotus. See also A. Landgraf, "Zur Lehre
von der Konsekrationsgewalt des von der Kirche getrennten Priesters in 12.
Jahrhundert," *Scholastik* 15 (1940), 204–227 (= *Dogmengeschichte des Frühscholastik*,
III/2).

[55] Hölbock, ibid., cites Peter Lombard in this sense.

The *Ecclesia* or Christian Community

alone, but in the name (*in persona*) of the whole church"[56]; "We can also understand the phrase, 'For whom we offer, or who themselves offer' in this sense, that all the faithful make the offering, not only the priests. For that which is brought about in a special way by the ministry of priests is also done in common through the intention [*vota*] of the faithful."[57]

To be frank, with Innocent as well as with Odo of Cambrai and Stephen of Autun, the *votum* of the faithful seems to be interpreted in a way that is *moral* rather than truly *liturgical*. From this time on, this tendency becomes rather general, as we see attested in the commentary of Albert the Great (otherwise beautiful and profound).[58] What is common to the whole community, to the whole body that is the church, is the service of the prayer—the chants and the responses made chorally. St. Thomas also distinguishes between what the priest does *in persona totius Ecclesiae*, namely, the liturgical prayers, and what he accomplishes *in persona Christi*, namely, the consecration of the bread and wine.[59]

II. WHAT IDEA OF THE CHURCH IS CONVEYED BY THIS THEOLOGY?

a) Most of the texts we have cited here are anterior to the treatises on the sacraments that were the fruit of the first scholastic period ("Frühscholastik") in the twelfth century. It was then that the theology of sacramental character was developed on the basis of the New Testament, the events and texts of the early church, and above all the teaching of

---

[56] *De sacro altaris mysterio*, III, 5 (PL 217:844C). More than a half-century earlier, there is a similar formula in the *Summa Sententiarum*, tr. 6, ch. 9: "nullus in ipsa consecratione dicit *offero*, sed *offerimus* ex persona totius Ecclesiae" (PL 176:146).

[57] Op. cit., III, 6 (col. 845D).

[58] *De Missa*, III, 7: "specialiter enim voto offerunt illi qui se et sua deferunt ad altare. Et ideo specialiter illi in altaris oblatione continentur et offeruntur: quia sicut sacerdos offert mysterio, ita illi offerunt spirituali voto" (ed. Borgnet, XXXVIII, 108).

[59] Cf. St. Albert, *IV Sent.*, dist. 24, art. 20 (XXX, 56–57): "hoc esse officium communitatis et totius corporis Ecclesiae in devotione Deo servientis, et non officium ministrorum et ministri sint, ac subinde totum conventum fidelium *posse* esse chorum et respondere precinentibus in laude Dei . . . quia hoc officium de se commune est omnibus christianis." St. Thomas, *Summa Theol.*, III, q. 82, above all art. 1 and 6.

At the Heart of Christian Worship

St. Augustine against the Donatists.[60] There developed, particularly in the writings of St. Thomas Aquinas, the idea of a cultic and liturgical power attached to the characters of baptism and confirmation.[61] In the scholastic systems of the thirteenth century this cultic power becomes the foundation for the participation of the faithful as actors in the liturgy, even if not as the primary subject of liturgical action conceived organically and holistically. The preoccupation of this period was exactly the *power* that each one had or didn't have to do something.[62]

However, the older authors we have already cited did not appeal to a liturgical power possessed by each individual, nor to a power to celebrate that belongs to the faithful. For them, the affirmation of a universal participation was rooted in the fact that the faithful live in the unity of the church and are members of the Body of Christ.[63] Their point of view was both mystical and corporate, and it depended directly upon the fact that the faithful are only one body in Christ. The

[60] For the early church, see the work of F. J. Dölger; for St. Augustine, see N. M. Häring, "St. Augustine's Use of the Word Character," *Medieval Studies* 14 (1952), 79–97; *idem*, "Charakter, Signum und Signaculum: Die Entwicklung bis nach der karolingischen Renaissance," *Scholastik* 30 (1955), 481–512; for the 12th and 13th centuries, see F. Brommer, *Die Lehre vom Sakramentalen Charakter in der Scholastik bis Thomas von Aquin inklusive* (Paderborn, 1908); F. Gillmann, "Der 'sakramentale Charakter' bei den Glossatoren . . . ," *Der Katholik*, IV-F, 5 (1910/1), 300–314; "Zur Lehre vom 'sakramentalen Charakter,'" ibid., IV-F, 6 (1910/2), 215–218; J. Lécuyer, *Le sacerdoce dans le mystère du Christ* (Paris: Cerf, 1957), 270f.; G. Galot, *La nature du caractère sacramentel: Etude de théologie médiévale* (Brussels and Paris: Museum Lessianum, 1957).

[61] See G. Thils, "Le pouvoir cultuel du baptisé," *Ephemerides Theologicae Louvanienses* 15 (1938), 683–689. Cf. St. Thomas, *Sum. Theol.*, IIIa, q.82, art. 1.

[62] The text of Albert the Great cited above is significant in this regard (n. 59), where we have emphasized the word *posse*; cf. his *IV Sent.*, dist. 17, art. 58 (Borgnet, XXIX, 754); dist. 24, art. 5 (XXX, p. 36); St. Thomas, *IV Sent.*, dist. 18, qa. 2, ad 1; dist. 24, q. 1, qa. 2, ad 3 and 4; *Contra Gentiles* IV, 74; *Supplement*, q. 34, ad 3, etc.

[63] In the documentation gathered by Schulte, see in particular texts by Isidore, Felix of Urgel, Beatus, and Bede. This same view was often expressed: see, for example, B. Botte, L. Charlier, A. Robeyns, B. Capelle, *Le sacerdoce des fidèles: Cours et conférences des Semaines liturgiques XI* (Louvain, 1933); F. Holböck, op. cit., (n. 53), 227–228. Pius XII in *Mediator Dei* brought together the point of view of the early church with that of the scholastic period but not without allowing Scholasticism to cast a cryptic shadow upon the early church's witness.

The *Ecclesia* or Christian Community

deepest motivation of the point of doctrine that interests us here is essentially christological.

The fundamental intuition that inspired the ancient authors was the link between *caput* and *corpus*, Christ as Head and the church as his Body. The one does not exist without the other; they cannot be separated. Ever since Cyprian, the mixing of the water with the wine in the chalice [at the Offertory of the Mass] was seen to be significant—it is the symbol of the Christians joined to Christ.[64] Everything that Christ did to save us, he did as our head or leader. He did this for us, therefore, holding us in himself through it all[65] but in such fashion that he did it more on our behalf than in our place. So his Body, following him, is obliged to do the same through his power still active in the church. The ancient authors blend here, in a manner that is very profound, the theme of the Spouse with the theme of the Body, passing from one to the other by using the idea of Augustine, *Sponsus et Sponsa, una caro*, the husband and his spouse becoming one flesh.

The church was born from the side of Christ on the cross, according to the symbols of water and blood, just as Eve came forth from the sleeping Adam.[66] The church is thus, by its nature (by birth), linked to the sacraments and vowed to sacrifice. She is the Spouse and the Body of Christ-the-Priest, and definitively united with him so as to continue the unique and everlasting sacrifice that she offers day after day, with him and by his power. This is the foundation of the traditional idea of liturgy, put forward in our day by the encyclical *Mediator Dei* and by the council's constitution *Sacrosanctum Concilium* (which we will examine later on).

---

[64] St. Cyprian, *Epist.* 63, 12 and 13; St. Isidore, *De eccl. off.*, I, 18, 4f. (PL 83:755f.: "quae copulatio et coniunctio aquae et vini sic miscetur in calice Domini ut comistio illa ab invicem non possit separari, sicut nec Ecclesia a Christo potest dividi . . ."); Paschasius Radbertus, cited above in n. 45.

[65] See, again, Cyprian, *Epist.* 63, 13 and 68, 5 (Hartel, 711–754).

[66] Documentation is given in the classic article of Fr. S. Tromp, "De nativitate Ecclesiae ex Corde Iesu in Cruce," *Gregorianum* 13 (1932): 489–527 (found in German in *Zeitschrift für Asz. und Mystik* [1934]: 233–246). These ideas play a decisive role in the liturgical theology of the High Middle Ages. Cf. Isidore, *Quaest. in V.T.: in Gen.* (PL 83:217); and R. Schulte, op. cit., 34, 42, and 45; Felix of Urgel (in Schulte, 88); Beatus and Etherius (*idem*, 90); Bede (106–108); Theodulphus of Orleans (173); Angelomme of Luxeuil (178–179)—and the synthesis offered by Schulte, 187; Rupert of Deutz, *De Trinit.*, bk. XLII; *In Reg.*, bk. I, ch. 10 (PL 167:1077).

This mystico-christological point of view is what provides balance to the vision of the priestly role of the faithful. It is not a question of a simple link between two terms: *the faithful* and *hierarchical priests*. There is a third term, Christ, who embraces the other two and connects them organically. The whole body is priestly;[67] but it is so precisely insofar as it is the Body of the First and Sovereign High Priest, Jesus Christ,[68] who never ceases to act in the celebration of his Spouse as the First and Sovereign Celebrant.[69] It is he, first of all, who offers, and the church offers only because she is his body and because she follows him faithfully in everything. Jesus offers himself and he offers us. The faithful, his members, offer him as well, and themselves along with him.

But the *number* of faithful or the breadth of extension of the church does not affect the notion of the "Body of Christ" from the point of view of the liturgical celebration. The genuineness of the celebration is found in each concrete expression of the mystery of Christ in and by a Christian community, an *ecclesia*. From this point of view, there is no essential difference between the universal church and any particular

[67] See the dossier gathered by P. Dabin, *Le sacerdoce royal des fidèles dans la tradition ancienne et moderne* (Brussels and Paris: Museum Lessianum, 1950); J. Lécuyer, op. cit. (n. 60), pp. 171–228. The authors studied by Schulte often refer to the faithful as "members of the High Priest—or Sovereign Priest" (Agobard: 177), or they say that the faithful participate, as sons and daughters of the church, in the priesthood of the High Priest (Theodulphus: 173).

[68] Cf., for example, St. Gregory, *Hom. in Ev., II, hom. 31*, 8 (PL 76:1231D–1232A); Beatus and Etherius, *Ad Elipandum* (PL 96:936AB and CD; 1011); Bede, *De tabernaculo 3*, 12 (PL 91:492D); *Exp. in Lc.* (314C and 305D); *Explan. Apoc.* (PL 93:192C); and cf. Schulte, 107–108, for numerous other references.

[69] For the first three centuries, cf. G. Dix, *The Shape of the Liturgy* (Westminster, MD: Newman Press, 1945), 252–253. It is Christ who acts in all the sacraments: St. Augustine, *In Ev. Ioan.*, tr. V, 18 (PL 35:1424); it is Christ who offers and consecrates: Braulio of Saragossa (+ 651), Schulte, p. 81; Remy of Auxerre, *In Hebr.* (PL 117:874C); Florus of Lyons, *De act. miss.*, 43: "in oblatione divini sacrificii sacerdotes exhibent offerendi et supplicandi ministerium, sed Deus largitur benedictionis donum per unum et verum sacerdotem, per quem et oblata sanctificat, et sanctificata acceptat" (PL 119:44A; see also ch. 60, col. 52BC); Paschasius Radbertus, *De corp. et sang. Dom.*, 12, 2 (PL 120:1312); Pseudo-Alcuin, *Confessio fidei* IV, 1 (PL 101:1087); cf. M. Lepin, *L'idée du sacrifice de la Messe*, 2nd ed. (Paris, 1926), pp. 138–139, 179 (for William of Paris). For recent church teachings, cf. encycl. *Mediator Dei* (AAS 1947, p. 528); Vatican II, Constitution on the Sacred Liturgy, *Sacrosanctum Concilium*, 7; the Decree *Presbyterorum Ordinis*, 5.

The *Ecclesia* or Christian Community

genuine local assembly (cf. n. 154 below). It is this fact that justifies how certain early texts, speaking of the offering of the Eucharist by the *ecclesia*, seem to point to the local assembly, while others clearly seem to speak of the universal church. And sometimes these texts are phrased in such a way that it is impossible to be sure whether they mean the local or the universal.

The church is considered as the Body of Christ and as such is united in him. She is thus understood more in her mystical reality than in her social constitution or according to the juridical structure of the worship that she celebrates here below. (We cannot, however, oppose or separate these two points of view, as I will explain.) This is so true, that this *ecclesia,* which we describe as the subject of the eucharistic offering, includes the saints of heaven and the angels.[70]

This is an astonishing claim. Do the angels really offer the Eucharist? We can recall a great many ancient texts claiming the participation

---

[70] Tertullian talked of the angel who presides at baptism (*De bapt.*, 4–6). The angel of the *Supplices* of the [Roman] Canon, often interpreted as Christ himself, appeared in a number of medieval authors so as to imply a ministry of the angels in the celebration of the Mass (cf. B. Botte, "L'Ange du sacrifice et l'épiclèse au moyen âge," *Rech. Théol. anc. méd.* 1 [1929], 285–308; A. J. Jungmann, *Missarum sollemnia*, 2nd ed. [Vienna, 1949], vol. II, p. 281f.). A text of St. Gregory, "quis fidelium habere dubium possit in ipsa immolatione hora ad vocem sacerdotis coelos aperiri, angelorum choros adesse, summa et ima sociari . . ." (*Dial.*, IV, 58: PL 77:425), was often cited in the Middle Ages; cf. M. Lepin, op. cit., 40–41. *L'expositio antiquae liturgiae gallic.*, wrongly attributed to St. Germanus of Paris, says: "dum sacerdos oblationem confrangeret, videbatur quasi angelus Dei membra fulgentis pueri cultro concaedere (. . .) quia tunc coelestia terrenis miscentur, et adorationem sacerdotis coeli aperiuntur" (PL 72:94). Bede, who was afraid if he missed a ceremony that the angels taking part in it would be astonished at his absence (*Monumenta Germaniae Historica, Epp.*, IV: 443), wrote also: "Jesus qui altaribus sacrosanctis . . . adesse non dubitatur, astantibus sibi ministris coelestibus" (*Expos. in Lc.*—PL 92:597D); these very expressions were repeated by Florus of Lyons, *De act. miss.*, 66 (PL 119:60AB). See also Bede, *In Cant.*, bk. 5 (PL 91:1183A-C). Bernold of Constance, in his *Micrologus*, edited under Pope Gregory VIII (ch. 11—PL 151:984B), echoes the common belief about "supernorum civium ordines . . . eisdem mysteriis . . . interesse creduntur." Toward the end of the 11th century the idea was widespread that the Church of Saint Denis [Paris] had been consecrated by Christ himself, assisted by heavenly angels: Suger thought that this miracle might be repeated in 1144 (cf. *De consecr. Eccles. S. Dionysii*, ch. 6; L. Liebmann, "La consécration légendaire de la basilique de St-Denis," *Le Moyen*

At the Heart of Christian Worship

of the saints of heaven in the liturgical action. Nothing shows more clearly than this that the church is imagined here as essentially a communion in the actual life of Christ. From this point of view, perhaps, we should be led to give to expressions like *offerre* a meaning somewhat less precise than some contemporary explanations.[71]

b) Since the Fathers speak in such a variety of ways about this Body of Christ (*ecclesia*) which is the subject of liturgical celebrations, it is important to identify and recognize these differences. Here I will aim to clarify their thought.

First, there are two aspects which are related one to another but are not totally the same. On the one hand, the Body is the totality of the faithful, the *ecclesia*, the "we" when we say "we Christians."[72] On the other hand, the *ecclesia* is even more than that. It represents a reality in

---

Âge, 3rd series, 6[1935] 252–264; E. Panofsky, *Abbot Suger* [Princeton, 1946], 114; M. Aubert, *Suger* [St. Wandrille, 1950], 159). There were many other similar legends (cf. J. Leclerq in *Rev. Mabillon* 33 [1943] 74–84, to which even St. Thomas makes allusion in *Sum. Theol.* III, q. 64, art. 7). A Benedictine author of the 12th century writes that St. Benedict, for whom no early witness claimed ordination, had been ordained "invisibiliter et divinitus . . . a Pontifice et Episcopo episcoporum," that is, by Christ in person (cf. J. Leclercq, "Un débat sur le sacerdoce des moines au XIIe siècle," *Studia Anselmiana* 41 [1957] 111–112). In the 12th century people thought that the Virgin Mary and the saints took part in the Mass and that sometimes the angels served Mass (cf. F. Heer, *Die Tragädie des hl. Reiches* [Vienna-Zurich, 1952], 193). In his notes, Heer makes reference to *Heinrich von Melk* (v. 1160), ed. V. R. Heinzel (Berlin, 1867), 111. Peter Lombard (*IV Sent.*, dist. 13) claims that a priest who leaves the church lacks the power to consecrate, since the angels *qui huius mysterii celebrationi assistunt* will refuse to give him their necessary collaboration. The idea that the angels celebrate the glory of God along with us is traditional (cf. G.M. Colombas, *Paraiso y Vida Angelica* . . . [Monserrat, 1958], 226f.). For these same ideas in the Eastern Church, cf. R. A. Klostermann, *Probleme des Ostkirche* . . . (Göteborg, 1955), 48–50.

[71] The encyclical *Mediator Dei* proposes to give a precise definition of the meaning of this term: *Acta Apostolicae Sedis* (1947): 555. English translation, *Mediator Dei: Encyclical Letter of Pope Pius XII on the Sacred Liturgy*—Vatican Library Translation (Washington, DC: N.C.W.C., 1948), nos. 93, 35. R. Schulte addresses the meaning of *offerre, consecrare, conficere* in early church texts, especially with reference to Isidore (45f.).

[72] For Ante-Nicene antiquity, cf. K. Delhaye, *Ecclesia Mater chez les Pères des trois premiers siècles* . . . , Préface by Y. M.-J. Congar—*Unam Sanctam* 46 (Paris: Cerf, 1964). For St. Isidore, the subject of *offerre* is often "nos" or "christiani" or "fideles" (Schulte, 36), as is likewise the case in the Spanish-Visigothic liturgy (ibid., 61f. and 74f.), as well as in Bede (113).

The *Ecclesia* or Christian Community

itself to which we can attribute characteristics that cannot be verified of Christians taken individually (or as a simple collectivity).[73]

The church is Spouse, the church is Mother, the church is Temple. We can see in a similar way that "every soul is the church," that the liturgy freely passes back and forth in its prayer between the individual believer and the church.[74] It is also true that each Christian soul is spouse, temple, and exercises a spiritual maternity. But the church is Spouse in a unique way. She is the new Eve, born from the side of Christ on the cross. This idea, used already by Tertullian, appears countless times in the ancient authors, to the point that it would be difficult to find one from whom this image is absent (see n. 66 above). Likewise, the church in herself is sinless, while the faithful are weak and sinners. They need the church precisely in order to heal their wounds. The church as church remains always united to Jesus Christ.[75]

What does this mean? In becoming reintegrated into the unity of the church from which sin has alienated them, the faithful become more perfectly church. So we can see that even if it is the same reality and mystery which is realized in each one of the faithful individually, in the collectivity of the faithful, and in the *ecclesia* as such, that reality and mystery have a depth of meaning and a fullness of significance in the church that is unlike anything else.[76] The church is the *person* to whom the Spirit is always promised. She is the *milieu* or the organism into which each one is grafted by baptismal incorporation.

---

[73] For Bede, the existence of the church often appears to be anterior to its members (Schulte, 113–116).

[74] For the theme "every soul is the church," see: Origen, Ambrose, Augustine, Bede (*In Cant.*, bk. 5, n. 26: "et ecclesia omnis, et anima quaequae fidelis," PL 91:1184D); Bernard, Peter Damian ("quaedam minor ecclesia": *Liber Dominius vobiscum* 10, PL 145:239), etc. Numerous texts are found in H. de Lubac, *Catholicisme* (Paris, 1938), 151f.; *Méditation sur l'Eglise* (Paris, 1950), 270; *Exégèse médiévale*, vol. I/2 (Paris, 1959), 559, 562, 586f. For prayer passing from the individual to the church, see "mozarabic liturgy" in Schulte, op. cit., 71 n. 374; 72 n. 380; and 75 nn. 388 and 389; also Peter Damian, op. cit., which gives a justification of the whole discussion.

[75] There are several texts supporting this, taken from the Spanish-Visigothic Liturgy, in Schulte, op. cit., 70. The prayer before the communion of the priest, *Domine Iesu Christe*, comes from the Gallican Liturgy: "ne respicias peccata mea sed fidem Ecclesiae tuae."

[76] These ideas are tied up with the theology of penance, the history of which has been studied by B. Poschmann. See the treatment of the same themes in

Likewise, if we follow the thinking of the Fathers about the spiritual maternity of the faithful, we come upon this question: how can you attribute maternity to Christians who are themselves children of the church? St. Ambrose and St. Augustine gave this answer: the faithful, taken separately or individually, are sons and daughters of the church; but if taken together, inserted corporately into its unity, they form the *Ecclesia-Mater*, and as such they give birth to souls.[77]

The reason is always the same: the Holy Spirit is bestowed and operates within the unity of the church. St. Augustine particularly developed this doctrine that is at once ecclesiological and pneumatological. It is the heart of his ecclesiology. For Augustine, someone can belong to the church insofar as it is a means of grace, *communio sacramentorum*, but that will be spiritually "useful," bear fruit spiritually, and

---

J. A. Möhler, *L'unité dans l'Eglise*, (Appen. XIII); B. F. M. Xiberta, *Clavis Ecclesiae: De ordine absolutionis sacramentalis ad reconciliationem* (Rome, 1922); B. Poschmann, *Paenitentia secunda: Die kirchliche Busse im ältesten Christentum bis Cyprian und Origines* (Bonn, 1940), and his article in *Münchener Theologische Zeitschrift*, 1950, fasc. 3; Karl Rahner, "La doctrine d'Origène sur la pénitence," *Recherches de Science Religieuse* 37 (1950), 47–97, 252–286, 422–456 (as well as the last two articles here); "Vergessene Warheiten über das Bussakrament," *Geist und Leben* 26 (1953): 339–364, 363; *De poenitentia: Tractatus historico-dogmaticus*, 3rd ed. (Innsbruck, 1955), 382f.; M. Schmaus, "Reich Gottes und Bussakrament," *Münch. Theol. Zeitschrift* 1 (1950): 20–36 (p. 31); *Kathol. Dogmatik*, vol. III/2 (1941), 387, and vol. IV/1 (1952), 527f.; C. Dumont, "La réconciliation avec l'Eglise et la nécessité de l'aveu sacramentel," *Nouvelle Revue Théol.* 81 (1959), 577–597; this article cites (in the same sense) E. Schillebeeckx, *De Christusontmoeting als sacrament van de Godsontmoeting* (Antwerp, 1957), 152; K. Rahner, "Busse," *Lexikon für Theologie und Kirche*, vol. 22 (1958), cols. 826–838. According to this theology, it is the integration or reintegration of the sinner into the *unitas* of the church that confers the Spirit and forgives our sins. We find texts of St. Augustine saying this: "Ecclesiae caritas, quae per Spiritum Sanctum diffunditur in cordibus nostris, participum suorum peccata dimittit, eorum autem qui non sunt eius participes, tenet" (*In Ioan. Ev.*, tr. CXXI, 4–PL 35:1958); "Pax Ecclesiae dimittit peccata et ab Ecclesiae pace alienato tenet peccata" (*De bapt.* III, 18, 23–PL 43:150); "quos civitas Dei recipiendo efficit innocentes" (*C. Crescon.*, II, 13, 16–PL 43:476). Cf. also K. Adam, *Die kirchliche Sündenvergebung nach dem hl. Augustinus* (Paderborn, 1917), 101–116.

[77] St. Ambrose, *Expos. in Luc.*, VIII, 73: "filii singuli, universi parentes" (PL 15:1879); St. Augustine: references found in my preface to K. Delhaye (op. cit., in n. 72), 8 n. 3.

The *Ecclesia* or Christian Community

offer salvation only if (through these means and even beyond them) he or she participates by way of *caritas* [charity] in the *unitas* [unity] of which the Holy Spirit is the principle. This is the aspect of the church as *communio sanctorum*—the communion of saints, where the faithful orientate themselves toward ecclesial unity by a "social love," living by the Holy Spirit in both *caritas* and *unitas*.[78]

This theology inspired a schema for ecclesiology that was common in the West in both ancient and medieval times. To give an example, in the twelfth century theologians commonly distinguished two stages in the building up of the church.[79] The church is seen first as a *congregatio fidelium*, a community gathered together in and through faith. Then it is constituted as the Body of Christ by the Holy Spirit. The Body of Christ is there when the Holy Spirit is there; these two are correlative realities. The christological principle from which the church takes its structure is completed by a pneumatological principle from which it obtains its source of life. The Holy Spirit is actually the principle of our communion with Christ and, in Christ, among ourselves. The Holy Spirit is the principle by which the faithful form themselves into an *ecclesia*, and thus become the organic unity of the body of Christ, the subject of liturgical actions.[80]

c) This entire theological perspective must be understood in the context of communion through the Holy Spirit. However, that certainly does not imply a misunderstanding of the hierarchical structure of the church, nor a purely spiritual vision of ecclesiology that is exclusive of, negative toward, or ignorant of the existence of a public ministerial priesthood. Nonetheless, it is true that the category or the value by which the church is grasped here is, first of all, that of its spiritual communion.

---

[78] See F. Hoffmann, *Der Kirchenbegriff des hl. Augustinus* (Munich, 1933), 263f., 266–267; also refer to the two preceding notes, as well as my General Introduction to the *Traités antidonatistes* of St. Augustine (Paris, 1963), 95f.

[79] I think here of texts like St. Augustine, *De pecc. mer. et remiss.* I, 24, 34 (PL 44:128); Paschasius Radbertus, cited in n. 45; Rupert of Deutz, *De div. off.*, II, 6: "quod cum sint multi, sic per unam fidem unumque Spiritum in unum corpus Ecclesiae sint coniuncti" (PL 176:38D); Hugh of St. Victor, *De sacram.*, bk. II, chs. 1 and 2 (PL 176:215–217). See also F. Holböck, op. cit. (n. 53), pp. 215–217.

[80] Stephen of Autun, *De sacramento altaris*, 13: "singula enim membra sibi invicem et capiti et corpori cohaerent quamdiu vegetantur Spiritu Dei" (PL 172:1289); according to Honorius Augustodunensis, it is the Holy Spirit who creates the unity of the three "bodies" of Christ: *Eucharistion seu de corp. et sang. Dom.*, ch. 1 (PL 172:1250).

At the Heart of Christian Worship

The Fathers and the High Middle Ages considered first of all the heavenly (or eschatological) reality (*res*) of the church, of which the *ecclesia peregrinans* [pilgrim church] is merely the beginning. This is evident even in the language they used. The ancient period doesn't distinguish between the church militant and a glorious church triumphant, as theologians will do in the second half of the twelfth century. Rather, they speak of a single church, one part of which is found still in exile—*peregrinans*, on the way—while another part is rejoicing already with the angels in the peace and blessings of the City of God.[81]

Only under the pressure of heresy and of the reflective analytical thinking proper to Scholasticism will a theology of the church on earth come to be elaborated. In the twelfth century there are treatises on the sacraments, on the sacrament of holy orders among others, defined in terms of the granting of a *power*. Popular heresies and lay spiritual movements, generally anti-ecclesiastical or anti-hierarchical, required a clarification of the conditions for the church to exist as a historic organization instituted by Christ.[82] The Reformation of the sixteenth century, by denying the very existence of a hierarchical priesthood and of a hierarchical, divinely instituted pastoral power derived from the apostles, brought the church not only to develop and affirm its institutional reality more strongly but also to introduce this institutional aspect into the very definition of the church militant (cf. St. Peter Canisius, St. Robert Bellarmine).

The High Middle Ages has not yet come to this. In addition, we sometimes find a certain imprecision in the way in which its theologians speak of the church and its priestly function.[83] Nevertheless, the Fathers and the High Middle Ages appreciated the sacramental, institutional, and hierarchical reality of the church as intensely as we. They knew and recognized as much as we do the reality and the role of the hierarchical priesthood. Without this priesthood, there would be

[81] See my article "Eglise et Cité de Dieu chez quelques auteurs cisterciens à l'époque des Croisades" in *Mélanges offerts à Etienne Gilson* (Toronto and Paris, 1959), 173–202 (190 and 202).

[82] See the ending of my article "Ecclesia ab Abel," in *Abhandlung über Theologie und Kirche: Festschrift für Karl Adam* (Dusseldorf, 1952), 79–108.

[83] An example is Florus of Lyons, whose understanding of *ecclesia* is sometimes the *circumstantes*, i.e., the faithful as distinct from the priest; sometimes the united local congregation, priest *and* faithful; and sometimes the whole church, including the angels and the blessed: cf. R. Schulte, op. cit., 162f.

The *Ecclesia* or Christian Community

the faithful, no doubt; but there would not truly be the "church."[84] In a certain way, they go even further than we in conditioning the spiritual life upon the sacramental and hierarchical institution. Precisely to the degree that the heavenly reality (*res*) exists for them in the pilgrim church, without the distinctions that later theology will develop, they find supernatural life and salvation within the visible church and its structures, understanding that outside of it there is only perdition and emptiness. It will be helpful to clarify further a number of questions that remain vague here, including the question under study.

III. HOW THIS VISION OF THE CHURCH WAS CHANGED AND SOMEWHAT OBLITERED

From a contemporary perspective, the history of ideas in ecclesiology shows us that we have passed from an ecclesiology of the *ecclesia* to an ecclesiology about *powers*, from an ecclesiology of communion and sanctity to an ecclesiology of institutions and the means of salvation founded by Christ. The development of ideas is often conditioned by a need to clarify and to insist on certain aspects in order to answer questions or to respond to contradictions. In any case, such a history begins with a consideration of some complex reality in a global way, and this can be the moment for a rich synthetic intuition. But then we distinguish and latch onto elements that best lend themselves to clarification.

At first we look at some evidently powerful influence in history, and then at the corresponding Christian reality as affected by that powerful influence. We look then at the Christian reality in itself and observe its manner of development. The early history of the idea of the maternity of the church, such as that written by J. C. Plumpe,[85] or the history of grace in the twelfth century, such as Z. Alszeghy[86] analyzed it, are two good examples of what I mean. In brief, we can note a tendency to pick out certain influences and to develop them with particular attention.

---

[84] The idea that there would be no *corpus* without the *caput* is used in this sense by Jonas of Orleans, *De instit. laicali*, II, 20 (PL 106:210).

[85] *Mater Ecclesia: An Inquiry into the Concept of the Church as Mother in Early Christianity* (Washington, 1943).

[86] *Nova creatura: La nozione della Grazia nei commentari medievali di S. Paolo* (Rome, 1956), esp. 80, 128, 156, 256 and the conclusion, 259f.

At the Heart of Christian Worship

Ecclesiology passed from a state where "church" was hardly at all considered in an institutional way, but was rather seen in the context of the mystery of salvation and of the communion of life with the blessed, to a state where the theory of the institution and institutional powers structured everything. Doubtless it would be legitimate to do a history of ecclesiology under the angle of the ideas of *corpus* and *caput*, body and head, at least as far as the West is concerned. The link between these two aspects has been examined quite a bit, although principally by developing more and more the consideration of *caput* and its value as somehow constitutive of *corpus*.

As far as ecclesiology goes, after the thirteenth century, attention passed from Christ-*Caput* to pope-*caput*.[87] As far as the sacraments go (especially holy orders, the theology of which became systematic in the twelfth century), they come to be considered more as *things* in themselves, separating them too much from the living person of Christ and from the Holy Spirit.[88] By contrast with the early church, the sacraments came to be considered less as acts of the church insofar as it prolongs Christ's presence, and they then lost touch with our communion in him and with him.

Certainly the decisive value of ordination has always been recognized. However, for the early church, it was the existence of the Mystical Body, the church, that made the sacraments and other ecclesiastical acts possible. As H. von Soden has said,[89] for Cyprian, the true sacrament was the church. We could call that, if you wish, a communitarian or *sobornost'* [communion] vision. From there, theology passed to a theology of powers considered in themselves and seen as sufficient in themselves. The very fact of possessing power permitted one to perform the sacraments and other ecclesiastical acts. St. Augustine's effort to link the sacraments to Christ, thus making them independent of the personal dispositions of the minister, bore fruit in new and different conclusions for another ecclesiology, where *unitas* and *caritas* no longer provided the balance that it did for Augustine himself.

----

[87] H. X. Arquillière made this observation with respect to the rapport between a text of Gregory the Great and a remark of Boniface VIII: *L'Augustinisme politique . . .* , 2nd ed. (Paris, 1955), 133 n. 5; *Saint Grégoire VII* (Paris, 1934), ch. IX.

[88] Cf. R. Graber, *Le Christ dans ses sacrements* (Paris, 1947), 11f., referring to J. Jungmann, *Die Frohbotschaft und unsere Glaubensverkündigung* (Ratisbon, 1936).

[89] "Der Streit zwischen Rom und Carthago über die Ketzertaufe," in *Quellen und Forschungen aus italienischen Archiven und Bibliotheken* 12 (1909), 41f.

The *Ecclesia* or Christian Community

Beginning with the twelfth century we can observe a correlative change of course in understanding the notion of *ordo* as designating the hierarchical priesthood. *Ordo* was a notion that previously had been organic and corporate or collegial, but that now passes over to meaning the power given by ordination that is personally possessed by an individual.[90] Is there a tendency here to isolate the ministerial priesthood? In a way, such a tendency is already observable from the fourth century on.[91] But is hierarchical priesthood now given a new value with respect to the *ecclesia*?

For the Fathers, the principal and most excellent part of the church was genuinely spiritual persons, the martyrs, the ascetics, and the saints. They were the ones who most of all realized the qualities of "Spouse"—of the maternity attributed to the church. After Gregory VII, however, these qualities are transferred conceptually to the institution and to hierarchical persons as such.

The pope and the priest become the *homo spiritualis*,[92] and the notion of the *Ecclesia-Sponsa-Mater* becomes transposed from the *mystical perspective* of the spiritual generation of Christians by holy souls and by the community to the *perspective of church authority*, that is to say, of the priesthood. The Spouse has the authority of her Consort, the *Mater* becomes a *Magistra*.[93] Hierarchical personalities take a higher and higher profile. The Augustinian theme (even more generally, the African theme) of Peter as figure of the church does not completely disappear, but it is more and more eclipsed by that of the *potestas* [power] personally possessed by the pope, "the vicar of Jesus Christ."

[90] Cf. P.-M. Gy, "Remarques sur le vocabulairre antique du sacerdoce chrétien" in *Etudes sur le sacrement de l'Ordre—Lex Orandi* 22 (Paris: Cerf, 1957), 125–145 (130–131). We can observe a trace of the ancient collegial meaning of *ordo* in St. Thomas, *IV Sent.*, dist. 4, q. 1, art. 2, sol. 1.

[91] See G. Dix, op. cit. (in n. 9), 132f.

[92] I intend to explore this point elsewhere with the seriousness it deserves.

[93] This idea is proposed in the False Decretals from the mid-9th century; it is often found in Gregory VII (see the references in *Sentire Ecclesiam: Festschrift H. Rahner* [Freiburg, 1961], 203 n. 25), in the Gregorian writers, in St. Anselm (see *Spicilegium Beccense*, I [Le Bec and Paris, 1959], 371f.), in John of Salisbury, etc. See A. L. Mayer (Pfannholz), "Das Bild der Mater Ecclesia im Wandel der Geschichte," *Pastor Bonus* 53 (1942): 33–47; "Das Kirchenbild des späten Mittelalters und seine Bezeihungen zur Liturgiegeschichte," in *Vom christl. Mysterium: Ges. Arb. z. Ged. v. O. Casel* (Dusseldorf, 1951), 274–302 (284f.).

At the Heart of Christian Worship

In the theology of penance it is the power of the priest, not the role of the *ecclesia*, that dominates. For a while two ideas of the church coexist, sometimes one, sometimes the other becoming dominant. On the one hand, the church is seen above all as the community of the faithful given life by the Holy Spirit. On the other hand, the church is seen above all as the ensemble of persons who hold powers and priestly prerogatives, and who exercise the functions that flow from them.[94] We could find a number of passages where *ecclesia* really means specifically the clergy.

It is clear that if the liturgy is the worship of the "church," the idea of liturgical action can hardly be unaffected by the evolution that we have just evoked with these few examples. Josef Jungmann was right to claim that in order to answer the question, "What is the liturgy?" we have to ask first, "What do you mean by *ecclesia*—church?"[95] His own answer is interesting: the *ecclesia* is the spiritual assembly of brothers and sisters (gathered in the faith), brought about by an act of the Lord and by his presence in their midst.

This answer goes back to an idea that is biblical and that also represents the most ancient Tradition. This is the Tradition that is found integrated into the liturgy and into its own usage of the word *ecclesia*. Jungmann's answer also retrieves the liturgy from a current, dominant for centuries, that linked the value of a liturgical action to an institution and to the ruling power of an authority, rather than to the activity of a community. Jungmann gave as an example the case of the priest saying his Breviary.[96]

Someone asked Fr. Karl Rahner what the well-known formula "to pray in the name of the church" meant. Rahner reacted by saying that it

[94] B. Tierney, *Foundations of the Conciliar Theology* (Cambridge, 1955), 23–24. In my *Jalons pour une théologie du laïcat*, p. 71 n. 40, I have given a series of texts (which could easily be amplified) where *Ecclesia* is used in the sense of "hierarchy, clergy, pope . . ."

[95] "Was ist Liturgie?" *Zeitschrift für Theologie und Kirche* 55 (1931): 83–102; reprinted in *Gewordene Liturgie* (Innsbruck-Leipzig, 1941), 1–27; cf. also *Questions liturgiques et paroissiales* (1959): 272f.

[96] Jungmann proposed this definition of the liturgy: "Liturgie ist der Gottesdienst der Kirche, das heisst: nicht nur der Gottesdienst den dir Kirche ordnet, auch nicht nur der Gottesdienst den die Kirche halten lässt, sondern vor allem *der Gottesdienst den dir Kirche hält*" (*Gewordene Liturgie*, 19). He should have put the words "die Kirche" in quotation marks, since they mean sometimes public ecclesiastical authority, sometimes the Christian community structured by the hierarchical priesthood—the "plebs sacerdoti adunata et pastori suo grex adhaerens," as the Constitution *Sacrosanctum Concilium* 26 puts it, in citing St. Cyprian.

The *Ecclesia* or Christian Community

is a fiction to speak about a "church" that is independent of its sanctified members. There is nothing more to add, beyond our union with Christ through grace; so there can't be, said Rahner, a surplus value that accrues to an act called an act of the church, beyond the reality of grace itself.[97] This position is analogous to one that he took on the question of the multiplication of eucharistic celebrations. But perhaps he is considering this too much from the perspective of the individual's union with God by devotion and grace, and not paying sufficient attention to the Traditional idea of the *ecclesia* and to the Holy Spirit present in *caritas* [charity] as the personal link of unity within the community of the *ecclesia*.

It seems to me that "praying in the name of the church" means something real for two reasons. First, it can signify praying the kind of prayer that the People of God has made its corporate prayer. Certain particular formulas, certain historical forms, have been sanctioned by those who have presided as pastors over the People of God, and these formulas have a unique ability to involve the faithful and organize their life. The matter of the judgment by authority concerning the authentic value of prayer falls into place here. But if it is a question of the prayer that the People of God as such pray, this prayer, by its form and content, needs to be homogeneous with the articles of faith and the worship that characterize this people. It needs to be coherent with revelation, the sacred mysteries, etc. Particular, local devotions normally are foreign to this unique quality of ecclesial prayer.

Second, "to pray in the name of the church" can mean to be involved in an act of prayer arising from a group which represents the church. *In nomine* [in the name of] is traditionally equivalent to *in persona (Ecclesiae)*—acting as church. A group of Christians gathered according to their customary practice *are*, for their part, the church and in communion with the whole church. This group is however not the whole; its prayer is the prayer of *a* church. It will not be the prayer of *the* church unless it verifies the qualities noted before, namely, a public witness and a recognized identity.

The process of development that we have been describing brought about the weakening of the priestly role of all the faithful, particularly in their offering of the Eucharist. The historical circumstances are clear enough. In Gaul at the end of the sixth century, people stopped

[97] K. Rahner, "Thesen über den Gebet 'in Namen der Kirche'," in *Zeitschrift für Theologie und Kirche* 83 (1961): 307–324; cf. also *Schriften zur Theologie*, vol. 5 (Einsiedeln, 1962), 471–493.

speaking Latin[98]; from the eighth century in the Frankish kingdom (in Rome in the eleventh century), the Canon of the Mass is recited by the priest in silence.[99] Other practices also accentuated the progressive mediation of the priest. This is evident in a number of the Explications of the Mass from around the year 800.[100] The altar is put at a greater distance from the people; in the ninth century, in place of the simple "*qui tibi offerunt*—who offer to you" of the Memento of the Living, the formula "*pro quibus tibi offerimus vel qui tibi offerunt*—for whom we offer or who themselves offer to you" was introduced.[101] In the twelfth century we see the priest begin to repeat the parts of the Mass that the choir or other ministers have sung.[102]

The sense of the celebration as an act of the *ecclesia* has been lost. The Mass has become the act of the priest, at which the faithful *assist*. When the Protestant Reformers desired to restore the community value of worship (*Gemeinde*), they did it under catastrophic conditions, not only denying the reality of the public priesthood of the ministers, but also in thinking only about the *communion* of the faithful, without recognizing their *offering* in terms of sacramental sacrifice.[103]

The idea of the priesthood of the faithful subsequenty underwent a devaluation at the hands of Catholic theologians. They reacted to Wyclif and the Reformers of the sixteenth century, who admitted only a priesthood that is uniquely and unilaterally the priesthood of the

[98] Cf. F. Lot, "A quelle époque a-t-on cessé de parler latin?" *Bulletin du Cange* 6 (1931): 97–159.

[99] C. A. Lewis, *The Silent Recitation of the Canon of the Mass* (Rome and St. Louis, 1962).

[100] The exposition *Primum in ordine* often speaks of the "sacerdos-clerus-plebs"; the exposition *Quotiens contra se* does so also, and it presents the Canon as something that the priest alone does; cf. R. Schulte, op. cit., 125–126 and 131–132.

[101] Jungmann, *Missarum sollemnia*, 2nd ed. (Vienna, 1949), vol. II, 204; A. Kolping (art. cit. in n. 28): 376 and 147; see also J. A. Jungmann, "Die Abwehr des germanischen Arianismus und der Umbruch der religiösen Kultur im frühen Mittelalter," in *Liturgishes Erbe und pastorale Gegenwart* (Innsbruck, 1960), 4f. Note that the addition "*pro quibus . . .*" is not found in the Roman Mass as it is exposed by Bernold of Constance under Grergory VII (*Micrologus*, ch. 23–PL 151:993B). See also P. Riché, *Education et culture dans l'Occident barbare: VIe-VIIIe siècles* (Paris, 1962), 546.

[102] Cf. N. M. Denis-Boulet in *L'Eglise en prière*, ed. A. G. Martimort (Paris, 1961), 299–300; and also L. Bouyer in *Dieu Vivant* 19 (1951): 87.

[103] Cf. G. Dix, work cited in n. 9, 136.

The *Ecclesia* or Christian Community

faithful. As a result, the Catholic position became this: the hierarchical celebrant is the one who really offers the Mass in the name of the church. The faithful only offer spiritually and mediately through the priest.[104]

Cajetan, in responding to Luther, claimed that the priestly dignity of the Christian community comes from the fact that certain ones are chosen and ordained from out of its midst, in order to become properly and personally priests. The faithful have a priestly character only *similitudinarie*, in a moral sense, through the exercise of the virtue of religion.[105] Theologians of that time, then, spoke of the faithful having only a "metaphorical share of the priesthood,"[106] a formula that the Second Vatican Council explicitly refused to adopt or encourage.

Even throughout the evolution traced here in a general way and illustrated by some particular examples, the traditional Catholic ideas continued to move forward in history. Their permanence was assured in the first place by the practice of the liturgy itself, that Holy Ark of the Tradition. The liturgy conserves within itself, even during periods that can barely understand it, the full substance of the mystery of God. Wherever the Latin liturgy was celebrated, people continued to say each day, "*Orate, fratres, ut meum ac vestrum sacrificium*—Pray, brothers [and sisters], that my sacrifice and yours . . . ," "*Haec dona, haec munera, haec sacrificia*—these gifts here present, this offerings, these sacrifices," pointing in this way to the offering of the faithful people. They continued to say "*qui tibi offerunt*—who themselves offer," "*oblationes servitutis notrae, sed et cunctae familiae tuae*—gifts of our loving service, but also of your whole family," "*nos servi tui et plebs tua sancta*—we your servants and also your holy people . . ."[107]

We can profitably look at a collection of theological interpretations given by important figures of this time. Nicholas of Cusa wrote: "*[fideles] simul cum ipso sacerdote hostiam offerunt*—[the faithful] together with the priest offer the sacrifice";[108] Adrian of Utrecht (Pope Adrian

---

[104] So Gabriel Biel explains, in a treatise that was widely disseminated at the end of the 15th and the beginning of the 16th centuries, *S. Canonis Missae Expositio*, lect. 22 and 29.

[105] Cajetan, *Jentaculum III* (French transl. by J. Coquelle and P. de Menasce in *Nova et Vetera* 14 [1939]: 274–283). See my *Jalons*, 240–241.

[106] See *Jalons*, p. 241 (references). Cf. S. Tromp, *Corpus Christi quod est Ecclesia II: De Christo Capite Mystici Corporis* (Rome, 1960), 317f.

[107] D. R. De Andrade, "Oblatio Capitis et Membrorum," *Revista Ecclesiatica Brasiliera* 22 (1962): 850–863.

At the Heart of Christian Worship

IV) said, "*Omnis missa fit vice universalis Ecclesiae et eius commissione—* Every mass is performed in the name of the universal church and by its commission";[109] and Benedict XIV spoke of the "co-offering" of the faithful in the Mass.[110]

But general affirmations of this kind were not sufficient. Given the technical precision of Scholasticism and the need to respond to the errors of the Reformers, it was necessary to be more precise. More than at other times perhaps, theology here depended on the state of the church's life, *following* its practice more than directing it. For instance, all this is needed as background to account for the classic explanation, given as a formula, by St. Robert Bellarmine. He said that the sacrifice of the Mass is offered by three "offerers": Christ, the priest, and the church. Christ offers by the ministry of the priest, who becomes in this way the representative of the Prime Mediator, at the head of the community for whom he offers. The church, which is to say the faithful, does not perform the eucharistic sacrifice by exercising a priestly act, but only by offering to the priest the matter for the sacrifice (the oblations or holy gifts), or by uniting themselves in will and desire to the act of sacrifice that the priest performs.[111]

I wonder if, in such an explanation, *all* the traditional values are really maintained. Clearly this kind of thinking is framed in terms of *power* rather than of *communion*. The priesthood of the minister is seen in its relationship not with the *Body* but with the *Head*, Christ, whom

---

[108] Cited by J. A. Jungmann, *Missarum Sollemnia*, 2nd ed. (Vienna, 1949), vol. I, 242, n. 44.

[109] *Quaest. in IV Sent.* (Paris, 1528), fol. 28b, cited by M. Lepin, op. cit., 230 n. 2.

[110] *De S. Missae sacrificio*, II, ch. 13, n. 12. For the specific context (communion given to the faithful with hosts consecrated at the same Mass), cf. *Questions liturgiques et paroissiales* (1950): 168–169.

[111] "Ecclesia non offert ut Sacerdos [Christ] per ministrum, sed ut populus per sacerdotem. Itaque Christus per inferiorem offert, Ecclesia per superiorem. Sacerdos enim quatenus talis major est reliquo populo, quippe qui, ut mediator quidam pro populo apud Deum intercedit, nec est proprie in ea re minister Ecclesiae, sed Christi principalis Mediatoris. Ex quo etiam sequitur, ut Ecclesia non proprie sacrificet exercendum actum sacerdotalem, sed tantum offerat sacerdoti rem sanctificandum, aut curet fieri sacrificium, aut certe consentiat in sacrificium et voluntate ac desiderio offerat, cum sacerdos offert." R. Bellarmine, *Controv. de Eucharistia*, bk. VI, ch. 4 (also: *De sacrif. Missae*, II, ch. 4); *Opera*, ed. Vivès, vol. IV, 373.

The *Ecclesia* or Christian Community

he represents in his role as Head and Mediator. The priest's action is considered perfect in itself; the *ecclesia* joins itself to his ritual action but not in any way so as to constitute its nature. The Mass is complete without the effective participation of the faithful or of a Christian community. This understanding created the problem which the Chancellor Bismarck, at the end of the nineteenth century, summarized in these terms:

> The two churches, Protestant and Catholic, have very different structures. The Catholic Church exists and fulfills itself through its clergy; it can subsist without a community—the Mass can be said without a community. The community is a useful object to affirm the function of the Catholic Church as a Christian society, but it is in no way necessary for the existence of the church. On the other hand, in the Protestant Church, the community is the complete foundation of the whole church. Any worship is unthinkable without the community. The entire structure of the Protestant Church depends upon the community.[112]

Clearly we can't remain at *that* point—and today we have the means to go beyond that Counter-Reformation vision. There has been a liturgical movement. It was able to give new life to texts and perspectives from the early church, powerfully contributing in this way to the renewal of a vision of the church that moves beyond legalism and reawakens its awareness of its profound nature as the Body of Christ. The liturgical movement restored to the life of the church the actions and the practice of a living participation of the faithful in liturgical action. "Active participation" became its key idea, on the authority of Pope St. Pius X,[113] a mandate repeated also by his successors.[114] There has been the teaching of *Mediator Dei* and of Vatican II. In the last part of my work here, I will attempt to integrate the developments of the modern period with the richness of the ancient Tradition.

---

[112] *Politische Reden*, vol. XII, 376.

[113] Cf. E. J. Lengeling, "Was besagt 'Active Teilname'," *Liturgisches Jahrbuch* 11 (1961): 186–188. So also *L'Eglise en prière*, ed. A. G. Martimort (Paris, 1961), 92.

[114] In particular, see Pius XI, Apost. Constitut. *Divini Cultus*, AAS 21 (1929): 39–40; Pius XII, encycl. *Mediator Dei*, AAS 39 (1947): 552, 555, 559, and his discourse of Sept. 22, 1956, to the Assisi Congress, AAS 48 (1956): 724. Cf. *Jalons*, 283.

At the Heart of Christian Worship

IV. A SYNTHESIS OF CONTEMPORARY CHURCH TEACHING WITH TRADITIONAL DOCTRINE

The fundamental question is the nature of the liturgy. But the nature of the liturgy is tightly linked to the nature of the church, the liturgy being the highest expression of the authentic nature of the church, as the constitution *Sacrosanctum Concilium* 2 clearly says. The question is fundamentally ecclesiological. With what idea of church are we operating? We might also ask ourselves: *"Pro quo supponit vox 'Ecclesia,'"* what meanings do we give to the word "church" when we say the church offers the Eucharist; and who is the subject of the church's liturgical actions?

We have to try to answer this question in rereading one after the other the two great documents of the magisterium which can give us the most help, the encyclical *Mediator Dei* of November 20, 1947, and the council's constitution [*Sacrosanctum Concilium*] of December 4, 1963. In fact, we might have been able to—perhaps should—make an appeal to the great *didascalia* [teaching] of the church which is the liturgy itself, the primary monument and witness of the Tradition. However, to go beyond what we have already done here and undertake a new exploration of the primitive Tradition would take us too far afield. It will be more profitable to carefully examine these two documents that are more didactic and more structured, in which the magisterium has interpreted and clarified the meaning of the Tradition.

We can observe the progress made between the first and the second of these documents, as to their awareness of the content of the Tradition. The constitution *Sacrosanctum Concilium* was given its formulation substantially by the Pontifical Preparatory Commission. Possibly if it had been composed and discussed after the dogmatic constitution *Lumen Gentium* [On the Church], it might have accentuated even more the points on which we can observe an advance over the encyclical *Mediator Dei*, from which it takes its fundamental teaching (sometimes even word for word).

As the constitution *Sacrosanctum Concilium* (26–32) says, the liturgy is an action that is at once hierarchical and communitarian. Exploring the interrelationship of these two essential values allows for the development of the necessary nuances. The great power of *Mediator Dei* is to have affirmed these two values together, but especially the communitarian value of liturgical action, based on the ecclesiology of the encyclical *Mystici Corporis* of June 29, 1943. From that point of departure, *Mediator Dei* was able to go beyond the juridical definitions and extrinsicist vision of the liturgy conceived as a "decorative ceremony"

The *Ecclesia* or Christian Community

49

or understood as "the ensemble of laws and prescriptions by which the ecclesiastical hierarchy organizes the regular execution of the sacred rites."[115]

Mediator Dei 20 defined the liturgy as "the public worship which our Redeemer as Head of the Church renders to the Father as well as the worship which the community of the faithful renders to its Founder, and through Him to the Heavenly Father. It is, in short, the worship rendered by the Mystical Body of Christ in the entirety of its Head and members."[116] The richest passages in which *Mediator Dei* speaks most positively of the liturgical action of the faithful, particularly in offering the Eucharist, are christological. In these texts, the faithful are considered as participating in the mystery of Christ by their union with him, their Head, their High Priest, and their Principal Celebrant:

> Sacraments and Sacrifice do, then, possess that "objective" power to make us really and personally sharers in the divine life of Jesus Christ. Not from any ability of our own, but by the power of God, are they endowed with the capacity to unite the piety of members with that of the Head, and to make this, in a sense, the action of the whole community. (MD 29)

> All the faithful should be aware that to participate in the Eucharistic Sacrifice is their chief duty and supreme dignity . . . together with Him and through Him let them make their oblation, and in union with Him let them offer up themselves. (MD 80)

> By the waters of baptism, as by common right, Christians are made members of the Mystical Body of Christ the Priest, and by the "character" which is imprinted on their souls, they are appointed to give worship to God. Thus they participate, according to their condition, in the priesthood of Christ. (MD 88)

> Now it is clear that the faithful offer the sacrifice by the hands of the priest from the fact that the minister at the altar, in offering a sacrifice in the name of all His members, represents Christ, the Head of the Mystical Body. Hence the whole church can rightly be said to offer up the victim through Christ. (MD 93) [*What follows explains the people's offering by the vota fidelium: the people offer because they are linked to Christ through and in the priest who represents the Head of the Body.*]

[115] *Mediator Dei*, AAS 39 (1947): 532. In the following passages, references to *Mediator Dei* will be indicated with reference to the text identified in n. 71 (above) and also found at www.vatican.va.

[116] AAS, 528–29. Cf. J. H. Miller, "The Nature and the Definition of the Liturgy," *Theological Studies* 18 (1957), 325–356.

At the Heart of Christian Worship

[New methods of participation in the Mass] foster and promote the people's piety and intimate union with Christ and His visible minister and . . . arouse those internal sentiments and dispositions which should make our hearts become like to that of the High Priest of the New Testament. . . . [T]hey also show in an outward manner that the very nature of the sacrifice, as offered by the Mediator between God and man, must be regarded as the act of the whole Mystical Body of Christ. (MD 106)

All of that is expressed in terms of christology (Christ as Head) and of the theology of the Mystical Body. However, when the encyclical *Mediator Dei* speaks in terms of *ecclesia*, it generally takes the word to mean the hierarchical institution, insofar as this is distinguished over against the faithful, and consists of priests, ordained in the line of the apostles, who exercise on behalf of the faithful a mediation in the name of the Christ-Head whom they represent.[117]

Before speaking of the Mystical Body in the manner we have just observed, *Mediator Dei* presented the hierarchical priesthood as an authority *over* the faithful, a mediation for their benefit more than a *ministry within* the body. This is why, from the beginning, it affirms the perpetuation of the priestly office of Jesus Christ by ordained priests. It is on this basis that the encyclical says: "The Church, faithful to the mandate received from its founder, continues the priestly function of Jesus Christ."[118] The priest represents the people before God because he represents Christ as Head.[119]

---

[117] "The Divine Redeemer has so willed it that the priestly life begun with the supplication and sacrifice of his mortal body should continue . . . in his Mystical Body which is the Church. . . . In obedience, therefore, to her Founder's behest, the Church prolongs the priestly mission of Jesus Christ mainly by means of the sacred Liturgy" (MD 2–3). "For He has not left mankind an orphan . . . , He aids us likewise through His Church . . . which he constituted the 'pillar of truth' and dispenser of grace . . ." (MD 18). "The Church has, therefore, in common with the Word Incarnate the aim, the obligation and the function of teaching all men the truth" (MD 19). "Like her divine Head, the Church is forever present in the midst of her children. She aids and exhorts them to holiness . . ." (MD 22). The "church" is taken in this same sense of a mediating institution in a number of texts of *Mediator Dei* (39, 69f., 119–120).

[118] MD 3.

[119] MD 84. Note 83 of the encyclical refers to the text of Bellarmine that we just cited above.

The *Ecclesia* or Christian Community

The encyclical correctly wanted to reject the idea that all the people might be the true celebrant, with the ordained priest as merely their delegate. We absolutely have to respect this teaching of *Mediator Dei* as dogmatically fundamental. However, we can't fail to notice a difference if we compare the manner in which the encyclical speaks about the celebration of the different sacraments and the part that the Christian people take in them, on the one hand, and the way in which the same subject is treated in the Dogmatic Constitution on the Church (*Lumen Gentium* 11), on the other.[120]

---

[120] Here are the texts that I have in mind:

MD 22: "Like her divine Head, the Church is forever present in the midst of her children. She aids and exhorts them to holiness, so that they may one day return to the Father in heaven clothed in that beauteous raiment of the supernatural. To all who are born to life on earth she gives a second, supernatural kind of birth. She arms them with the Holy Spirit for the struggle against the implacable enemy. She gathers all Christians about her altars, inviting and urging them repeatedly to take part in the celebration of the Mass, feeding them with the Bread of angels to make them ever stronger. She purifies and consoles the hearts that sin has wounded and soiled. Solemnly she consecrates those whom God has called to the priestly ministry. She fortifies with new gifts of grace the chaste nuptials of those who are destined to found and bring up a Christian family. When at last she has soothed and refreshed the closing hours of this earthly life by holy Viaticum and extreme unction, with the utmost affection she accompanies the mortal remains of her children to the grave, lays them reverently to rest, and confides them to the protection of the cross, against the day when they will triumph over death and rise again."

Lumen Gentium 11: "The sacred character and organic structure of the priestly community are brought into being through the sacraments and the virtues. Incorporated into the church by Baptism, the faithful are appointed by their baptismal character to Christian religious worship; reborn as sons and daughters of God, they must profess publicly the faith they have received from God through the church. By the sacrament of Confirmation they are more perfectly bound to the church and are endowed with the special strength of the Holy Spirit. Hence, as true witnesses of Christ, they are more strictly obliged both to spread and to defend the faith by word and deed.

"Taking part in the Eucharistic sacrifice, the source and summit of the Christian life, they offer the divine victim to God and themselves along with him. And so it is that, both in the offering and in Holy Communion, in their separate ways, though not of course indiscriminately, all have their own part to play in the liturgical action. Then, strengthened by the Body of Christ in the Eucharistic communion, they manifest in a concrete way that unity of the

At the Heart of Christian Worship

The ecclesiology of the two documents is not exactly the same. *Mediator Dei* has a beautiful theology of the liturgy, closely linked to the doctrine of the Mystical Body of *Mystici Corporis*, but it does not have an ecclesiology of the People of God, nor the order that *Lumen Gentium* established in its second and third chapters, nor the idea of servant-minister that runs through all the texts of Vatican II. *Mediator Dei* has a profound doctrine of the participation of the faithful, but it only goes halfway toward a healthy idea of the *sobornost'* [collegiality in the Holy Spirit] that the Tradition calls for. In this sense, the constitutions *Sacrosanctum Concilium* and *Lumen Gentium* seem to me to have taken a new step in the right direction. We can perceive this in the way in which the different documents address the question of a private Mass celebrated in the absence of the faithful or without a community.

Mediator Dei proposes two points with respect to private Masses:[121] (1) At the altar the priest acts as the representative of Christ, Head of Christians, and does so in the name of the faithful and with such power that "it is in no wise required that the people ratify what the sacred Minister has done"; (2) nonetheless, because of the dignity of so great a mystery, the priest should have a minister serve the Mass in conformity with canon 813.[122] *Mediator Dei* does not see in this server

---

People of God which this most holy sacrament aptly signifies and admirably realizes.

"Those who approach the sacrament of Penance obtain pardon through God's mercy for the offense committed against him, and are, at the same time, reconciled with the church which they have wounded by their sins and which by charity, by example and by prayer labors for their conversion. By the sacred Anointing of the Sick and the prayer of the priests, the whole church commends those who are ill to the suffering and glorified Lord that he may give them relief and save them (see Jas 5:14-16). And indeed, it exhorts them to contribute to the good of the People of God by freely uniting themselves to the passion and death of Christ (see Rom 8:17; Col 1:24; 2 Tim 2:11-12; 1 Pet 4:13). Those among the faithful who have received Holy Orders are appointed to nourish the church with the word and grace of God in the name of Christ. Finally, in virtue of the sacrament of Matrimony by which they signify and share in (see Eph 5:32) the mystery of the unity and fruitful love between Christ and the church, Christian married couples help one another to attain holiness in their married life and in accepting and educating their children. Hence in their state and rank in life they have their own gifts within the People of God (see 1 Cor 7:7)."

[121] MD 96. Cf. AAS, 560–561 and 562–563. See also Acts of the Council of Trent, session XXII, ch. 6: Denziger 944 (1747).

[122] MD 97. Cf. the Roman Synod of 1960, can. 571 (cf. MD 76, 61, n. 1).

The *Ecclesia* or Christian Community

some sort of representative or witness of the community. The conciliar documents don't go much further than this either.[123] Are we still in the situation described by Bismarck—a Catholic Church with no need of a congregation? Doubtless no, since each private Mass integrates the mystery of the adoration of Christ and a spiritual presence of the whole church. But is that enough?

The constitution *Sacrosanctum Concilium* follows the same theology of the liturgy as *Mediator Dei*. From the point of view of its ecclesiology, it is anterior to *Lumen Gentium*. Yet even in following closely the ideas of *Mediator Dei, Sacrosanctum Concilium* seems to me to set itself apart by some important nuances. Unless I am mistaken, the difference is here.[124] *Mediator Dei* passes directly from the ordination of the

---

[123] On this question of private Masses, two documents following *Mediator Dei* and even *Sacrosanctum Concilium* hold the same position as Trent and *Mediator Dei*, using however this phrase: "the Mass, even if it is celebrated alone . . . is an act of Christ and *of the church*" (Paul VI, encycl. *Mysterium Fidei*, Sept. 3, 1965, AAS 57 [1965], p. 761); "it is an act of Christ and *of the church*" (Decree *Presbyterorum Ordinis* 13, which makes reference in a note to *Sacrosanctum Concilium* 26 and 27. This last, SC 27, justifies the preference given to communal celebrations and adds: "This applies with special force to the celebration of Mass (even though every Mass has of itself a public and social character) . . ." I can testify from my personal experience that this particular note was *intentionally* added by the commission of the council.

[124] The point that I am raising here is extremely important, both for the equilibrium of our ecclesiology and for the dialogue between Protestant and Catholic theologians. Protestant ecclesiology moves from the apostles to the community of the faithful. The ministries, instituted or willed by the Lord in a general way, arise from the community as concrete experiences and are only vocations within the community. On the other hand, Catholic ecclesiology moves from the college of apostles to the instituted ministries that derive from the apostles, and then to the community—the apostles being (cf. *Ad Gentes* 5) in a representative way at one and the same time both the new People of God and the beginning of the (priestly) hierarchy. On this point, see M. Carrez, "Apostolat et Peuple de Dieu," *Verbum Caro* 71–72 (1964): 42–55; J. Ratzinger, "Les implications pastorales de la collégialité des évêques," *Concilium* 1 (1965): 33–55. In the texts of the early church, all this sometimes remains undetermined. St. Bede attributes to the church everything that has been transmitted by the apostles (cf. R. Schulte, op. cit., 109 n. 614; 116 n. 670; 117 n. 676). On the other hand, Florus of Lyons says that Christ transmitted the celebration of his sacrifice to the apostles and to the church (ibid., 160). J. Pascher, "Ekklesiologie in der Konstitution des Vaticanum II über die hl. Liturgie," *Liturg. Jahrbuch*, 14

---

apostles by Christ to the hierarchical priesthood, whereas *Sacrosanctum Concilium* passes from the mission of the apostles—a perpetuation of the mission of Christ—to the church, that is, to the *ecclesia congregata*.[125] The church, from its very beginning, has practiced a worship consisting of word and sacraments; this is clear from the witness of the apostolic period. *Sacrosanctum Concilium* 7 also affirms that Christ is always present within his church, "*Ecclesiae suae semper adest,*" and introduces its definition of the liturgy, taken from *Mediator Dei*, but in an ecclesiological context already somewhat different, for it is that of the church as the Body of Christ:

> Christ, indeed, always associates *the church* with himself in this great work in which God is perfectly glorified and men and women are sanctified. The church is his beloved bride who calls to its Lord, and through him offers worship to the eternal Father.

> The liturgy, then, is rightly seen as an exercise of the priestly office of Jesus Christ. In the liturgy the sanctification of women and men is given expression in symbols perceptible by the senses and is carried out in ways appropriate to each of them. In it, complete and definitive public worship is performed *by the mystical body of Jesus Christ, that is, by the head and his members.*

> From this it follows that every liturgical celebration, because it is an *action of Christ the priest and of his body, which is the church,* is a preeminently sacred action. No other action of the church equals its effectiveness by the same title nor to the same degree.[126]

A parallel text of Pius XI allows us to grasp the importance of this text's ecclesiology, because for Pius XI, *ecclesia* designates a

---

(1964): 229–237, studies the concepts and images of the ecclesiology used by *Sacrosanctum Concilium* in an extremely interesting way: Spouse (born from the wounded side of Christ), Body, People of God. He does not, however, treat the point under question here.

[125] The approach of the decree *Presbyterorum Ordinis* 2 is comparable to that of recent studies on the priesthood, such as R. Salaün and E. Marcus, *Qu'est-ce qu'un prêtre?* (Paris: Cerf, 1964), 137; L. Lochet, "Situation du prêtre dans l'Eglise," *Christus* 48 (Oct. 1965): 408–507.

[126] SC 7. I have italicized the words which indicate the ecclesiological meaning of the text. Cf., SC 83: "*illud sacerdotale munus per ipsam suam Ecclesiam peragit*—for it is through his church itself that he continues this priestly work."

The *Ecclesia* or Christian Community

hierarchical authority, as is frequently the case in *Mediator Dei* also. By contrast, it is instructive to analyze the meaning of *ecclesia* in *Sacrosanctum Concilium*. I don't claim to have made an exhaustive inventory, but the following examples are doubtless the principal ones, and they are significant.

The church is defined in SC 26 as "*unitatis sacramentum*, that is to say, the sacrament of unity, namely, the holy people united and organized under their bishops," with a reference to St. Cyprian.[127] This means a People of God who are thus structured and ordered. This church is essentially priestly and vowed to the worship of God. It is born on the cross, as Eve was drawn from the side of Adam; and therefore it is by its nature destined to be associated with the sacrificial worship that Christ rendered to the Father. The church is associated with Christ completely as Church-Spouse of the Body of Christ: "Christ, indeed, always associates the church with himself in this great work in which God is perfectly glorified and men and women are sanctified. The church is his beloved bride . . ." (SC 7; cf., SC 83). Here we are in harmony with the deepest themes of the Tradition.

Most particularly, in designating the authority that presides over the faithful, *Sacrosanctum Concilium* 14 and 21 employ the expression *Mater Ecclesia*, in these two cases in relation to "*populus christianorum—* the Christian people." Compare this with SC 4, 60, 102, and 122 (in these last two cases, one can't say clearly whether the expression is taken in a larger sense perhaps). Also, *Sacrosanctum Concilium* speaks of "*animorum pastores—*pastors of souls";[128] the government of liturgical activity is said to depend not on "the church," as Pius XI or Pius XII would still have said, but "*ab Ecclesiae auctoritate—*on the authority of the church" (SC 22; cf. above, n. 128).

One can hardly doubt that there is an underlying intention in all this, since the coherence of the passages makes the intention clear. We find a confirmation in what *Sacrosanctum Concilium* has to say about the Divine Office in 83 and the following paragraphs. There again, it takes up a notion already present in *Mediator Dei*. It characterizes the Office by its public character—it is an *instituted* form of prayer, "*oratio publica—*public prayer" (84, 90, 98). But *Sacrosanctum Concilium* insists

---

[127] *De Eccl. cath. unitate*, ch. 7 (Hartel, pp. 215–216); *Epist.* 66, 8, 3 (Hartel, 732–733).

[128] SC 14. Cf. my "Quelques expressions traditionnelles du service chrétien" in *L'Episcopat et l'Eglise universelle—Unam Sanctam* 39 (Paris: Cerf, 1962), 101–132.

At the Heart of Christian Worship

strongly on the communitarian character—virtually universal—of the praise of which Christ is the Principal Celebrant (SC 83, where one reads "Since the divine office is the voice of the church, of the whole mystical body, publicly praising God . . .").

Père Roguet aptly commented:

> The Council is not content to repeat the classic doctrine of the deputation of certain persons to the Divine Office; it enlarges and completes the picture. It understands the public prayer of the church as belonging to all the "states of perfection" (no. 98), and above all it underlines that all the faithful participate with the priest in this public prayer and invites them to become involved as often as possible (no. 100).
>
> Such a view of the Divine Office is more acceptable for the Oriental churches who separate the prayer of the priest from that of the assembly much less than we do in the West; and this wider scope is likewise demanded by a healthy view of the church. Understood in this way, the Divine Office has the two-fold character already noted in number 7 with respect to the liturgy in general: it is at once the voice of the Spouse addressed to Christ, and the prayer of the Whole Christ to the Father. All those who exercise this prayer in God's presence do so in the name of the church and fulfill the glorious role of the Spouse of Christ—precisely the deep meaning of the traditional expression "office of the church" (no. 85).[129]

Have we come closer than *Mediator Dei* to the values of the idea of *sobornost'* (that presence and participation of all the members of the church in its life and its corporate acts)? Yes, I think so. On the one hand, in *Sacrosanctum Concilium* 14 the active participation of the

---

[129] *La Maison-Dieu* 77 (1964/1): 162. The decree *Presbyterorum Ordinis* touches upon the question of the prayer of the Divine Office for priests. It situates the question within the status of the priest who is at one and the same time the minister of Christ, Head of the Body, and also the representative of the ecclesial community—itself representative and mediator for the world (*pars pro toto*). So we read the following: "By praying the Divine Office, priests themselves should extend to the different hours of the day the praise and thanksgiving they offer in the celebration of the Eucharist. By the Office they pray to God in the name of the church for the whole people of God entrusted to them and in fact for the whole world" (PO 5); and, "In reciting the Divine Office they lend their voice to the church which perseveres in prayer in the name of the whole human race, in union with Christ who 'always lives to make intercession for them' (Hebrews 7:25)" (PO 13).

The *Ecclesia* or Christian Community

faithful is founded upon: (1) the very nature of the liturgy as the activity of the Mystical Body; and (2) "the right and the duty" of the Christian people insofar as they are "a chosen race, a royal priesthood, a holy nation, a redeemed people" (1 Pet 2:9; cf. 2:4-5). In addition, SC 31 prescribes that "when the liturgical books are being revised the rubrics should indicate the people's parts."

Elsewhere, in the very important section on the norms drawn from the nature of the liturgy insofar as it is the hierarchical action of the community (SC 26f.), we find the two following values presented in this order: (1) the value of "church" taken as a unity or community, ". . . of the whole body, the church";[130] (2) the value of the organic distribution of activities among the members of this body "in different ways, depending on ranks, roles and levels of participation." From these principles flow some important consequences. First, a communal celebration must be preferred to a private one because, among other reasons, each member in the body accomplishes a meaningful role (SC 27). It follows that the part in the celebration assured by a member of the assembly is a genuine ministry[131] and that this part should be done in such a way so as not to be repeated or redone by the presider, that is, by the priest who here represents the Head, *caput*.[132] This is a small step, perhaps, one which was reintroduced under Pius XII in the restoration of the Paschal Vigil. But it is part of a Tradition which ought never to have been broken.

This is a simple practical law that should always have been self-evident. However, few prescriptions of *Sacrosanctum Concilium* have had so great an ecclesiological significance. We shall see this as we move along. We said above that the history of ecclesiology might have

[130] I think, and I could demonstrate, that this is how we should translate *corpus Ecclesiae* here and almost everywhere else.

[131] On the theme of ministries, see my contribution in *Le diaconat dans l'Eglise et dans le monde—Unam Sanctam* 59 (Paris: Cerf, 1966), 121–141.

[132] SC 29. In this perspective, the word "participation," although it means that each one should contribute his/her own part, may seem insufficient. At least, it needs to be given its full force. You can find in *La Maison-Dieu* 77 (1964/1): 55–56 the historical exposé of the suppression of this doubling. Cf. *Novus Rubricarum . . . Codex*, 1960: "The Mass requires by its very nature the participation of all those who are present to it, according to their particular status." The decree of Feb. 9, 1951, on the Paschal Vigil, ch. 4, no. 15, says the same thing: see the commentary of Dom L. Beauduin in *La Maison-Dieu* 26 (1951/2): 106–107.

At the Heart of Christian Worship

been written under the angle of the fate of the schema *corpus-caput*, body-head. Often enough, the term *head* absorbed the term *body*. Can we now begin to overcome this abuse that has gone on for centuries?

Clarifications and Synthesis

Let us now take the perspective of an organic look at the liturgy, whose purpose is the salvation of the faithful. When we speak about an organism, we are talking about a vital unity of activities and of objectives, brought about by the collaboration of multiple members or organs, each of which has its own proper activity. The member's activity is both partial (in the sense that it performs a particular service) and total (in the sense that this service is for the benefit of the whole and ensures the integrity of the life of the whole).

The Fathers often employed the example of a chorus and of the harmony in which each one plays or chants his or her part.[133] That kind of harmony is the ideal for liturgical acts. In the celebration of the Eucharist, in particular, the priest should not desire to *do* everything or to *say* everything. Evidently he remains the one who alone speaks out loud to accomplish the consecration and pronounce the *anaphora* [Eucharistic Prayer]. However, too juridical a perspective here, with regard to the sacraments as well as with regard to the church, might lead one to fail to see something of great importance. Effectively, from a purely canonical point of view, the community or the faithful contributes nothing to the strict validity of the Mass, which depends upon the ritual power of the public or hierarchical priesthood.[134] However, we should note that, from the point of view of strict validity, a priest, in order to consecrate, must still make reference to the faith of the church and desire to do what the church believes.[135]

But the eucharistic celebration cannot be reduced to a valid consecration. It is a liturgical act, and it achieves its objective only if it ensures at one and the same time the two ends of glorifying God and of sanctifying the faithful. The Mass is not something that belongs to the

---

[133] See, for example, St. Ignatius of Antioch, *Eph.*, IV, 1–2; St. Augustine, *En. in Ps.*, 149, 7 (PL 37:1953).

[134] So I subscribe to *Mediator Dei's* solemn rejection of the following opinion: "some go so far as to hold that the people must confirm and ratify the Sacrifice if it is to have its proper force and value" (MD 95).

[135] This point has been explained by A. R. Van de Walle, "Rencontre du Christ et communauté liturgique, principes préliminaires dogmatiques," *Concilium* 12 (1966): 23–33.

The *Ecclesia* or Christian Community

priest; it belongs to the church of which the ordained priest is only a minister (servant). The church must be present, one way or the other.[136]

In this perspective of the shared activity of a single body, the Fathers insisted on the character of dialogue between the priest and the assembly, and especially upon the *Amen* pronounced by the faithful. When the presider of the celebration says to the assembly, "The Lord be with you," and when the assembly responds to him, "And with your spirit," they communicate something of mutual importance. They mutually confirm the presence of the Lord *who unites them* and who is the Supreme Celebrant of the holy mysteries. Before entering into the sacred "action," and, in the Roman rite, after having received the gifts of the faithful and having asked them to pray that this sacrifice—which is also theirs—should be acceptable to God, the priest introduces the Preface by the dialogue which (found in all the liturgies) may well go back to the Apostles.[137] "*Sursum corda*—Lift up your hearts. *Habemus ad Dominum*—We have lifted them up to the Lord." "*Gratias agamus Domino*—Let us give thanks to the Lord our God. *Dignum et iustum est*—It is right and just!" Here is a commentary of St. John Chrysostom on the meaning of this dialogue at the Preface:

> In the course of the sacred mysteries, the priest addresses a wish to the people, and the people a wish for the priest; for the "And with your spirit" is nothing less. Likewise, the Eucharistic Prayer is their common prayer, for the priest does not give thanks (does not "eucharis-

---

[136] The ancient norm was that the priest does not celebrate alone. Cf. St. Cyprian, *Epist.*, 5, 2: "Presbyteri quoque qui illic (in prisons) apud confessores offerunt singuli cum singulis diaconis per vices alternant." Canon 813 of the CIC [1917] cited by *Mediator Dei* (see n. 122 above) makes reference to the Council of Basel (!), session XXI, ch. 8 (*Conc. Oecum. Decreta*, ed. G. Alberigo et al. [Rome, 1962], 467) and to a decretal of Pope Alexander III, C. 6, X, I, 17 (Friedberg, II, col. 137). The meaning of this rule is ecclesial, not simply a question of dignity or solemnity. After completing this essay, I discovered the study of G. De Broglie, "La Messe, oblation collective de la communauté chrétienne," *Gregorianum* 30 (1949): 534–561. He distingishes two things: the priest acting alone performs the external act that constitutes the sacrifice only insofar as he is the minister of the church; so it is the whole church that acts through him, and in this way the action proceeds from the church as a whole. Moreover, by joining themselves intentionally and affectively to the sacrifice of the Mass, the faithful show that this sacrifice is also theirs.

[137] The Old Testament or Jewish antecedents are incomplete: G. Dix, op. cit. (in n. 9 above), p. 118. This liturgical dialogue is found first in Hippolytus.

tize") all by himself, but the people give thanks along with him. For he does not even begin [the Eucharistic Prayer] until after receiving from the faithful their agreement, when they say, "It is right to give him thanks and praise . . ."

Now see here: if I tell you all that, it is so that even the simplest among you should be attentive, so that you learn that we are—all of us—one single body, and there is between us no other difference than that which exists between one member and another.[138]

Or again, observe this statement of James of Edessa from the end of the seventh century:

The priest points out to the faithful in what direction [to lift up their hearts], and they, having given their consent and declared that his intention is [right and just], they along with him, he along with them, become one single body of Christ, following one same idea . . .[139]

The Amen, borrowed from Jewish ceremonial, shows up even in the New Testament[140] and then among the most ancient witnesses to the rites of consecration of the Eucharist[141] or of Holy Communion.[142] Unanimously, the Fathers and the ancient authors give to the Amen a strong meaning of consent and commitment. "Your Amen is your signature," says Augustine, and the commentators follow him in saying

---

[138] *Com. in 2 Cor.*, hom. 18 (PG 61:527). Concerning the *Dominus vobiscum—Et cum spiritu tuo*, see the carefully researched essay concerning possible biblical antecedents by W. C. van Unnik, "*Dominus vobiscum*: The Background of a Liturgical Formula" in *New Testament Essays: Studies in Memory of Th. W. Manson*, ed. J. B. Higgins (Manchester, 1959), 270–305. The context for the formula is that the presence of the Holy Spirit is assured to the assembly by the holy offering of the spiritual sacrifice; the minister needs to receive the same reassurance as one who stands in the line of those chosen by God to carry out this service.

[139] Assemani, *Bible et Orient*, I, 480, cited by G. Dix, loc. cit., n. 137.

[140] Cf. I. Cecchetti, *L'Amen nella Scrittura e nella Liturgia* (Vatican, 1942); *L'Eglise en prière*, ed. A. G. Martimort (Paris: Cerf, 1961), 130f.; and my *Jalons*, p. 289 (numerous references).

[141] Cf. Justin, *I Apol.*, 65 and 67.

[142] Cf. Hippolytus, *Trad. Apost.*, 23—*Sources Chrétiennes* 11 (Paris, 1946), 54–55.

it.[143] In pronouncing their Amen, whether together at the end of the Canon, or individually when they receive Holy Communion, the faithful, together with the priest, bring about the unity of the celebrating subject. They do not give him a power that he had already and that they didn't have. Rather, together they accomplish something new—something more than a ceremony. They cooperate by their faith, say Odo of Cambrai and Stephen of Autun (see n. 51 above).

Something happens. In this way, the community comes to be; and the organism of fraternal harmony to which the presence of the Lord has been promised is realized. This is a mystery that goes beyond any question of juridical validity; and it achieves the very objective of liturgical action, namely, the glorification of God and the sanctification of the faithful.

The action of the priest could be "valid" without the Amen of the community, but it would not have its full meaning. And should the faithful refuse to give their deep assent, the priest's action could not produce its effects of unity in charity. Worship brings about the glory of God *among human beings*: the Mass does not obtain its spiritual effect without the community.[144]

We have to recover the meaning—then the reality—of this structure of mutual consent that marks the entire life of the church. It was

[143] St. Augustine, *Serm.* 272, 334, 362 (PL 38:1247, 1469, 1632); Florus of Lyons, *De act. miss.*, 74 (PL 119:65C); and see my *Jalons*, loc. cit., then, in addition to Cecchetti (in n. 140); see also J. Diaz Castañeda, *El Amen de la Misa: Su valor catequistico y pastoral* (Barcelona, 1965). The kiss of peace signifies the same reality: cf. Innocent I, *Epist.* 25, 1 to Decentius (PL 20:553), cited in Gratian C. 9 D II, *De cons.* (Friedberg, I, col. 1317) and Innocent III, *De S. Altaris myst.*, VI, 5: "qua constat populum ad omnia quae in mysteriis aguntur atque in Ecclesia celebrantur, praebuisse consensum" (PL 217:909).

[144] Cf. St. Thomas, III, q. 82, art. 7 ad 1; art. 9 ad 2; art. 10 ad 2. Cf. G. Philips, " La partecipazione dei fideli al Sacrificio della Messa," in *Eucharistia* (Rome, 1957), 359–405, p. 370, which has in mind (also 393) the case of a priest who is excommunicated or deposed; J. Lécuyer, "Théologie et sacerdoce chrétien," in *La tradition sacerdotale* (Le Puy, 1959), 241–266 (262f.). In the 12th century the author of the *Summa Sententiarum*, tr. VI, ch. 9 (PL 176:146) and Peter Lombard (*IV Sent.*, d. 13) thought that such a priest could not consecrate because he was not able to say. "*Offerimus . . .*" That is, he was not within the church. But Alger of Liège replied that he is not entirely separated; he is still in or of the church precisely because of his power to consecrate (*De sacr. corp. et sang. Christi*—PL 180:842B). Concerning this question, cf. F. Holböck, op. cit. (in n. 53), 232–238; A. Landgraf, cited above in n. 54.

At the Heart of Christian Worship

an unexpected discovery when, preparing my book *Lay People in the Church*, I made an extended research into the great documents of the Tradition. It became clear to me that the living structure of the church was a structure where the community ought to cooperate in the decisions and the acts of those who exercise authority among them, at least by their consent.[145] The community should even cooperate, first of all, in designating its own leaders. By contrast with what is now going on, the ancient Tradition considered the consent of the elected leader secondary, but considered the will of the people to be necessary.[146] This great "structure of consent" represents an aspect of the church's life which has been forgotten as a result of the unilateral development of authority and of a too narrowly juridical conception of the church. Where do we find ourselves today, for example, with respect to the state of things expressed by this text of Hippolytus?

> Let them ordain as bishop the one who has been chosen by the people. When his name has been pronounced, and he has been agreed upon by all, the people will gather together with the college of presbyters and bishops who are present on Sunday. At the consent of all, let these lay hands on him . . .[147]

This consent, mentioned three times by Hippolytus, what does it mean? Does it have a place in the realization of the church—People of God and Body of Christ? If liturgical actions are nothing other than something that a priest does, then there is no need for consent. But if liturgy is the work of the whole church, then consent has an essential role.

This is even more evident if we reflect on the ministerial nature of the presbyteral or episcopal priesthood. Certainly neither the bishop nor the presbyter is merely an emanation or a delegate of the community in some modern democratic sense. It is important to insist that if the church is priestly as a whole, if it is ontologically *anterior to the distinction between the simple faithful and the ordained ministers*, it is still

---

[145] See my *Jalons*, especially 329f.; my article "Quod omnes tangit ab omnibus tractari et approbari debet," *Revue de l'histoire du Droit* (1958): 210–259; G. Dix, essay cited in n. 9 above, 130–131. On the role of acclamations in elections and councils, etc., see Th. Klauser, "Akklamation," in *Reallexikon für Antike und Christentum* I, col. 216–233.

[146] See my article "Ordinations invitus, coactus, de l'Eglise antique au canon 214," *Revue des Sciences philosophiques et théologiques* 50 (1966): 169–197.

[147] *Sources chrétiennes*, 11 (Paris, 1946), 26–27.

The *Ecclesia* or Christian Community

nonetheless fully priestly only through its ordained ministers who, alone, can accomplish the Eucharist and transmit the priesthood. This is the part of the undeniable truth of the position of Cajetan and of others reported earlier (cf. nn. 104–106).

We have to recognize that if the church, by its most profound nature—signified by its birth from the side of Christ on the cross and as Spouse of Christ—is essentially priestly and vowed to continue the worship of its immolated and risen Savior, it is such effectively only because it counts among its members bishops and priests who are ordained to celebrate the Eucharist in succession to the apostles. There is no fullness of church without Eucharist, nor without the reality of such an ordained priesthood.[148] It is in this priesthood that the sacramental Memorial of the Cross has been left by Christ to the church, his Spouse, as the Council of Trent explained.[149]

However, this theology situates the hierarchical priesthood *within* the church, not above it. The church celebrates at the hands of its priests (cf. Trent, cited above). When we define church as Spouse of Christ or as the Great Sacrament,[150] we understand by "church" the totality of the People of God, ordered and structured in unity. *In order that it may become what it is called to be*, the church has been constituted by its Lord with a hierarchical priesthood within it. The priesthood is therefore a *service of the church*, in which and for which it exercises a *ministry*.[151]

One could show—I have done this elsewhere[152]—how the two forms or titles of participation in the priesthood of Christ are necessary one

---

[148] Cf. LG 17. The application of the term "church" meant exactly that up to Vatican II, which has opened a new chapter in the understanding of the church. Cf. *Chrétiens désunis: Principes d'un 'oecuménisme' catholique—Unam Sanctam* 1 (Paris: Cerf, 1937), 301–307, 381–382; also my "Note sur les mots 'confession,' 'Eglise' et 'Communion,'" in my *Chrétiens en dialogue—Unam Sanctam* 1(Paris: Cerf, 1964), 211–242.

[149] Sess. XXII, ch. 1: Denziger 938 (1740).

[150] SC 5; LG 1, 9, and 48.

[151] St. Augustine insisted especially on this point in using the word *ministerium*: cf. D. Zähringer, *Das kirchliche Priestertum nach dem hl. Augustinus* (Paderborn, 1932). Probably the "*ministerio sacerdotum*" of Florus (cf. n. 40) and of Innocent III (n. 44) was intended to mean the same thing.

[152] For example, the following: "Structure du sacerdoce chrétien," *La Maison-Dieu* 27 (1951): 51–85, reprinted in *Sainte Eglise* (Paris: Cerf, 1963), 239–273; or explaining in the wake of *Mediator Dei* the manner in which the faithful offer

to the other and complete one another, in order to accomplish the worship that God expects from his people. This is how the Fathers understood things, as is evident in the definition of the church given by St. Cyprian (cf. n. 72) or in the admirable words of St. John Chrysostom on the laity, whom he calls "the priestly *pleroma* [fullness]" of the bishop.[153]

Once again, observe that the history of ecclesiology is dominated in the West by the schema *corpus-caput*, body-head. This formula has been applied to the relationship between the church and papal power in an almost unilateral manner: the body depends on the head, but the head (while still being part of the body) does not depend on it. The pope's supreme decisions are considered to be valid *"ex sese, non ex consensu Ecclesiae*—on their own authority, not by reason of the church's consent."[154] In the schema *corpus-caput* there is always the possibility that the *caput* might act alone, since it has the power to do so. This is in fact the aspect of ecclesial reality that has been the most affirmed, and which has been strongly underlined by the two Vatican councils.

But this simply cannot suffice as being the whole of ecclesiology, not even the whole of what one ought to say about the pope in ecclesiology. We have to respect the truth articulated by the Fathers—St. John Chrysostom, for example, when he said that the body is the fullness of the head, and the head the fullness of the body.[155]

The schema *corpus-caput* also applies to the question of the appropriate participation of the faithful and of the presbyterate or the episcopate in the priesthood of Christ. Catholic doctrine holds that the

---

the Eucharist (*Jalons pour une théologie du laïcat*, 269–300). In addition to the theological studies noted there (277, n. 313), there are these also: R. Erni, *Der Gemeinschaftskarakter der Eucharistie: Das Opfer der Kirche* (Lucerne, 1954); *Opfer Christi und Opfer der Kirche*, ed. B. Neunheuser (Dusseldorf, 1960); J. L. Murphy, "The Church Offers the Mass," *American Ecclesiastical Review*, 142 (1960): 164–177, 234–246.

[153] *In Philip.*, ch. 1, hom. 3, 4 (PG 62:204); cf. *Jalons*, 299 n. 359. Chrysostom also writes, "the body is the fullness of the head, and the head the fullness of the body": *In Ephes.*, ch. 1, hom. 3, 2; *In Cor.*, ch. 2, hom. 6, 2 (PG 62:26, and 339); *In Rom.*, hom. 24, 2 (PG 60:623–624).

[154] Vatican I, sess. IV, cap. 4 (Denziger 1839 [3074]); explained by Vatican II, *Lumen Gentium* 25.

[155] St. John Chrysostom, *In Ephes.*, ch. 1, hom. 3, 2 (PG 52:26); *In Colos.*, ch. 2, hom. 6, 2 (PG 62:339); *In Rom.*, hom. 24, 2 (PG 60:623–624). Cf. St. Cyprian: "l'évêque est dans l'Eglise et l'Eglise dans l'évêque" (*Epist.* 66, 8—Hartel,

priesthood is constituted in its hierarchical degree by a new participation in Christ's priesthood, namely, not only by *living* in Christ but also by *communicating life* as Head.[156] Christian priesthood in its hierarchical degree is a priesthood of the Head of the praying and offering community. It can also act on its own (*ex sese*). The Mass *can* be celebrated without a community. We have to see there, in a profound sense, not only the privilege of a "power" given to a person but the consequence and the sign of the fact that the church does not give itself its own being; it receives its being from Jesus Christ, its Head.

But if, for reasons we have explained already (n. 156), Christ is the Head or Leader who exists *above* the Body, the priest (or the pope) is the head *within* the body. The priest (or the pope) exercises the service of a certain kind of "headship." One of the tasks for our time has to consist in restoring to this "within" its full significance.

With respect to the liturgy, that means that the integral subject (*pleroma*) of liturgical action is the *ecclesia*,[157] even when, on the plan of

---

p. 732); St. Augustine also sees Christ as at once completing the church and the church completing Christ in a way: *De Trin.*, XV, 19, 34 (PL 42:1084); *En. in Ps.*, 67, 25 (PL 36:829–830). This understanding of the insertion of the priest within the church, and of the church as the sacrament of salvation, is strongly emphasized by R. Salaün and E. Marcus, *Qu'est-ce qu'un prêtre?* (Paris: Cerf, 1965), *passim* and especially 88f., 137, 162.

[156] Cf. MD 92–93 on this point of Christ as Mediator; also *Lumen Gentium* 10 and 28; *Presbyterorum Ordinis* 2, 3, 6. A clarification is needed here, however. Protestants object that there cannot be a participation in the role of Christ's Headship. It is important, then, to distinguish between the role of *Caput* or Headship in the order of supernatural life—as the Source of this life, on the one hand, and a headship in the order of external authority, on the other hand. Christ is Head in the two orders for the church, and he is so in a manner which is truly primary; however, the hierarchical ministers are also "heads," but only in the second sense—by ordination and by participation in the Headship of Christ. So in Christ the quality of Principle or Head and that of Mediator are identical; while in the church, mediation (to the degree that there is such) is not that of a Principle and Head, but only that of a simple ministry.

[157] One might ask if this *subject of liturgical action* is the Christian community in its totality, or whether it pertains to the members actually present at a celebration. The documents (MD 92–93; SC 33) seem to favor the first hypothesis. Cf. the position of Stephen of Autun, cited above in notes 49 and 51. Moreover, we know that each local eucharistic assembly realizes the mystery of the church in such fashion that the whole church is substantially present in each individual celebration under this aspect of mystery: *Lumen Gentium*, 26; *Ad Gentes*, 20.

At the Heart of Christian Worship

juridical powers, the ordained priest acts alone. Even there, he is the minister of the *ecclesia*, without being, however, merely its delegate. His role has been willed and instituted by the Lord. But the ultimate and transcendent subject of liturgical action is Christ himself, who by his Holy Spirit gives unity and life to his Body, which he has constituted as priestly in its entirety. As we have seen, Christ has structured his Body, even with respect to this very priestly quality, as flock and shepherd, people and leader, community and presider.

Fr. Yves M.-J. Congar, August 1966

ॐ

Agenda for Personal and Group Reflection

Questions for the Individual Reader

1. St. Augustine's teaching, reported here, is that the church, reproducing the true sacrifice of Christ, offers itself as well as the mystery it celebrates upon the altar. The fundamental unity of the whole church as Body of Christ is maintained in its liturgical action as well. Is this new information for you? How well known is this biblical and patristic teaching in the contemporary church—in your parish?

2. Congar reports that "the Fathers and the High Middle Ages considered first of all the heavenly reality (*res*) of the church, of which the Pilgrim Church is merely the beginning." How does this retrieval of classical theology help you appreciate the way in which the liturgy *transforms* the assembly by the very fact of *embracing* them in the mystery of Christ's sacrifice?

3. Congar insists that "to pray in the name of the church" does not mean just praying in the name of all who are actually gathered in the parish assembly, but in the name of the entire membership of the Body of Christ. How can this awesome thought help you to deepen your own understanding of the meaning and significance of your participation in the church's liturgical action?

4. The council decreed that all ministers, clergy and laity, should do their part and only their part: "In liturgical celebrations each person, minister or layman, who has an office to perform, should do all of, but only, those parts which pertain to his office by the nature of the rite and the principles of liturgy" (SC 28). What is the theological significance of this decision, in the light of Congar's historical study? What about the

The *Ecclesia* or Christian Community

faithful who passively observe the Mass ritual and do not participate by offering their own active role in the celebration?

Questions for Group Discussion

1. Congar shows how the celebration of the Eucharist (according to the New Testament) manifests the solidarity between Christ as the one Priest of the new covenant and the baptized as his body in this world. From this point of view, what do you find to be the strongest argument or explanation to help people understand the *corporate* character of eucharistic celebration?

2. Congar makes very clear that the fundamental expression of the royal priesthood of all the baptized (ordained and non-ordained alike) is the personal self-offering of the faithful of themselves as a living sacrifice in every dimension of their ordinary lives. What is the link between this ordinary priesthood of every day and the priestly action of the eucharistic assembly? How important is it for people to understand the nature of the link between these two realities?

3. In Congar's view the offertory procession—ancient in its origins— has been a powerful symbol of the faithful's role in the Mass. From what you have learned here, what are some essential points to make in developing a catechesis of the offertory procession for the faithful?

4. Congar makes a strong argument about the importance of thinking through the relation of *caput* and *corpus*—head and body. Although in the most fundamental sense, Christ is the only organic head of the mystical body, nonetheless, the pope (for the whole church) and the ordained presbyter (for the Sunday assembly) stand as *caput*—head. What are some other contexts in which there are parallel relationships between groups of the faithful and the de facto leader in given situations? Does this relationship help you to appreciate the nature of the "internal ministries" that take place within families, groups, or religious communities?

Chapter 3

The Structure of Christian Priesthood

Translator's observations: *This important reflection on the meaning of Christian priesthood first appeared in the French liturgical
journal* La Maison-Dieu *in 1951. It may well have been a by-product
of Congar's work* Lay People in the Church, *published in French
the previous year. In that work, he illuminated the royal priesthood of
the baptized, sometimes called the common priesthood, as a theological
theme in order to develop positively the ecclesial and liturgical role
of the laity in the church and in the world. Pressed at the time of the
council to collect and publish a number of his articles on ecclesiology, he
republished this essay in* Sainte Eglise *(The Holy Church: Studies and
Approaches to Ecclesiology)* in 1963.*

*After establishing that the very idea of priesthood is related to sacri-
fice, he goes on to show the radical difference between the substitution
sacrifices of the Old Testament and the self-offering of Christ (and his
members) that is the one sacrifice of the New Testament. He develops
further here an idea which we saw in the previous chapter, the idea of
the priesthood of a holy life.*

*We find Congar once again using a theme that appeared in chapter
1, the movement from the exterior to the interior, seen both in the Bible
and in the Christian life. Additionally, he develops here an image that
is very powerful, the movement from Christ as* Alpha *to Christ as*
Omega—*the first being Christ's unique divine initiative in the incarnation, and the second being the plenitude of the Body of Christ incor-
porating the lives and sacrifices of all his members.*

*This essay studies in great detail the teaching of Pius XII in his
encyclical on the liturgy,* Mediator Dei, *teasing out the full theological significance of that text for the royal priesthood of the people of
God. These are ideas that even today need to be examined, studied, and*

* "Structure du sacerdoce chrétien," in *Sainte Eglise: Etudes et approaches
ecclésiologiques—Unam Sanctam 41* (Paris: Editions du Cerf): 239–273.

internalized by both clergy and laity in order to achieve a comprehensive understanding of the documents of Vatican II.

Sacred Scripture, the liturgy, the major ancient Christian writers, as well as the magisterium—all contain numerous affirmations about the priesthood of Christians. All these sources have already been studied in considerable detail. In this study I presuppose the value of these well-known texts and draw upon their findings.[1] Consequently, I will not follow the kind of inductive methodology here that proceeds from an analysis of important texts so as to create a doctrinal synthesis. Rather, I want to develop an overall perspective on Christian priesthood. Starting with the most general ideas, I will aim to articulate their concrete applications. Above all, my objective is to bring order to the major elements of the question. A careful study of this question, based upon critically important texts, should shape my conclusions according to the thought of St. Augustine, the theology of St. Thomas, and the doctrine of the encyclical *Mediator Dei*.

Priesthood's Relation to Sacrifice

Priesthood, in the most general sense, is related to sacrifice. I would define priesthood as the quality that makes it possible for us to present ourselves before God for the sake of obtaining God's grace by offering a sacrifice which pleases God. In this way we enter into communion with God. It is true that there are other definitions of sacrifice, in particular along the lines of the idea of *mediation* (in certain texts of St. Thomas) or the idea of *consecration* (in the French school of spirituality). In the

---

[1] Limiting myself to a number of solid studies written in French and easily accessible, let me suggest the following: Lucien Cerfaux, "Regale Sacerdotium," *Revue des sciences philosophiques et théologiques* 28 (1939): 5–39; the articles by B. Capelle, B. Botte, L. Charlier, and A. Robeyns in *La Participation active des fidèles au culte* [Louvain Liturgical Week 1933] (Louvain, 1934); P. Dabin, *Le sacerdoce royal des fidèles dans la tradition ancienne et moderne* (Bruxelles and Paris: Museum Lessianum, 1950) = a collection of texts in chronological order that is vol. 48 in this theological collection; articles by Père J. Lecuyer on priesthood in the writings of the Fathers (Hilary, John Chrysostom, and others).

For a more detailed list of suggestions, see ch. 4 of my *Jalons pour une théologie du laïcat—Lay People in the Church* (Eng. transl. 1967). See also P. Glorieux, *Théologie et sacerdoce* (Chambery, 1938); Y. M.-J. Congar, "Un essai théologique sur le sacerdoce catholique: La thèse de l'abbé Long-Hasselmans, textes et remarques critiques," *Revue des sciences religieuses* 25 (1950): 187–199 and 288–304.

At the Heart of Christian Worship

latter case, there is the idea of priesthood as an expression of love and adoration toward God or that of apostolic love as a ministry of salvation toward human beings (Canon Masure). But the idea of mediation is bigger and less precise than the idea of priesthood. For example, there are mediations through revelation that are not priestly as such. Further, the idea of mediation, when applied to priesthood, restricts priestly action to its public or liturgical form. That is a dubious approach which results in an arbitrary prejudice against the genuinely priestly character of the faithful, a quality clearly attested to in the Holy Scriptures.[2]

The idea of consecration concerns more the question of the spirituality of the priestly function rather than the definition of priesthood as such. As for the idea that includes the apostolate in the notion of priesthood, it can't just be dismissed, for it does find a basis in several passages of the New Testament. However, the way it is presented by the authors we refer to here, it looks more like a description of the activity of clerics rather than a definition of priesthood. This idea of apostolate needs to be grounded in a more formal perspective. In my view, the concept of sacrifice is the apt one to provide such a perspective.

In terms of the Bible, the idea of priesthood is tightly linked to the idea of sacrifice, whether because the priestly character of Christ (even when not expressly invoked) is suggested by his status as victim,[3] or because priesthood is expressly defined by its sacrificial function.[4] Further, there is no shortage of texts from the Fathers (especially St. Augustine), from theologians (especially St. Thomas), and from the magisterium (I think especially of Trent), which clearly link priesthood to sacrifice.[5]

---

[2] The principal biblical texts concerning the priestly character of the people of God or of the faithful are these: Exod 19:3-6; Isa 61:6; 1 Pet 2:4-5, 9-10; Rom 12:1 (cf. 6:13); Heb 13:15-16; Rev 1:5b-6; 5:9-10; 20:6 (cf. 22:3-5). Next come some texts containing liturgical expressions: Rom 15:16; Eph 2:18-22; Phil 2:17; 3:3; Heb 4:14-16; 7:19; 8:1; 10:19-22. Also perhaps these texts as well: Luke 1:75; and the texts related to St. Paul's collection, namely, Rom 15:27 and 2 Cor 8:4; 9:12.

[3] See 1 Pet 1:19; 2:24; 3:18; John 17:19.

[4] Cf. Heb 5:1; 8:3; cf. 2:17; 9:11-14; 10:11.

[5] "*Ideo sacerdos, quia sacrificium*—thus priest, because sacrifice" (St. Augustine, *Confessions*, bk. X, ch. 43, n. 69 [PL 32:808]; cf. *Enarrationes* in Ps 109, n. 17 [37:1459]; in Ps. 130, n. 4 [37:1706]; in Ps. 149, n. 6 [37:1952]). "*Dicit sacerdos quia se obtulit Deo Patri*—he is called priest because he offered himself to God the Father" (St. Thomas Aquinas, *Commentary on Hebrews*, ch. 5, lesson 1). "*Sacerdotium et sacrificium ita Dei ordinatione conjuncta sunt, ut utrumque in omni lege*

The Structure of Christian Priesthood

71

Sacrifice in the Context of Ordinary Life

Accordingly I will take my point of departure from this notion of sacrifice. This question has been and still is being critically discussed. Nonetheless, by taking sacrifice in a broad perspective and also according to its most common meaning as well as with reference to ordinary experience, we discover the meaning of the Scriptures, considered not so much in certain particular texts or in certain episodes or institutions, but rather in their overall meaning. This will soon become clear.

In everyday usage we tend to speak about sacrifice either too narrowly or too broadly. It is too narrow when we teach children the path of "little sacrifices," because we thereby identify the word with something painful. It is too broad (but nonetheless interesting) when we say of a young woman who remains unmarried in order to take care of her aging father or mother that she "sacrificed herself to her parents." In a similar vein, we sometimes speak of a soldier who "sacrificed his life for his country." In these two cases "to sacrifice oneself" consists in placing oneself in a perspective that clarifies a person's relation to others and shows what that means, what he/she is for them.

It is a question of relating ourselves to things greater than we are. If they are *good* for me, it is because they represent an absolute goodness beyond discussion, and they require that eventually I prefer them to my own self or, at least, to the selfish part of myself.[6] Precisely because there is selfishness inside us, it is demanding and painful to face up to what we are supposed to do for our neighbor. Sin inclines us to consider things selfishly or too much according to our personal interest. This egotism gives to our efforts to live for what is greater than ourselves—to our sacrifice—an aspect of painful detachment. But such efforts to live beyond ourselves can also succeed in bringing us our heart's delight. This is what happens each time we truly love. Note in the account given here, however, how the qualities of expiation and satisfaction are present at the heart of sacrifice, understood in its largest and most positive sense.

---

exstiterit—Priesthood and sacrifice are both so joined by their being ordered to God, that they existed in both laws [covenants]" (Council of Trent, session 23, ch. 1 [Denziger, 957]).

[6] By way of confirmation, look at this unexpected example: "People ought to appreciate the value of life, but also ought to know how to subordinate it to ideal goals or ends that are collective, such as justice, human freedom, national independence, and peace itself. We call this subordination a 'sacrifice' in practical terms" (Léon Blum, *A l'échelle humaine*, 120).

At the Heart of Christian Worship

When it is a question of our relation to God, who is our Creator and from whom we receive the whole of what we are and have, the fitting "sacrifice" to offer is ourselves—the totality of our being, our actions and our possessions. That obviously takes a lifetime. This lifetime literally won't be complete in its offering of life itself until it includes our death as well. But this lifetime of self-offering is expressed concretely in particular acts and in things. By offering them, we are able to express our orientation to God who is the author of our life and our true fulfillment. Seen like this, our sacrifices have their "soul" and their "matter"—their spiritual and their material dimensions.

The "soul" of our sacrifice is the free and loving embrace of our relation to God, that is, of our absolute dependence on God. We exist by God's gift, and we express our orientation toward God by conforming our will to his. This "soul" is the spiritual movement of the human being toward God. When we talk of the human creature's return back to God—of the virtue of religion, of interior sacrifice, as St. Thomas does;[7] or of the invisible sacrifice, as St. Augustine does[8]—these are all just different names for the "soul" of every sacrifice. For these great teachers, the essential fact is this: the *external* action is *added* to the sacrifice, but that is not what first of all identifies a sacrifice.[9]

As for the "matter," it encompasses everything that is suitable to be offered, "every good work, every work of virtue," as St. Thomas puts it.[10] But the "matter" is also exterior things, as we can see in all the world religions and in the Bible itself. From this perspective, we end up defining religious sacrifice with St. Augustine as "every action done with the objective of uniting ourselves to God in a holy communion."[11]

[7] For example, see the *Summa Theologiae* 1a2ae, q. 101, a. 2; 2a2ae, q. 81, a. 2; q. 82, a. 4; q. 85, a. 2; q. 93, a. 2; 3a, q. 22, a. 2.

[8] *City of God*, bk. X, ch. 6 (PL 41:283); ch. 19 (41:297), etc.

[9] See St. Thomas Aquinas, *Summa Theologiae*, 2a2ae, q. 85, a. 2; cf. a. 4 and with q. 81, a. 7; q. 93, a. 2, obj. 2; q. 94, a. 4, ad 1; *Contra Gentiles* III, 120—This teaching is taken up by the encyclical *Mediator Dei*.

[10] *Summa Theologiae*, 2a2ae, q. 81, a.4, ad 1; q. 85, a. 3; and cf. q. 124, a. 5; *Commentary on Psalms*, 19, 4.

[11] From the great text of *The City of God* cited here later. This definition was used by St. Thomas (2a2ae, q. 85, a.2; a. 3, ad 1; 3a, q. 22, a. 2; q. 48, a. 3; *III Sentences*, d. 9, q. 1, a. 1, qa 2, ad 1; *in Boetii de Trinitate*, q. 3, a. 2) and also by the encyclical *Mediator Dei*.

The Structure of Christian Priesthood

The Priesthood of a Holy Life

Since priesthood is correlative to sacrifice, there is a form of priesthood that corresponds to this very general form of sacrifice, but it is also deeply personal and interior. This is the priesthood of self-offering, the offering of one's very life; it is the priesthood of a holy life, the priesthood of justice. This is the meaning of the text of St. Irenaeus that some have complained about as if he were rejecting the existence of a hierarchical priesthood: "*Omnes enim justi sacerdotalem habent ordinem*—All the just are in a priestly order."[12] He wrote that with respect to David eating the loaves of proposition, but his intention is genuinely universal. Later on, we will look at how the New Testament represents this perspective. For the moment, let's stay with the idea of a priesthood of justice that corresponds to the offering of a holy and virtuous life.

To the degree that we can accept that there is virtue and religion outside the people of God represented by Israel (and so also by the church), we can admit that a natural priesthood of a holy life also exists as an authentic reality. The Bible gives us the example of Abel (Gen 4:4) whose sacrifice is even mentioned in the Canon of the Mass. Most of the time, this natural priesthood goes beyond a purely interior and personal attitude and becomes expressed in the public rites of some office, whether that of father or patriarch,[13] tribal leader or king.[14]

In any case, even when it is institutionalized in a public, hierarchical, and ceremonial fashion, all natural priesthood is linked to the sacrifice which constitutes the people's will to relate what they are and what they have to the Creator of everything. All of that is expressed in natural priesthood, and it will one day lead to the revelation of the true priesthood of Jesus, the cause of our praise and thanksgiving. Jesus brought all of that to the cross, giving transcendent value to what, without him, could never reach all the way to the holy of holies.

---

[12] *Adversus Haereses*, IV, 8, 3 (PG 7:995).

[13] Such is the case of Noah (Gen 8:20f.; cf. Sir 44:17); Abraham (Gen 13:4); Isaac (Gen 26:25); Jacob (Gen 35:1); Job (Job 1:5); Manoah, the father of Samson (Judg 13:19); Jethro (Exod 2:16; 18:1, 12); and possibly of Melchizedek (Gen 14:8f.).

[14] This is the case of Gideon (Judg 6:19f.), Saul (1 Sam 13:9f.; 14:34-35), David (2 Sam 6:13f; 24:25), Solomon (1 Kgs 9:25), and Ahaz (2 Kgs 16:12f.).

At the Heart of Christian Worship

God himself provided for us the homage that he wanted to receive from human beings. God not only created us but also devised a plan to include us in his grace. God's goal for us is the gift of perfect communion with him through the indwelling of God in us and of us in God. The corresponding means to achieve this divine plan had to be the institution of a sacrifice and of a priesthood of grace suitable to bring about this perfect communion. In sum, there is a positive divine economy of sacrifice and of priesthood. The Bible gives evidence of this world of self-gift and of grace.

It is enough to read the Book of Leviticus to discover what this ritual structure was like at its beginning. Further, in order to understand how God wanted to orientate it, read the prophets and the psalms of the Exile. Finally, to appreciate the consummation of this whole economy in Jesus Christ, read the Letter to the Hebrews and the Book of Revelation.

I will not treat the priestly institutions of the Mosaic Law in detail here, however worthy of consideration they are. What is important at this point is to observe the meaning of God's plan and its realization in the Christian understanding of the priesthood. Let us pay attention here to two essential points:

1. The sense of God's plan, as the Bible reveals it to us, moves from the *exterior* to the *interior*. In the end, God wants no other sacrifice than the offering of the very person of the believer. We find at the time of the prophets two series of texts with opposite meanings. On the one hand, God declares that he is disgusted with the sacrifices offered in conformity with the law of Moses.[15] On the other hand, God lets us understand through the prophets themselves that, in the purified Israel after the Exile, there will again be sacrifices and even the whole apparatus of external rites.[16] Even better, the prophet Malachi

---

[15] "What to me is the multitude of your sacrifices? says the Lord; I have had enough of burnt offerings of rams and the fat of fed beasts. . . . When you come to appear before me, who asked this from your hand? Trample my courts no more; bringing offerings is futile; incense is an abomination to me. . . . Your new moons and your appointed festivals my soul hates; they have become a burden to me, I am weary of bearing them. When you stretch out your hands, I will hide my eyes from you; even though you make many prayers, I will not listen" (Isa 1:11-15). Cf. Jer 7:21-23; Ps 50:10-13; etc.

[16] Cf. Isa 56:7; 66:20f.; Jer 33:11; Ps 51:21; and the whole of Ezekiel.

The Structure of Christian Priesthood

announces that, in contrast to the spoiled offerings made by the priests of the postexilic restoration, there will be a new incense and a pure oblation (1:11).

Don't be astonished to watch God both refuse and demand sacrifices through the mouth of the prophets. We realize that this "yes" and "no" uttered simultaneously indicates the dialectic of transcendence which is at the heart of the prophetic mission. The "yes" and the "no" are both true, because the "no" has reference to sacrifices under a certain aspect that must be negated and surpassed, while the "yes" addresses sacrifices at a deeper level of reality that pertains to a new state of affairs.

Further, the prophets clearly explain the meaning of this dialectic. God wants sacrifices, but not like those offered to him that are accompanied by injustice. He wants mercy and not external observances; he wants heartfelt piety and not halfhearted performance of the rites.[17] Finally, God wants not the offering of external things—animals and firstfruits—but the offering of the very person:

> Not for your sacrifices do I rebuke you: your burnt offerings are
>   continually before me.
> I will not accept a bull from your house, nor goats from your folds.
> For every wild animal of the forest is mine, the cattle on a thousand hills.
> I know all the birds of the air, and all that moves in the field is mine.
> If I were hungry, I would not tell you; for the world and all that is in it
>   is mine.
> Do I eat the flesh of bulls, or drink the blood of goats?
> Offer to God a sacrifice of thanksgiving, and pay your vows to the
>   Most High. (Ps 50:8-14)

> Sacrifice and offering you do not desire (O Yahweh) . . .
> Burnt offering and sin offering you have not required.
> Then I said, "Here I am . . . I delight to do your will, O my God."
>   (Ps 40:6-8)

St. Paul applies this text from the psalms to Christ, and even puts it in his mouth as the expression of his intention in coming in human flesh:

---

[17] Cf. Hos 6:6; Amos 5:24-25; Isa 1:16f.; Mic 6:6-8; Ps 40:7, 9, 10; Ps 51:18f.; Ps 69:31f.; Ps 141:2; etc.

At the Heart of Christian Worship

When Christ came into the world, he said: "sacrifices and offerings you have not desired, but a body you have prepared for me; in burnt offerings and sin offerings you have taken no pleasure. Then I said, 'See, God, I have come to do your will, O God' (in the scroll of the book it is written of me)." When he said above, "You have neither desired nor taken pleasure in sacrifices and offerings and burnt offerings and sin offerings" (these are offered according to the law), then he added, "See, I have come to do your will." He abolishes the first in order to establish the second. (Heb 10:5-9)

In Jesus Christ, the worship that God wants is perfectly realized. This new worship surpasses the entire system of the law still linked to the immolation of external things. It proposes as the only real sacrifice that of persons who lovingly conform their will to the will of God.[18]

2. St. Paul wrote elsewhere that everything in the nature of promises from God in the Old Testament has become "Yes" in Jesus Christ (2 Cor 1:20). Christ is the center and the summit of everything. From Adam and Abraham, all through the history of Israel, everything moves toward Christ until everything is fulfilled and the *Alpha* of everything has become our own *Omega*.

The Fathers of the Church examined in detail the sacrifices and the priesthood of the Old Testament, explaining their value as those things "which happened to them in figures" (cf. 1 Cor 10:11). They foretold the coming of Jesus Christ, in whom alone they would find their "truth." He is—he alone—the true sacrifice, the authentic altar, the true priest, and the true temple. These different themes are clearly exposed in the Holy Scriptures,[19] but thanks to the Epistle to the Hebrews, none of them is more fully explained than the theme of Jesus as the unique priest.

Already in the Old Testament, although a priestly character was affirmed of the whole people, there was a contraction of the priesthood into the person of the high priest, at least in the sense that the high priest represented the entire people as if he contained them within himself. There was between him and them a kind of equivalency of

[18] With regard to this whole theme, see also G. Hebert, *Le trône de David* (Paris, 1950), ch. 4; and also my article "Pour une prédication et une liturgie 'réelles,'" *La Maison-Dieu* 16 (1948): 75–87.

[19] For the theme of Jesus as the True Temple, cf. the studies by A.-M. Dubarle, "Le signe du temple," *Revue biblique* 48 (1939): 21–44; and by Jean Daniélou, *Le signe du temple* (Paris, 1942).

The Structure of Christian Priesthood

religious function.[20] On the great Day of Atonement, the high priest alone entered into the presence of God, fulfilling in an impressive and solemn rite his role of representing the whole people in order to offer the sacrifice of expiation and to reestablish the people's communion with God the most high.

We should reread in parallel here chapter 16 of Leviticus and the Epistle to the Hebrews, above all Hebrews 8:1-10; 13. We are at the heart of the dispensation of priesthood that God had sketched out prophetically in Israel before fulfilling it in Jesus Christ. As on the Yom Kippur of the liturgy of Aaron, when it is a question of reconciling human beings with God, it is Jesus Christ alone who, carrying them all in himself, is at once the only perfect victim and the only priest able to enter the holy of holies. "No one has ascended into heaven except the one who descended from heaven, the Son of Man" (John 3:13).

In the order of properly divine blessings, when it is a question of entering God's own heart and of bringing human beings into communion with God and into the temple of eternal life, only the Son of God made man can be the adequate priest and the adequate victim. This is the teaching of the Letter to the Hebrews, for which an abundance of Pauline and Johannine texts provide a rich and glorious synthesis.

Perhaps no one has given a richer interpretation of this synthesis than St. Augustine in a series of dense and sumptuous texts which we will cite here, especially two staggeringly beautiful chapters of *The City of God*. There he defines sacrifice not only on the level of theology or ideas, but in the framework of the whole of salvation history or, if you will, in the framework of the entire trajectory of God's plan, starting at its beginning and ending in the city of the saints.[21]

Sacrifice really doesn't seem completely true to Augustine except when it is *total*, and only if it follows through to its full and ultimate

---

[20] We find clues of this sort in the prescriptions for the Day of Atonement, clues that benefit from the interpretation afforded by the Letter to the Hebrews: the high priest carried the names of the tribes on his shoulders and on his heart (Exod 28:12, 29); on his forehead he wore the words expressing the consecration of the whole nation: *Holy to Yahweh* (Exod 28:36f.). This symbolized his carrying before God the faults of the whole people as well as his own wish for expiation (Num 18:1). The same offering was made for the unintentional faults of the high priest as for the faults of the whole assembly of Israel (Lev 4:3, 13-14), etc.

[21] *The City of God*, bk. X, chs. 5 and 6 (PL 41:281–284).

At the Heart of Christian Worship

fruition. Adopting the prophetic dialectic outlined above, Augustine shows first of all that "true sacrifice consists in every action done with a view to uniting us to God in a holy communion, that is, every action referred to our ultimate end—that one Good capable of making us genuinely happy."

Then, seizing upon this idea of a movement of total attachment which leaves no room for the misery of alienation from God, and going back to the idea of so many biblical texts which identify true sacrifice with mercy, Augustine shows that total sacrifice is the realization of the attachment to God of ". . . the entire redeemed city, that is, the assembly and society of the saints." This alone forms the ". . . total sacrifice which is offered to God through the Great Priest who offers even himself for us in his passion, so that we may be the body of such a head." Elsewhere, commenting on the passage in the Epistle to the Hebrews which we cited above, "Sacrifice and offering you did not desire, but a body you prepared for me . . . ," Augustine shows that this body, matter for the sacrifice and the object of the priesthood of Christ, is at once the personal body of Christ, his communion-body (or mystical body) that we form along with him, and—forming the link between the first and the second—his sacramental or Eucharist body.[22]

As a result, the Augustinian synthesis links the following ideas together for us: (1) The *content* of the sacrifice is *us*: "*Totum sacrificium ipsi nos sumus*—we are ourselves [within] the whole sacrifice."[23] (2) In order that this sacrifice might achieve its full reality, we all together form one single Body of Christ. ". . . this is the sacrifice of Christians—many become one Body in Christ."[24] (3) The Eucharist is the sacrament and sign

---

[22] *Enarrationes* in Ps. 39, nn. 12 and 13 (PL 36:442). It would not be too difficult to justify exegetically this theological commentary of Augustine by making a study of the New Testament use of *sôma*, which is at once the body of Christ sacrificed on the cross and in the Eucharist, as well as the body-temple or sanctuary that is the church. Cf. C. F. D. Moule, "Sanctuary and Sacrifice in the Church of the New Testament," *Journal of Theological Studies* (1950): 29–41; cf. 31–32.

[23] *The City of God*, bk. X, 6; cf. X, 19, and his *Sermon 19*, ch. 5, n. 3 (PL 38:133–134); *Sermon 48*, ch. 2, n. 2 (38:317): "*Quaerebas quid offeres pro te, offer te. Quid enim Dominus quaerit a te, nisi te?*—You wanted to know what to offer for yourself; offer yourself. What indeed does the Lord seek from you then, other than yourself?"

[24] "*Hoc est sacrificium christianorum: multi unum corpus in Christo*": *The City of God*, bk. X, 6—a formula much used in the Middle Ages.

The Structure of Christian Priesthood

of this—a sign that is expressive, dynamic, and effective. The Eucharist not only contains the sacrifice of Christ on the cross, which already includes our sacrifice, but it also is the sacrament of the entire sacrifice that the communion-body makes of itself: ". . . so it becomes clear to the church that in the Eucharist which it offers, the church itself is offered."[25]

This Augustinian synthesis is so abundant that it has made me anticipate some of my later points which will concern the properly Christian economy of sacrifice and of the sacrifice in the time of the church between the Ascension and the Parousia, which is—using the categories with which we have become familiar—between our Alpha and our Omega.

Priesthood in the "Time of the Church"

A priest of the diocese of Marseille, Abbé G. Long-Hasselmans, who unfortunately was unable to complete his very interesting study on the priesthood (see n. 1 above), posed the problem in a striking way in these terms, which will need considerable explanation:

- Only one is *priest* (*hiereus*).

- All are *priest* (*hiereus*—written in the singular).

- Some are *priests* (*prebyteroi*).

There are three points here. The first is the great affirmation in the Letter to the Hebrews that there is only one priest, Jesus Christ. The second is another clear biblical affirmation concerning the priestly character of all Christians (see n. 2 above). And third, there is still another affirmation that is rooted in the experience of the earliest days of the church. From the last years of the second century or the beginning of the third century, we find terminology bearing on the existence of a hierarchical priesthood.

My perspective here is not to formulate these questions from a historical or text-study point of view, but rather from a speculative perspective, trying to understand the reasons, the links between them, and to put them in a coherent perspective. From this point of view, Abbé Long puts the matter well. It is a question of how to articulate

---

[25] "*Ubi ei [Ecclesiae] demonstratur quod in ea re quod offert, ipsa offeratur*": Cf. *Tractatus 26 in Joannem*, ch. 6, nn. 15 and 17 (PL 35:1614), and the Easter sermons edited by Dom G. Morin in *Miscellanea Agostiniana*, vol. I (Rome, 1930).

and harmonize the three propositions, how to understand the meaning of the priesthood during the time of the church.

I hope to shed light on the question by considering the general conditions of the Christian economy or of the time of the church. Here are two brief points along these lines.

a) As a rule, within the whole economy of grace (and particularly within the economy of Christ's ministry), a gift is given first of all to one person or to a small number, so as to be extended to many others thereafter. This is the law of *pars pro toto* [a part for the whole] as the Protestant exegete W. Vischer liked to stress. When it is a question of Jesus Christ, the plan of God's grace is such that the spiritual gifts that were given to him in absolute fullness are communicated from him to us in such a way that even though everything comes fully from him ("He will glorify me, because he will take from what is mine and declare it to you" [John 16:14]), nonetheless these gifts are truly appropriated and are actually *acted out by us*.

This is so because we are *persons*—beings existing with a proper self. Even though we receive everything from God by participating in God's own being, nevertheless we do not cease being ourselves. We do not become God. We retain the power to exercise actions which are genuinely our own. This explains how, even though we receive everything from God, we nonetheless *add* something. (We are able to contribute something, since we have been made according to the *image of God*, that is, God's *interlocutor*—nothing less than God's partner . . .).

Understanding all this leads us to appreciate the fundamental identity as well as the fundamental difference between the mystery of Christ and the mystery of our own life, between his Passover and ours.[26] Everything begins from his Passover and everything moves toward our own. The two belong to the same mystery. Once again what we read in John 3:13 proves to be true: "No one has ascended into heaven except the one who descended from heaven, the Son of Man." We cannot go up to heaven except in Jesus Christ; we cannot pass over into the intimacy of the Father—which is also the holy of holies of the Letter to the Hebrews—unless we have become members of Christ, become his communion-body.

[26] For this decisive point, I recommend the wonderful book by F.-X. Durwell, *La Résurrection de Jésus, mystère du salut* (Le Puy and Paris, 1950).

The Structure of Christian Priesthood

Christ is our Alpha and our Omega, as we read in the Book of Revelation (1:8; 21:6; 22:13). But Christ is our Alpha all by himself, even though he is such for our sake (*hyper êmôn*, for our benefit), whereas we are the Omega along with him and he cannot be that without us. The resurrection of Christ and his entry into his glory are not the total completion of the Christian economy, even if, in one sense, they achieve everything. These mysteries are actually a point of departure. Between his resurrection and personal triumph over death, on the one hand, and the accomplishment and restoration of all things—his total and definitive victory—on the other hand, there exists a period of time about which Christ himself said that the Father alone in his omnipotence knows "the times and the seasons" (Acts 1:7-8). This is precisely the time of the church, the time that begins with the event of Pentecost.

There is great meaning here, and the meaning is very clear. All of this signifies that the mystery of Christ is only completed fully through our entry within it; his Passover is completed in ours. If the two are fundamentally identical, nonetheless, the second—our passover, our mystery—is not a pure and simple repetition of the first. Every fruit comes out of the seed, the whole body proceeds from its "head"; everything that will be found in the Omega will have come forth from the Alpha.

Nonetheless our cooperation, our personal agency, even our contribution as persons with freedom is needed, although all of that has been done *for* us and given *to* us. We must surrender ourselves to the mystery in such a way that, at one and the same time, we receive everything from the fullness of Christ,[27] and he finds his plenitude in us.[28]

This insight constitutes a rule of thumb that serves as the key to a number of problems fundamentally related to one another, such as the development of dogma, the Tradition, the liturgy, and the collaboration of the faithful and of the church in the redemption given by Christ.[29] In all of these cases, there is a *repetition* in time of a unique

---

[27] Cf. John 1:16; Eph 1: 23; etc.

[28] Eph 1:23 (*tou pleroumenou* is a passive form. Cf. the commentary by Armitage Robinson. The encyclical *Mediator Dei* supports this understanding also); cf. 1 Cor 12:13; Col 3:11. For the integration of these two meanings—Christ filling us up + Christ being brought to complete fullness in us—cf. Dom Warnach, *Die Kirche im Ephesersbrief* (Munster, 1949), 13 and n. 69.

[29] Both Pius XI (in his encyclical *Miserentissimus Redemptor* of May 8, 1928, *Acta Apostolica Sedis*, 170–171, making explicit reference to the priesthood of Christians) and Pius XII (in his encyclical *Mystici Corporis* of June 29, 1943)

and original gift. The repetition does not *create* anything, yet nonetheless it adds, it "fills up what is lacking," as St. Paul says (Col 1:24).

From the point of view of sacrifice and the priesthood, we explain the fact this way. If the sacrifice and priesthood of Christ are unique and capable of achieving for all time the sanctification of those who are called to sanctity, if they contain every sacrifice and the entire priestly quality of human beings, nonetheless they need to be *enacted* and celebrated by human beings.

In order to pass *from* the state of plenitude that belongs uniquely to the only Son *over to* the fullness of the body, the sacrifice and priesthood of Christ need to be appropriated by the faithful. *Only One is priest*, but he allows many to be priests in him and through him; only one sacrifice has efficacious value, but it gives value to all of our sacrifices. It *contains* them, but they give it a new kind of fulfillment and abundance by actualizing its transcendent value. Without the participation of the members, the sacrifice of Christ would not be total.

b) Christ is the principle, or the Alpha, of everything, and he is also—once realized and established in plenitude—the end, or the Omega, of everything. But he is also the *way* that joins the beginning to its end, and that he remains, as long as the Alpha is not entirely transformed into the Omega, as long as the fruit of the redemptive incarnation is not complete.

In the dialectic between the gift and its application that we have quickly sketched in the preceding section, there should be added a dialectic between *reality* and *means,* in order to describe the Christian status of sacrifice and priesthood. This is also a dialectic between interiorized life and exterior mediation. When the end term is fully reached where Christ will be in the plenitude that conforms to the plan of God, or otherwise put, when the Alpha will have brought about its Omega, there will no longer be any need for an order of means or any need for Christ to exist for us as the *way*. He will then hand over the kingdom to his Father, says St. Paul, and God will be all in all (1 Cor 15:28). Following the mystery of Christ's personal resurrection, as long as our own passover is in a state of development, Christ gives himself to his church not only as being already and forever its life but also as a means to achieve this life.

---

developed this theme of Christians and of the church cooperating in the redemption of Christ.

The Structure of Christian Priesthood

Thus there are in the church two aspects that we must understand both how to unite as well as how to distinguish. The church is *life* in Christ. It is that already, and each day it becomes more so and will do so eternally. But the church is also the *means* to bring about this life; it is the structure for the means of grace, and it will be that as long as the totality of the Lord's life has not yet been accomplished and interiorized in the church according to the plan fixed by God.

Relative to these two aspects and governing their relationship, there exists a twofold rapport between the Lord and the church. The Lord is the soul and the life of the church, and in this way he is interior to the church by his Holy Spirit. But the Lord also rules and acts within the church by his power. He is the Vine, the one who lives in his branches and they in him, but he is also the Lord, the authority upon whom the ministries depend (Cor 12:5). These two perspectives complement one another, and St. Paul is able to demonstrate how at one and the same time the church is the *body* of Christ and Christ is the *head* of the church.

There is only one church that verifies this twofold aspect of the communion of redeemed life and the means of obtaining this life. The fact that these really are two different aspects does not create an obstacle. This is very important if we want to understand the character of life in the church in general and that of priesthood within it in particular. From one end to the other, we find in the church two levels of reality. Respecting and harmonizing this twofold structure is the secret of a Catholic ecclesiology—there is an order of communion and of life, on the one hand, and an order of means of grace and of sacraments, on the other hand. There are both *res* and *sacramentum*, as the vocabulary of St. Augustine puts it—spiritual reality and holy sign.

From the point of view of sacrifice and priesthood, we will have the perfect sacrifice of humanity incorporated within the sacrifice of Jesus Christ. On Calvary, Christ included our sacrifice within his own and he wishes to become totally one with us in heaven—one single filial being turned toward the Father, *unus Christus amans Patrem*—one single Christ loving the Father.[30] We exercise the priesthood that corresponds to this sacrifice of ourselves each time we refer our very selves to God in the charity of Christ.

[30] Following St. Augustine (*In Epistolam Joannis ad Parthos*, tr. 10, n. 3–PL 35:2055), who wrote: "*Erit unus Christus amans seipsum*—There will be one Christ loving himself."

At the Heart of Christian Worship

We recognize here in a properly Christian frame of reference the sacrifice and the priesthood of life itself, called also the sacrifice and priesthood of justice and of sanctity about which we have already spoken and to which the biblical texts fundamentally refer. But there also exists within the church another priesthood or, if you will, another title to sacrifice and priesthood. This is the active representation, the real memorial ritually enacted, in short, the sacrament of the sacrifice that Jesus Christ offered once for all on the cross. He had already anticipated this sacrifice on Holy Thursday under a properly sacramental form, which he confided to the church to celebrate "until he comes again" (1 Cor 11:26).

Here it is a question of the sacramental celebration, through the sacraments and particularly through the Eucharist, of Jesus' passing over to his Father. The Eucharist contains the very substance of Jesus in his passion. The role of the sacraments is to reproduce in a particular mode of being [as sign] that is precisely symbolic-real, what Jesus did for us in the days of his flesh. This allows the root to bear its fruits—to make the Christ Alpha produce within us over time the reality of life in such a way as to form the Christ Omega. Making real what they signify, the sacraments draw from what is his to provide nourishment for us in view of our insertion into him and of our growth even to the point of what is perfect for us. This is the supreme role of the Eucharist, the sacrament of the sacrificed body of Christ.

The Eucharist shares with the personal body of Christ and with his communion-body or mystical body the same name of *body*. The Eucharist is precisely the dynamic link which unites one to the other, drawing from the first to nourish the second, just as the stem nourishes the fruit by drawing from living roots. This traditional understanding of the Eucharist and of the sacraments in general has been admirably described by Père de Lubac in his book *Corpus mysticum* where, after having cited the uplifting texts of St. Augustine, he writes for himself: "The end term coincides with the beginning; the church meets its perfection in Christ."

"Only one has ever gone up to heaven," we can say it again, "the one who came down from heaven, the Son of Man who is in the heavens." But this Son of Man, who is our head and our whole substance, has become sacramentally present on earth as our means of life and our nourishment in order to join the body of his incarnation to his body of communion and glory across the time of humanity, giving transcendent value to the actions of those who live in him.

The Structure of Christian Priesthood

Two Sacrifices That Are Really Only One
We are now at the point of being able to clarify the meaning for the church of sacrifice and of priesthood.

a) We find ourselves in the presence of two sacrifices which are not foreign to one another and above all which are destined not to be separated. On the one hand, there is the sacrifice of Jesus Christ, namely, his return as Son to the Father, painfully achieved for us on the cross and sacramentally handed over to the church to be celebrated and to be lived. On the other hand, there is our own sacrifice, constituted by all the acts by which we order ourselves to God and turn ourselves back to him, the last and most decisive of these acts being our death.

In one sense, this sacrifice of ours must be something other than that of Christ. That can be seen from the fact that we are irreplaceable elements, both from the perspective of the matter involved—it is *our* life that God desires to incorporate—and from the perspective of the offering made—it is *we* who must make this offering. Once again, we are persons who exist in a being all our own; we are each one an image of God, an interlocutor, a partner of God. We can either give ourselves or refuse ourselves to God. But confronted with the reality of God, we know that we are not equal with God. Rather, God is our all, and the very fact that we can oppose God is a power that we have received and that we continue to receive from him.

Likewise, the sacrifice of Jesus Christ, with respect to our sacrifices, is a greater whole which envelopes them and contains them, and it is offered in order to give value to ours, since "one only has gone up to heaven . . . ," only one inherits the blessings of the Father—the Son— and we are inheritors of these blessings only if we are found to be in him and have become *filii in Filio*—sons and daughters in the Son, his co-inheritors.

This is why the two sacrifices that exist in the church, while being distinct, should not remain separate. Through the daily realization of our sacrifice, we develop ourselves to the point of our final destiny. This sacrifice of ours is subsumed and made one with his by its union with the sacrifice of Jesus Christ—a union which is exercised by faith, and by all the activities that faith and sacramental communion initiate and sustain. Then, united to the sacrifice of Christ, our own sacrifice— which is our proper agency and that by which we develop ourselves spiritually—fulfills the plan of the growth from Alpha to Omega, from the Christ who has alone made all things for us to the Christ brought to perfect fullness with us, in us, and through us. In this way the two

At the Heart of Christian Worship

sacrifices are organically joined together according to the offering of the church and the plan of God. This is at once a recognition of the distinctness and the unity of the two, their irreplaceable duality and their necessary oneness.

b) There is a type of priesthood that corresponds to each of these sacrifices. To the sacrifice of oneself, called also the sacrifice of justice and sanctity, corresponds an interior and personal priesthood—a priesthood of personal sanctity. The New Testament speaks about this kind of priesthood in describing spiritual worship, spiritual sacrifices pleasing to God (Rom 12:1; Phil 3:3; 1 Pet 2:5), holy and living offerings (Romans), a sacrifice of praise, the fruit of one's lips (Heb 13:15), the confession of faith (1 Pet 2:9), and works of mercy in the tradition of the prophets, such as charity, sharing, and almsgiving,[31] as well as the work par excellence of spiritual mercy which is teaching—the communication of saving truth by the word.[32] For the ministry of the Gospel that he exercises, St. Paul uses very strong liturgical expressions: not only *diakonia* (servant ministry) but *leitourgia* (a work of worship), sacrifice and offering (Rom 15:16, 31). We will examine these expressions later on.

Nowhere in the New Testament do we find an explicit reference to the worship and to the "royal priesthood" of the faithful at the Eucharist or in public rites or the liturgy of the church as such.[33] Often this reference has been explicated by the Fathers and even more by spiritual authors and modern theologians.[34] However, more often the Fathers of the Church and the medieval theologians such as Thomas

---

[31] Heb 13:16; cf. Hos 6:6 and 14:3, and with the expression of St. John Chrysostom speaking of the "altar of almsgiving" or the "altar of the poor": *In II Corinthios*, homily 20 (PG 61:540). There are countless texts of a similar kind in the Christian tradition.

[32] Cf. 1 Pet 2:9 and, by reason of what has been said, Heb 10:24. St. John Chrysostom calls the exercise of the ministry of the word "the greatest and the most august of sacrifices": *Sermo cum presbyter factus fuerit* (PG 48:694).

[33] An *explicit* reference, remember. It would be difficult not to see an implicit reference to the Eucharist in Heb 13:10; cf. 6:4; and 1 Cor 10:17-22. Further, the priesthood of the faithful seems to be clearly linked with baptism in Heb 10:19-22; cf. Gal 3:27.

[34] You may find such texts in the collection of P. Dabin (see n. 1 above) and further references in ch. 4 of my *Jalons pour une théologie du laïcat—Lay People in the Church*, trans. Donald Attwater (Westminster, MD: Newman Press, 1967).

The Structure of Christian Priesthood

Aquinas[35] point to a relationship between the "royal priesthood" of the New Testament, not so much with the sacraments and the Eucharist, but with what we have already called the personal priesthood of justice and holiness by which we offer ourselves to God. This priesthood develops in the Christian life as an expression of living in Christ through grace and through the virtues—as an expression of one's incorporation into the Mystical Body as the organism of grace.

There is an equally sacramental priesthood that corresponds to the *sacramental celebration* of the sacrifice of Christ. Here it is no longer a question of offering our sacrifice insofar as it is properly speaking our own—that of our holy life (we just barely dare to speak in such a way . . .) or at least of our life tending toward holiness, which consists precisely in conforming our life to God and in communion with God as the fruit of sacrifice. Rather, at question here is the very sacrifice of Jesus Christ, being extended to us in such a way so that it contains our own sacrifice in itself. Christ's sacrifice has been offered for us and is given under a form of sacramental celebration to the church, precisely to allow us to unite ourselves to it and to consummate the offering of ourselves in it. For the moment, however, our focus is not on this insertion of our offering within that of the Savior. We must first of all consider the miraculous gift that the church has received to celebrate the authentic memorial of the sacrifice of Jesus Christ between the time of his glorious ascension and his equally glorious return.[36]

Such is the marvel of the sacramental order (illustrated in such a remarkable way by what St. Paul says about baptism in the Letter to the Romans), that the sacrament achieves and repeats indefinitely in our space and time the active presence of the *acta et passa in carne*—what

---

[35] See St. Thomas Aquinas, *IV Sentences*, d. 13, q. 1, qa 1, ad 1; *Summa Theologiae*, 3a, q. 8, a. 1, ad 2. Also see Bernard Botte in *La Participation active des fidèles au culte*, 28 (see n. 1); also L. Charlier, *idem*, op. cit., 30f. For the period that goes from Berengar of Tours to Innocent III, see the concluding section of the practically exhaustive summary of F. Holböck, *Der eucharistische und der mystiche Leib Christi in ihren Beziehungen zu einander nach der Lehre der Fröhscholastik* (Rome, 1941), 227–239.

[36] In my view we have not yet satisfactorily shed all the light possible upon the implications of the phrase "Do this . . . in remembrance of me" (1 Cor 11:24-25; Luke 22:19). The expression makes reference to a Hebrew radical, *zkr*, used in the Old Testament in a way that makes the idea of memorial equivalent to the active manifestation of divine presence (cf., e.g., Exod 3:15, 20-22; Ps 111:4).

At the Heart of Christian Worship

Jesus did and what he suffered in his flesh, and most particularly the sacrifice or the Passover of Jesus which leads him into the presence of his Father. However, *everything* here must be seen as sacramental. If the sacrifice is *sacramentally* that of Christ himself, the priesthood also must be the same. The celebrant also must be in some way a sacramental reality—an organ or instrument of Jesus Christ. This is how there exists in the church, alongside the personal priesthood of sanctity, a sacramental priesthood permitting us to celebrate, until he comes again, the same sacrifice of Jesus Christ. It is nothing less than that!

The Nature of the Ministerial Priesthood

Until now we have been speaking about this sacramental priesthood in only the most general terms. But now it is time to give a more precise explanation of the ministerial priesthood so as to develop a more exact account of the structure of Christian priesthood.

The structure of Christian priesthood follows the general law and structure of the church (and for that matter, of every operation of God among us); that is to say, it is at once communal and hierarchical. Its structure has to do with the community in the sense that God has unceasingly treated human beings as a *people*, as an organic whole and thereby as an organized body. In Israel, the priestly quality of the people as a whole was not an obstacle to the institution of a hierarchical priesthood, as Korah, Dathan, and Abiram learned the hard way by failing to respect the order established by God (Num 16–17).

The structure is also hierarchical in the sense that God generally gives to certain ones the ministry of procuring blessings destined for a great number. God teaches using the words of the prophets and doctors, rather than by speaking to each individual directly in the intimacy of their conscience. God enjoys communicating to creatures the dignity of acting as causes along with him. But it is not just in the name of such general laws, however well founded they are in the facts and documents of Revelation, that we affirm here the existence of a hierarchical order in the sacramental priesthood given to the church. The New Testament itself contains texts which show us the functions of the ministry communicated to certain persons but not to everyone—and first of all to the apostles.[37]

---

[37] Thus we find that it was given to certain ones:
- to be sent (John 17:17-19; 20:19f.),
- to be *episcopes* such as Jesus is (1 Pet 2:15),

The facts recounted in the Acts of the Apostles and the epistles, as well as the oldest documents of Christianity, together bear witness to show us the celebration of the Eucharist reserved to ministers ordained by the laying on of hands—a tradition which reaches back finally to the apostles themselves.[38] But let us be content with this summary claim, since the purpose of this article is not to establish in precise detail all the evidence for the Catholic priesthood. Rather, what we are looking for here is a systematic organization.

With respect to the sacramental priesthood, which allows the church to celebrate the sacrifice of Jesus Christ, who is its most holy head and the principle of all its grace, we are led to distinguish two degrees in this priesthood corresponding to two very different positions. These two degrees are constituted by a sacramental consecration establishing the Christian in a sacramental identification with Christ. By baptism (and confirmation[39]) each of the faithful is made a celebrant of

---

- to be pastors (John 10; 1 Pet 5:2f.; John 21:15f.),
- to be the foundation for a church that is the house of God (1 Cor 3:11; Eph 2:20),
- to be "gate" (John 10; Rev 21:12-14),
- to strengthen and confirm (Luke 22:32),
- to preach and to baptize (Matt 28:19-20; Mark 16:15-16),
- to forgive sins (John 20:23) as God does (Mark 2:7; Luke 5:21; 7:49) and as God has given to the Son of Man to do (Matt 9:6; Mark 2:10; Luke 5:24),
- to "do this in memory of me" (Luke 22:19; 1 Cor 11:24-26).

[38] Cf. Clement of Rome, *Letter to the Corinthians*, 44, 4; Hippolytus, *The Apostolic Tradition*, or also the introduction to his *Philosophoumena* (or *Refutation of All Heresies*); as well as the study by Dom Gregory Dix in *Apostolic Ministry* (London, 1946).

[39] We find in the patristic, liturgical, and theological tradition the following: 1) the almost universal affirmation of a link between the priesthood of Christians and baptism; 2) very frequently a link between this priesthood and anointing; since the ancients, imbued with symbolic-sacramental understanding, would not have conceived that someone might become Christian and have a share in the priestly quality of Christ (royal and prophetic) without being anointed. However, within this fundamental position, we see also that the royal priesthood of Christians is linked sometimes to confirmation, sometimes (without explicating the point) to baptism, sometimes to the anointing given in the rite of baptism, and sometimes (and most often) to the post-baptismal anointing—for which it is difficult to say, for the later periods, if that means a rite of baptism or of confirmation. Cf. P. Dabin, op. cit., 44f.,

the mysteries of Christ, particularly of the Eucharist, in order to unite themselves and be nourished there. By the sacrament of holy orders, that is, by the apostolic imposition of hands in view of undertaking a ministry, certain ones among the faithful are ordained with the objective of actively accomplishing the Eucharist.

There is no doubt that Thomas Aquinas conceived matters this way. The format of his *Summa Theologiae*, as we know, involves the return of the human creature to God from whom he came forth. There is a kind of integration of matter or content between the spiritual agency of the human person (analyzed in great detail in the second part) and the "sacrifice" for which St. Thomas adopts the definition of Augustine. This sacrifice made by the faithful appears as extensive as the whole religious and moral life of the person, which for Aquinas is the object of the "royal priesthood." However, when St. Thomas, in the third part, considers Christ, who by everything that he does and suffers for us is the *way* of our return to God, he takes account of the unique character of the properly Christian economy of this return.

Jesus Christ, he says, "inaugurated the worship or the rite of the Christian religion in offering himself as an oblation and a self-gift to God."[40] This worship proceeds entirely from Christ and, adds St. Thomas, from his quality as priest.[41] Here we find ourselves in the *Summa* faced with the traditional view so splendidly formulated by St. Augustine, by St. Leo, and so much present in the ancient art of the East and, at least until the twelfth century, of the West as well. This Tradition was restored at last in the encyclical *Mediator Dei*: the priesthood of Christ, our unique high priest, alone the "*verus sacerdos*—the true priest,"[42] seated with his Father in heaven, continues on earth, in and through those who belong to him, the sacrifice and the adoration of his cross. To achieve that, he consecrates the members of his body to celebrate the worship for which he is himself the high priest. He allows them to participate in his own priesthood. This is the value, both litur-

---

and especially B. Welte, *Die Postbaptismale Salbung: Ihr symbolischer Gehalt und ihre sakramentale Zugehörigkeit nach den Zeugnissen der alten Kirche* (Freiburg-im-Breisgau, 1939).

[40] *Summa Theologiae*, 3a, q. 62, a. 5, with its citation of Eph 5:2; cf. q. 22, a. 2; *Commentary on the Psalms*, 44, 5; *Commentary on Hebrews*, ch. 5, lesson 1.

[41] 3a, q. 63, a. 3; cf. a. 6, ad 1.

[42] *Contra Gentiles*, IV, 76; cf. *IV Sentences*, d. 17, q. 3, a. 3, qa 2, ad 1 (*Summus Sacerdos*); 3a, q. 22, a. 4.

The Structure of Christian Priesthood

gical and priestly, that St. Thomas sees realized in the sacramental *characters* or consecrations of baptism, confirmation, and holy orders.[43]

The worship of Christ within his church, which constitutes the liturgy properly so called (this is also the definition given by the encyclical *Mediator Dei*), is clearly both social and communal. It is institutionalized and organized; it is a *rite*, as St. Thomas clearly says. The whole body celebrates it along with Christ, its head and sovereign Priest. However, the body is organized in such a way that, even if all the members are actively involved, only certain ones take the role of *giving* to others, while others take the role of *receiving*. Certain ones have the role of simply perfecting themselves, while others have the role of perfecting others.[44]

Here we find the link between the consecrations of baptism (and confirmation), on the one hand, and the consecration of holy orders, on the other hand—two degrees within the priestly quality by which the Body of Christ celebrates with its head the spiritual worship of the new covenant instituted through Christ's blood. The sacrament of holy orders is, in its priestly quality or its Christian liturgical power, the new and eminent degree, furnished with a certain power of action thanks to which certain ones within the body are ministers of the unique priest (*unus sacerdos*) for the others.[45]

Three Titles to the One Priesthood

The texts of St. Thomas, together with the whole doctrine that we have developed here, seem to impose a distinction. In the church there are not three priesthoods—because there can only be one, that of Jesus Christ—but three different titles to participation in the unique and sovereign priesthood of Jesus Christ.[46] Let me explain this distinction

---

[43] Cf. 3a, q. 63, a. 3; a. 6, corpus and ad 1. The doctrine about the character of baptism (and of confirmation) as a participation in the priesthood of Christ, (too briefly) sketched out by St. Thomas in the *Summa Theologiae*, tends to become a common teaching. It was taken up again by the encyclical *Mediator Dei*.

[44] Cf. *Summa Theologiae*, 3a, q. 63, a. 2; a. 3; a. 6; q. 65, a. 2, ad 2.

[45] "*Gradus eminens per potestatem spiritualem ordo nominatur*—Holy Orders is called an eminent status conferred by means of spiritual power": *IV Sentences*, d. 24, q. 1, a. 1, qa 2, ad 4.

[46] I agree here with the excellent specialist on the Thomistic treatise on the sacraments, Dom Bernard Durst, *Dreifaches Priestertum*, 2nd ed. (Nerresheim, 1947). Cf. H. Bouëssé, op. cit., 106–110.

At the Heart of Christian Worship

within the context of the organic unity that I have already affirmed. I will likewise undertake to characterize and distinguish each of the three titles with its appropriate name.

There is the priesthood of a holy and consecrated life, that is to say, the priesthood of the just, which is characterized by communion with God. It is personal and interior. It is called spiritual, not only because it concerns the order of the life of grace given by the Holy Spirit, but because it is about the interior, personal spiritual life of each one. I would, however, like to call this title of priesthood "real" as well, in order to point out, in accord with the great biblical idea espoused by St. Augustine, that it touches the ultimate reality envisaged by the movement of the entire economy of salvation and which is nothing other than human persons themselves (see n. 18 above). In this respect I will speak about the *spiritual-real* priesthood, but one might also say in biblical terms a *royal* priesthood or, following the Catechism of the Council of Trent, an *interior* priesthood.

The two other priestly titles have in common a relationship to visible exterior worship, specifically ecclesial and liturgical. One can call both of them exterior or liturgical, or even sacramental, since they are given by a sacrament and they exist in relation to sacramental worship. Despite these characteristics common to them, there is the difference between baptismal priesthood, on the one hand, and ministerial or hierarchical priesthood on the other. However, it is difficult to insist upon a limited vocabulary; each expression designates a certain aspect of these things, each has advantages and disadvantages. No one expression is sufficient to render the others totally useless.

Baptismal priesthood enables the faithful to take part in properly ecclesial acts of worship and thus in the holy liturgy of the church. Baptism makes them consecrated beings, members of the People of God within the new and definitive covenant. As such, they are constituted in the ecclesial order of the laity.[47]

The ministerial or hierarchical priesthood constitutes persons as ministers of sacramental worship that Christ celebrates with his members in his body which is the church. He empowers ministerial priests to celebrate the holy mysteries not only as participants but also actively as public ministers—ministers of the church. This last expression is correct

---

[47] A large number of official documents promulgated under the pontificate of Pius XII have returned to old and classic formulas such as *ordo laïcorum, ordo laïcatus*, etc. You can find references to these in my *Lay People in the Church*.

and full of significance; St. Thomas[48] and the most official documents of the church employ the term. We can't abandon it. However, it is essential to understand it and to be careful not to become confused by a misunderstanding, especially about two points closely related one to another.

On the one hand, one might consider priests only as instruments of this entirely priestly body of the church; in short, they would thus be seen as nothing more than persons ordained to a priesthood that is a priestly function received in the service of the community of the faithful. Abbé Long (see n. 1 above) seems close to taking such a position, as does also R. Sohm, a prestigious historian of early canon law. But it has been noted that the title of service for the community was not constitutive of ordination as such, even if this ordination has been done in view of such a service.[49]

In early Christianity there were ordinations which were, as today, a pure investment of priestly power without immediate reference to a ministry. The hierarchical priesthood is certainly destined to serve the People of God, but it is in itself a deep personal gift of spiritual power in the order of sacramental worship within the church, not the simple ordination for an instrumentality of service within the priestly body. By that very fact it is clear that the priest is not simply the representative or the delegate of the community of the faithful.

Perhaps he is the community's representative in certain acts, even within the liturgy, for the liturgy includes in large part a sacrifice of praise, worship lifted up by humankind toward God. However, in the properly sacramental actions of the liturgy, most especially in the consecration of the eucharistic gifts, it is first of all the worship of the Lord that the priest celebrates. He is more than anything the minister and sacramental representative of Jesus Christ; he celebrates, as theology says, *in persona Christi*—in the name of Christ, and thus has only a *ministerium*—a ministry.

Certainly, the faithful, by reason of their faith and their consent, have a real and properly liturgical role, but their participation and their consent cannot be considered that which assures validity to the operations of hierarchical priestly power. This power does not come

[48] Cf., e.g., *Contra Gentiles*, IV, 73; *IV Sentences*, d. 19, q. 1, a. 2, qa 2, ad 4; d. 24, q. 2, a. 2, ad 2; *Summa Theologiae*, 3a, q. 64, a. 1, ad 2; a. 8, ad 2.

[49] Cf. the work of V. Fuchs, *Der Ordinationstitel von seiner Einstehung bis auf Innozenz III* (Bonn, 1930).

At the Heart of Christian Worship

from below but from above, by reason of a sacramental ordination. The errors of the Synod of Pistoia about this point, about which lingering traces of misunderstanding continue in the discussion of this question, were very clearly condemned once again by the encyclical *Mediator Dei*.[50]

Without being able to explain myself here as fully as I would like, I still want to observe that the priesthood of Christ, as it is communicated sacramentally to the faithful in baptism, and to presbyters by their ordination, is not uniquely liturgical. The sacrifice of Christ, which they have been consecrated to celebrate, evidently had a supremely liturgical quality. But its essential content—and understand me, I mean its content as worship—was not anything other than the sacrifice, that is to say, the perfect referral to God, of the living Christ *containing us in him*.

Ultimately a Christian is not consecrated, nor is a priest ordained, for a liturgical-ritual celebration, even though this celebration is that of the body and blood of the Lord and has a decisive importance. The sacraments are for humans, for a reality of grace (*res*) in the hearts of persons. The priesthood exists, beyond any sacramental activity, to excite and stimulate participation in the sacrifice of Christ, so as to bring about the sacrifice of human persons united to the sacrifice of Jesus Christ. In this way the faithful accomplish and fill up the sacrifice of Jesus, their Alpha (their source). It would not be difficult to show how this way of looking at things is in conformity with classical theology.[51] In any case, it clearly corresponds to the texts of St. Paul which we will read here according to their original meaning (Rom 15:16 and Phil 2:17).

We can now adopt a perspective on the organic reality of priesthood in the church that is both unified and differentiated. We are talking about the organic union of the three titles to priesthood that we have distinguished within one single body of praise, which is the Mystical Body of Christ. The spiritual-real priesthood of justice and sanctity finds its fulfillment in the exercise of the baptismal priesthood.

---

[50] *Mediator Dei: Encyclical Letter of Pope Pius XII on the Sacred Liturgy* (Washington, DC: N.C.W.C, 1948), no. 162.

[51] What I say here applies not only to the priesthood of sacred ministers but to baptismal priesthood as well. Popes and theologians have often linked Catholic Action to the priesthood of the faithful. To study this, see my *Lay People in the Church*.

The Structure of Christian Priesthood

Through the baptismal priesthood uniting us to the Passover of the Lord, we enter efficaciously with Christ into the holy of holies and we become acceptable to the Father in our own self-offering.

This baptismal priesthood can only be exercised thanks to the ministerial or hierarchical priesthood. We become united to God in the highest degree in Communion, but we receive Communion from the hand of the ordained minister who is chosen to celebrate the sacrament. Thus the whole body cooperates in the work of its head, Christ, each member acting according to the gift they have received (Eph 4). Everything bespeaks order; everything likewise bespeaks hierarchy. But each one is active as well, and everything is for the sake of life itself.

We have to avoid giving the impression, as certain contemporary authors have done (sometimes under the somewhat dubious influence of M.-J. Scheeben), that the ritual action is the most important thing. Eager to give full value to the visible organism of the church, which is in effect the institution or means of grace, some theologians make sacramental character the most profound reality in the order of participation in Christ and in sacramental worship, a kind of end in itself. St. Thomas took great care to relate character and sacraments *ad cultum praesentis Ecclesiae*—to the worship of the church of the present day.[52] Nourished from an Augustinian source, Thomas knew full well that grace is superior to character in the order of union with God and that all the sacraments are made for the sake of the spiritual reality which they aim to produce in human believers as their proper fruit.

A Concluding Summary

The sketchy indications that we have given here will undoubtedly become clearer if, to conclude, we rapidly review the priestly activities of the faithful. They are exercised according to the twofold title of grace and of baptismal consecration.

a) For the faithful to be a priest is first of all to offer one's life, to make of one's own person a reality constantly directed to God. St. Paul insists especially on the offering of one's body.[53] The meaning of this, from a biblical point of view, is that the body is life itself insofar as it is tangible and visible. But our physical body also plays a decisive role in the orientation of our entire moral life. The "body" is not exactly

---

[52] *Summa Theologiae*, 3a, q. 63, a. 1, ad 1; a. 3, ad 3.
[53] Cf. Rom 6:12-13, 19; 12:2; cf. 1 Cor 3:16-17; 6:15, 19-20.

the "flesh" in the biblical sense of this word, but it is closely linked. Experience shows how much the attitude we take with regard to our body and to the bodies of others is of decisive importance for our relationship with God. It is there that one becomes either slave or free.

The spiritual ideal is that of a person freed from selfish concupiscence—what an ambition!—in such fashion as to be the servant of God and of others in a spirit of love. That is what Christian freedom means, and that is the idea behind this self-offering which genuinely merits the title of royal priesthood and which is so closely linked to a spiritual royalty. Here we begin to understand also the Christian tradition, still alive in the church, which sees martyrdom, virginity, and the monastic life as privileged realizations of our spiritual dominion—our dominion over the world and over ourselves, perfect acts of our royal priesthood. It seems to me that religious, especially those who are not clerics, should find in the royal priesthood an extremely profound and authentic principle of the spiritual life and of interior integrity, according to the sense in which we have briefly sketched the idea here. Their life is an exercise of this royal priesthood in a "pure state," so to speak.

This royal priesthood, however, has meaning for every Christian life according to the state in life of each person. The life of Christian spouses and Christian parents opens to them an area of choice. There is the priesthood of fathers and mothers of families which is situated at the conjunction of three types of priesthood that are blended together here: the natural priesthood of which we spoke earlier and which is identified with paternal authority; the priesthood of justice and holiness which is exercised in the specific conditions of one's own state, providing endless opportunities for offering oneself to God and offering conjugal and family life; and finally, baptismal priesthood whose sacramental consecration has a resonance in the consecration of one's marriage, since the natural contract of marriage becomes a sacrament on the basis of this baptismal consecration.

The Fathers often said that the family is the church in miniature. The family is also the place where the royal priesthood of the faithful is exercised day by day with as much richness as in a monastery. This is so in the life situation of spouses first of all, because their condition is a condition of mutual respect one for the other which, inspired by authentic love and a deep and free consent, becomes very truly a condition of "sacrifice" according to the meaning that we have explained. It is not in vain that St. Paul described marriage as a mystery capable of symbolizing the union of Christ with his church. In reality, nothing less than the love and the consent of Christ for his church have to be invoked here. It is a love and an assent which, from both sides, demand a commitment to a dying and rising. This is realized only in a new birth one to the other, a unity, that follows upon a death to the kind of life that one might have lived purely for oneself (see Eph 5:25, 31).

As to the priesthood of Christian parents, it is exercised—taking the word in a very broad sense—in the liturgy of the home, through common prayer before meals and at night, through the prayer of parents for their children (sometimes in joy and sometimes in tears), and through the introduction of children to prayer and to the faith, etc. Christian parents have the unique privilege of seeing their role as Christian witnesses and their natural authority coalesce so that they become one and the same. In raising up a young person to mature life, they are able to raise up a disciple . . . Christian families are literally cells of the church.

b) The baptismal priesthood develops its full liturgical value through participation in the celebrations of the church, particularly the celebration of the Eucharist. This is a question which can't be treated suitably in a few lines. Unfortunately, too often the matter is taken up with an attitude which does not favor a happy solution. There are obsessions which get in the way of understanding the true nature of the liturgy in the overall reality of baptismal priesthood.

The first mistake is to make a direct connection between the royal priesthood and the classic texts which presented it (1 Pet 2, etc.) with the offering of the eucharistic sacrifice. This temptation is strong in part because the liturgical texts of the Mass seemed to suggest it. There were tendencies of this kind before the Reformation and before the Council of Trent, and they were expressed again in the seventeenth and eighteenth centuries as well as at the present time by certain authors of some reputation.[54]

In our day explanations of this kind have been developed above all by the desire to give to young people involved in Catholic action a spiritual motivation drawn from the rediscovery of the Mystical Body and to emphasize the full ecclesial value of the laity that Catholic action has awakened.[55] It is not surprising that there has been a reaction

---

[54] On this point, see the interesting work of Dom A. Robeyns in *La Participation des fidèles au culte* (Louvain, 1933), 50–60.

[55] One example of a (well-documented) synthesis that passes directly from biblical texts concerning the royal priesthood to a theology of the offering of

against this. However, it is unfortunate that this reaction has given into an obsession contrary to the former tendency that is itself dangerously narrow.

Several authors have taken up the idea, developed by Cajetan in reaction to Luther, that the church is priestly because it has within itself a hierarchical priesthood, in their view the only true priesthood. Thus the faithful express a priestly quality by their submission to and their union with the hierarchical priesthood.[56] Others have reacted in fear that the idea of offering oneself at the Mass—an idea often expressed by a procession of gifts at the moment of the Offertory—detracts from the truth that there is at Mass only one genuine sacrifice, that of Christ sacramentally offered by the priesthood of hierarchical priests.[57]

Let me respond to these problems by putting things a bit differently, because it seems to me that the agency of the church which moves us in our growth from the Alpha to the Omega is not sufficiently appreciated here. It is, of course, above all a question of emphasis and nuance. But for my part, I react strongly against the insistence of some that we should not affirm the existence of any genuine priesthood except that

---

the eucharistic sacrifice is: E. Niebecker, *Das allgemeine Priestertum der Gläubigen* (Paderborn, 1936).

Then there is this example of a certain impatience with the limits of a doctrine of priesthood with respect to the laity. About 1932, after a theologian had explained the theology of St. Thomas Aquinas, which does not link the royal priesthood of the faithful directly with the offering of the liturgy, the head chaplain of the Catholic Action movement said to him: Well, then, how are we going to get our young people enthused?

[56] Cf. Cajetan, *Jentaculum III* (French translation by J. Coquelle and P. de Menasce in *Nova et Vetera* 14 [1939]: 274–283); Msgr. Gröber, archbishop of Freiburg-im-Breisgau, in his report of January 1943 (see *La Pensée catholique* 15 [1948]: 66); see also *La Maison-Dieu* 7 (1946): 100. Msgr. Gröber cites Palmieri, *De romanis Pontificibus*, 17, in this sense: "*Est enim Ecclesia regale et sanctum sacerdotium quia est regnum quod a sacerdotibus regitur, quodque ad cultum divinum per actus hierarchicos speciatim exhibendum ordinatur*—The church is a royal and holy priesthood because it is a kingdom ruled over by priests, and which is shown to be especially ordered to divine worship through hierarchical acts." I don't know a single exegete who would recognize in this text a legitimate interpretation of the biblical data on the royal priesthood.

[57] This is the understanding of Dom B. Capelle, "Le chrétien offert avec le Christ," *Questions liturgiques et paroissiales* (1934): 299–314; (1935): 3–7; "Nos sacrifices et le sacrifice du Christ à la messe," in *La messe et sa catéchèse* (Paris, 1947), 154f.

The Structure of Christian Priesthood

of public hierarchical priests and that the "priesthood" of the faithful is purely moral and metaphorical.

Unquestionably, the object of the royal priesthood is "moral," since it consists in the life of persons themselves. Certainly this priesthood is "spiritual," but we really have to understand the full meaning of this word. The "spiritual" character of the Christian is not a symbolic internalization of an external and material ritual, such as that of the Mosaic covenant, as explained by Philo.[58] It is the *reality* brought about by the new and definitive covenant. This is why we have called the royal priesthood "spiritual-real." We need consciously to let go of the obsession, for or against, to link this priesthood to the liturgical offering of the Eucharist, and at the same time let go of the tendency to see it exclusively in terms of a public liturgical form of priesthood and ritual.

The biblical and traditional teaching, which is perfectly explicit here, does not support either of these interpretations. I think we can escape from the tendencies described here by recognizing the three distinct priestly titles and recognizing that the first—that of the royal priesthood which is interior and personal—while being entirely spiritual, is not purely metaphorical but real in its own order. We must still clarify the relationship between the baptismal title and the hierarchical title to priesthood. In other words, we need to make clear what part the faithful take in the offering of the Eucharist.

There is an abundance of texts from the Fathers and from the literature from Middle Ages before the thirteenth century. A bit later (point iv) we will see how important this is. Let me present here a résumé of conclusions to be drawn from these sources:

i)   Christ offered himself once for all in sacrifice. In this offering he included the self-offering of us all.

ii) The church celebrates this sacrifice of Christ in the sacrament which he himself instituted. The Eucharist is at one and the same time the sign (first and principally) of the sacrifice of the cross, and (next) of the sacrifice of the church. This doctrine, formulated

---

[58] Even St. Ambrose, who was excessively influenced by Alexandrian exegesis and by Philo (he often transcribed entire books of his), saw the difference: "Philo limited himself to a moral sense, since his Jewish ideas impeded him from grasping spiritual things" (*De Paradiso*, IV, 25, cited by J. Daniélou, *Sacramentum futuri* [Paris, 1950], 45). We find this also in Origène: cf. H. de Lubac, *Histoire et Esprit* (Paris, 1950), 150–166, 267–270.

At the Heart of Christian Worship

in a masterful fashion by Augustine, is also the teaching of *Mediator Dei*, where we read: "It is obviously necessary that the external sacrificial rite should, of its very nature, signify the internal worship of the heart. Now the Sacrifice of the New Law signifies that supreme worship by which the principal Offerer Himself, Who is Christ, and in union with Him and through Him all the members of the Mystical Body, pay God the honor and reverence that are due to Him."[59]

iii) Insofar as the Mass is the sacramental "renewal," always identical and ceaselessly renewed sacramentally, of the sacrifice of Jesus Christ, it can only be celebrated by hierarchical ministers constituted as sacramental ministers of Jesus Christ. Insofar as it is a question of accomplishing a sacramental action, both exterior and public, of the eucharistic sacrifice, it is the action of the sacramental (ministerial) priesthood.[60] Or again, in the sense that the Mass is a sacrifice where the victim is truly immolated, it is properly the act of the sacramental priesthood, the act of the church inasmuch as such a priesthood exists within her.[61]

iv) However, this sacrifice of Jesus Christ is that of the head of the whole body which is the church. In addition, the whole body must unite itself affectively by faith, love, devotion, and a deep assent to the celebration. The encyclical *Mediator Dei* has a long development on this point. Further, even though it affirms that the faithful do not celebrate the visible rite of the offering in the same way and by the same title as the priests (namely, with the power to consecrate), it nonetheless insists in underlining the unity of the faithful, offering along with the liturgical minister and through him a liturgical act that is a critical value "which pertains to the liturgical worship itself."[62] This participation is

---

[59] *Mediator Dei*, op. cit., 93. (Cf. *Summa Theologiae*, 3a, q. 82, a. 4); later in the encyclical (103), St. Augustine is cited either directly or through the text of St. Robert Bellarmine.

[60] Expressions taken from G. De Broglie, "Du role de l'Eglise dans le sacrifice eucharistique," *Nouvelle Revue Théologique* (May 1948): 449–460; and "La messe, oblation collective de la communauté chrétienne," *Gregorianum* 30 (1949): 534–561.

[61] Expressions taken from B. Capelle, op. cit., *supra*.

[62] *Mediator Dei*, op. cit., 92: "Now the faithful participate in the oblation . . . because they not only offer the Sacrifice by the hands of the priest, but also to

expressed especially in the Amen which closes the Canon, but also in the response *"Et cum spiritu tuo*—and with your spirit" in the dialog which begins the preface, in the Communion, and in the gestures of the faithful, etc.[63]

When we read ancient texts, especially those of the High Middle Ages in the West, we are struck with the fact that they seem to say more than that. In these texts the faithful appeared to be genuine celebrants of the mystery. No more than today did those authors attribute to the faithful the power to consecrate the holy gifts. However, they seemed to think that this consecration could not be made without being rooted in the unity of faith and prayer of the faithful.[64]

Modern sacramental theology is interested in little more than the canonical conditions for the validity of the sacrament, and insufficiently concerned about the interior meaning of things.[65] It specifies very well

---

a certain extent, in union with him." Also, 104: Offering the Great Amen, let Christians "offer themselves, their cares, their sorrows, their distress and their necessities in union with their Divine Saviour upon the Cross."

[63] Many ancient texts address this point. I cite a certain number, as well as monographs touching this point, in my *Lay People in the Church*, ch. 4. As to the Amen, see the synthesis of A.-M. Roguet, *Amen, acclamation du peuple sacerdotal* (Paris, 1947).

[64] Here are few examples: *"Quidquid in divinis obsequiis a quolibet Ecclesiae membro reverenter offertur, id etiam fide et devotione cunctorum universaliter exhibetur . . .* —Whatever is reverently offered by any member of the church in divine worship can be shown to belong to the faith and devotion of everyone" (St. Peter Damian, *Liber Dominus vobiscum*, ch. 7 [PL 145:237]); *"virtute communionis in Ecclesia confici sancta mysteria per gratiam Dei*—the holy mysteries are confected in the church through the grace of God by virtue of communion in the church" (Odo of Cambrai, *Expositio in canonem missae* [PG 160:1057]); *"quotquot sunt de corpore Christi quod est Ecclesia salutantur et eorum suffragia postulantur, quorum fides per gratiam Dei adjuvat fieri tanta mysteria*—all those who belong to the body of Christ that is the church are helped and their prayers are lifted up, and their faith through the grace of God assists these great mysteries to be brought about" (Stephen of Autun, *De sacramento altaris*, ch. 13 [PL 172:1289]), etc. In patristic and early church ecclesiology, belonging to the mystical body is the principle of validity for sacramental actions or hierarchical acts.

[65] Translator's note: Congar first published this essay in 1951, when the assessment which he makes here happened to be generally true. This is, of course, no longer the case. Both the documents of Vatican II and the work of a

At the Heart of Christian Worship

the minimum of gestures, words, matter, and intention required for a valid celebration but is not concerned about the ecclesial meaning or the religious sense of the celebration. Between the eleventh and twelfth centuries and ourselves, the difference is not one of faith, not even one of doctrine, but rather a difference of manner in approaching these things and seeing them in a certain context—the context of synthesis.

What is ultimately at stake is ecclesiology, and more precisely, the atmosphere of the ecclesiology. This is why so often we treat problems posed by the liturgy in a wholly different perspective and in completely different categories than those characteristic of the creation of the texts and of the liturgical gestures which gave rise to these problems.[66] Briefly put (I treat all this in my *Lay People in the Church* where this point is one of the key ideas), today we have for ecclesiology a juridical theology of hierarchical powers, not a theology centered on the church.

Unquestionably, the hierarchical powers have their place in the church, an essential place and a decisive one. They assure that the church maintains its structure. However, although structured hierarchically, the church lives in all the people. "The laity," said St. John Chrysostom, "are the priestly fullness of the bishop."[67] The law of the church, if we consider it in its living reality and not only in skeletal form, is that there should be at one and the same time hierarchical administration and communication, and also community consent. As long as we have not restored this traditional perspective on ecclesiology, a host of liturgical and pastoral—even apostolic—problems will remain at a level of stalemate where canonical distinctions alone try to replace the reality of authentic life.

---

whole generation of great liturgical and dogmatic theologians have given us a rich biblical and historical appreciation for the sacraments as ecclesial realities that are at root personal exchanges between the members of the Body of Christ and their Head. Congar was addressing a period when seminary formation was still coming out of manuals in which there was little interest in anything other than matter and form, validity and liceity.

[66] In my bulletin on theology in the *Revue de sciences philosophiques et théologiques* (Oct. 1951), I have given the example of the problem we call today ceremonial concelebration.

[67] *Commentarium in Philip.*, ch. 1, homily 3, 4 (PG 62:204).

The Structure of Christian Priesthood

Unfortunately, the questions themselves have been ruined by bad solutions. We have to use good resources to pose good questions. In our case, the errors of the Protestants, the Gallicans, and the Jansenists, who more or less made the consent of the faithful a condition for the validity of hierarchical acts (and not only the fullness of their reality and of their expression in the life of the church), have unadvisedly given Catholics the obsession to avoid the appearance of favoring such a false idea. This explains why the encyclical *Mediator Dei*, which is so grand in its vision and so rooted in tradition, paradoxically draws from the idea of the priest celebrating as the minister of Christ the head in the name of his whole body, not so much the conclusion that the whole body takes part in the celebration but rather this—that the priest celebrant alone celebrates the sacrifice of the whole body and thus he can celebrate in the absence of the faithful . . .[68]

v) On the cross, Christ included all our sacrifices within his own. The eucharistic sacrifice is sacramentally the sacrifice of Christ—as the Council of Trent expressed it following the Fathers of the Church, the victim is the same and the priest is the same—but it is also the sacrament of the sacrifice of the church. The second way in which the faithful participate in the eucharistic sacrifice, following the teaching of the encyclical (MD 94f.), is to offer themselves as spiritual sacrifices with and through their sovereign Priest. The encyclical cites several of the rich, dense texts of St. Augustine in this regard: "On the table of the Lord lays our mystery." . . . "For in the Sacrament of the altar, the church is made to see that in what she offers she herself is offered."[69]

[68] Translator's note: In his essay, "The *Ecclesia* or Christian Community as the *Subject* Acting in the Liturgy," produced after the council, Congar compares the theology of *Mediator Dei* with that of *Sacrosanctum Concilium* (as we have seen), showing that the council's liturgy constitution would have been unthinkable without the advances that were developed in Pius XII's encyclical. His work here, however, is to compare the teaching of *Mediator Dei* with the broad retrieval of ancient texts and ancient teaching that are a true ressourcement of liturgical theology. In that perspective he regrets that Pius XII did not draw more fully on the consensus of the premedieval ecclesial tradition for a more dynamic role for the whole body in the work of enacting the church's sacraments.

[69] St. Augustine, *Sermon 172* and *The City of God*, bk. X, 6, cited in *Mediator Dei* 103.

At the Heart of Christian Worship

This is the content of the royal priesthood in the personal offering of life brought about by participation in the sacrament that the hierarchical priesthood celebrates. By their baptismal consecration, the faithful are constituted as legitimate co-celebrants in this sacrifice. In this offering made under the sovereign power of Christ the priest, the three titles to priesthood come into play, all three existing in the Body of Christ which is the church, which itself adds its own agency to the gifts given by its head.

The church develops and makes actual the offering which Christ made of her on the cross. The church fulfills in the body what had already been offered by the head. She brings Christ to fullness within her, all the while receiving from him the very grace by which she adds her own contribution to this fullness. This is how the body experiences the maturation and the growth of the One who, after having achieved everything and contained everything fully in himself, now desires that we should do the same *with him*. Thus the mystery of his Passover becomes the mystery of our own passover. So comes about the identity of the Omega with the Alpha as well as the real filling up of the one with the other.

᪥

Agenda for Personal and Group Reflection

Questions for the Individual Reader

1. The word and concept *sacrifice* is awe inspiring. Congar, however, shows us that Christ transformed all sacrifice by making of his divine-human life a perfect self-offering to God the Father. Can you understand how that divine initiative brings you into the circle of divine love and forgiveness? What is the link?

2. Congar speaks in this chapter of the priesthood of a holy life, which he calls "deeply personal and interior." This is the priesthood of each one of us—ordained or not—of our very life, in solidarity with Christ's self-offering. How does this idea relate to the category of the realized mystery (*res*) of the Eucharist that Congar described in chapter 1?

3. Congar argues that our "priesthood of a holy life" (along with the whole communion of saints) contributes to the development of Christ *Omega*. Does this idea realistically help you to appreciate the theological meaning of your own life in a deeper way?

The Structure of Christian Priesthood

4. Why is it that the ordained ministerial priest should not be understood only as a delegate or representative of the community? What values, essential to Catholic theology, would be lost by doing so?

Questions for Group Reflection

1. By showing the gradual purification of sacrifices in the Old Testament, moving them from ritual and exterior to personal and interior, Congar prepares the way for our understanding of the completely interior and self-giving sacrifice of Christ as the fulfillment of the bloody sacrifices of the temple. Compare the two covenants: how do they differ as to the nature of sacrifice and as to those who offer it?

2. According to St. Paul's teaching in Colossians 1:24, the repetition of Christ's sacrifice in the church's liturgical action does not create anything new objectively, but it "fills up what is lacking" with respect to the self-offering and solidarity of the faithful. How does this theological truth translate into the celebration of the Sunday Mass in your experience? Do the faithful need a deeper catechesis? What points need to be stressed?

3. Congar says that the church is life in Christ but also the means to bring about this life. In terms of the theological development of this chapter, how can you explain these two points?

4. Congar warns us not to allow ourselves to be drawn into the idea that "the ritual action is the most important thing." Is he right? With good theological understanding, how would you express what *is* the most important thing?

Chapter 4

Where Does the "Sacred" Fit
into a Christian Worldview?

Translator's observations: *This essay appeared in the same volume
of commentaries on the Constitution on the Sacred Liturgy as chapter
2.* At first glance, this topic might seem somewhat alien to the theme
of liturgical theology. However, it soon becomes apparent that Congar's
concern is a description of the world where the priesthood of personal
holiness is lived out. From that point of view, this chapter develops
themes that are extremely helpful for understanding what we might call
the liturgical spirituality of the council.*

    *In its own way, this chapter is a continued exploration of the con-
trast, developed in the previous chapter, between the old covenant and
the new covenant. The study here of the purity code (rules of what is
pure and impure) in Israel shows the similarities between the Hebrew
religion's idea of the sacred and the profane, on the one hand, and the
ideas about the sacred and the profane in the world religions. However,
as Congar correctly sees, the radical transformations of the new covenant unified, internalized, and concentrated the experience of the holy
in such a way as to do away with the distinction (at least the world religions' distinction) between sacred and profane.*

    *I am reminded of a marvelous phrase of Teilhard de Chardin, who
said, "God is inexhaustibly accessible to me in every moment of my experience." In that sense, everything can be a path to the sacred, even if
not everything is sacred as such. Once again, following the intuitions
of St. Paul's theology, Congar makes the body-person of Jesus Christ the
center of gravity of his theology of the sacred. Everything dispositive to
illuminating the way in which Christ is the fullness of all creation par-
takes of the Christian sense of the sacred.*

---

* Situation du 'sacré' en régime chrétien" in *Vatican II: La Liturgie après
Vatican II–Unam Sanctam* 66 (Paris: Editions du Cerf, 1967): 385–403.

It is a fascinating argument. It helps the reader to deepen even fur-
ther the theology of radical self-offering and consequent transforming
presence in the world that is at the heart of the new covenant of grace.

Few ideas are as ambiguous as the idea of the "sacred." Perhaps this
would not be so if you took the sacred in itself, in a more or less formal
sense. In that case you could always find a definition that is more or less
commonly accepted as, for example, the one given by the eminent dictionary *Littré*: "what is consecrated to a spiritual usage, whether speaking
of persons or things," and so what concerns a religion, and which merits
to be respected without question. By contrast, the "profane" is described
as "what has nothing to do with religion, what is contrary to the respect
that one owes to sacred things." The *Dictionnaire philosophique* of Lalande
doesn't tell us much more.[1] Its explanation is considerably influenced by
Durkheim—it takes a sociological, science-of-religion perspective.

Another example is Roger Callois, who has also enriched this topic,
but merely by showing the ambiguity that exists between the sacred
"of respect" and the sacred "of transgression."[2] Finally, the point of
view of Mircea Eliade, although interesting in itself, does not really
help us here either. The New Testament is dealing with something
completely different.

So let me explain the status of the "sacred" and the "profane" in the
economy [context, milieu; see translator's introduction to this volume]
of Gospel and Messiah. In recent years several interesting studies have
addressed precisely this theme. A. Kagame has demonstrated that the
pagan "sacred," suffused with "magic," holds God *at a distance*, while
the Christian "sacred" seeks to *approach* God.[3] P. Ayraud, taking the

---

[1] *A.* (In an immediate and general sense): something that pertains to the
order of things that are set apart, reserved and inviolable; that ought to be
the object of religious respect for a group of believers. *B.* (In a moral sense—
the usual meaning): "the sacred character of the human person." There is
added here, in this meaning, the idea of an absolute and incomparable value.
C. (In a weaker and more specialized sense): that which pertains to worship,
e.g., "sacred music." *Littré* is a classic reference tool in French—a more or less
definitive statement of accepted scholarship. Likewise, the *Dictionnaire philosophique* is the practical equivalent for philosophical questions.

[2] Roger Callois, *L'homme et le sacré* (expanded edition with three appendices on
sex, games, and war and their relationship to the sacred) (Paris: Gallimard, 1950).

[3] A. Kagame, "Le sacré païen, le sacré chrétien," *Recherches et Débats* 24
(1958): 126–145.

At the Heart of Christian Worship

Platonic and Augustinian (Bonaventurian) view of things, has pointed out that the "sacred" is not identified with the supernatural but exists also in the natural order of things—in creation. He defines the sacred as "the trace of the divine will that is found at the heart of essences."[4] However, if the sacred is understood in this way, it becomes nothing more than the dimension of *anything* that has to do with its orientation to its ultimate end. The *human person*, however, is the one who *deciphers* this relationship.

For my part, I would say that the "sacred" is what *we* discern in things, distinguishing them from what is ordinary, by formally referring them to *our* final end of union with God. This introduces into the notion of the sacred a relation to the *intention* and the *use* assigned by persons. It recognizes that people give meaning to the sacred in this way, as Joseph Gelineau has explained.[5] Pierre Colin, for his part, has shown that the sacred signs coming from Christ (the sacraments) require an investment of interpretation and cooperation on the part of believers.[6] The sacraments reach out from the church, where the community of believers assembles, and influence the whole of family life and work, giving them a new meaning that derives from a human community called to become the family of God in Jesus Christ.

The author who comes closest to the point of view that I want to adopt here—that of the history of salvation or of the stages of the "economy"—is doubtless Jean-Paul Audet. He writes, "Our experience of the divine, always *mediated* however pure it may be, takes on a kind of dignity that pertains to this mediation, a kind of grandeur related to the divine—this is the sacred!"[7] The sacred is the domain of realities (things, words, persons . . .) by means of which we experience the divine.

The "divine" here is the transcendent, personal God. Whenever the transcendence of God is not respected, the sacred falls into magic,

---

[4] P. Ayraud, "Le profane et le sacré," *Chrétiens dans le monde [Cahiers de la Pierre–qui–vire]* (March 1955): 41–49, esp. 45.

[5] Joseph Gelineau, "Langues sacrées, langues profanes," *La Maison–Dieu* 53 (1958/1): 110–129.

[6] Pierre Colin, "Le sens chrétien du sacré," *Christus* 7 (1960): 458–472.

[7] Jean-Paul Audet, "Le sacré et le profane: Leur situation en christianisme," *Nouvelle Revue Théologique* 79 (1957): 33–61; see also references to his works cited in the notes of this same article.

Where Does the "Sacred" Fit into a Christian Worldview?

the "divine" automatically becomes a means to attain a magic result.[8] There's more than one question that is raised by this idea: Does this quality of mediation exist everywhere, or are there privileged realities which are set aside for this mediation? Is the "sacred" immanent in things, or is it we who constitute it? Is the sacred, for example, the same as God?

What Do the Sacred Scriptures Tell Us?

Starting with the Old Testament, one fundamental fact strikes us from the moment we open the Bible. The ancient Eastern explanations for the origins of the world (cosmogonies) are explanations which insert the cosmos into a sacred divine order, where the presence and the lives of the gods are intermingled with the elements of the world. By contrast, in the Bible, the world is placed in a dependence upon God, but by means of a divine Word. This Word, while affirming the transcendence and freedom of God, nonetheless guarantees the reality of the world as a world of real things and of human beings.

The human being has dominion over things and assigns names to the animals (Gen 1:28-30; 2:19-20). The world is not "sacred" in itself, but it can and ought to be a symbol of the Creator for humans and because of them. Even history, including the history of the chosen people, subject as it is to the sovereign rule of God, is a *human* history where human freedom is truly expressed.

God's choice of Israel, through a covenant with them based upon the law, made them a special people, set apart from the idolaters who did not know God. On account of this, Israel in its entirety was a *consecrated* people, bound to observe certain obligations that indicated how the nation belonged to God, obligations that also defined the nation's connection with God. By means of these obligations, laws of purity established the people (and more particularly its ministers of sacred rites) in a state of purity that pleased God. These purity codes demarcated the conditions and the boundaries of the terrain by which one entered or rested in contact with God. These obligations had to do with persons, places, and times.

---

[8] See the explanation of this view in E. Hocedez, "Sacrement et magie," *Nouvelle Revue Théologique* 58 (1931): 481–506. A. Léonard provides a fuller analysis of the superstitious conscience in "La metamorphose du sacré dans la superstition," *Supplément de la Vie Spirtuelle* 28 (Feb. 1954): 5–29.

At the Heart of Christian Worship

The Pure and the Impure

According to the law, at least insofar as it was fixed in postexilic Judaism, every Israelite was obliged to observe complicated dietary restrictions based upon the idea of the pure and the impure.[9] Even unavoidable manifestations of sexuality made women impure (cf. Lev 12 and 15). Some illnesses, especially leprosy, also rendered someone impure (Lev 13–14). Likewise, contact with dead bodies (Num 18:11-16) made someone impure, in a way even more strict if someone was a priest, and above all the high priest (see Lev 21:11).

One important responsibility of priests was to teach the Israelites the distinction between the pure and the impure (Lev 10:10-11, Ezek 22:26; 44:23; cf. Hag 2:11-13). The priests were subjected to stricter obligations, especially when exercising their functions in the temple or when they were going to offer sacrifices (Lev 21). On the other hand, they were permitted to touch sacred things; for example, they could eat their part of the sacrifices, something forbidden to the "profane" (cf. the interesting use of this word in 1 Sam 21:4f.).

Even stricter obligations weighed upon the behavior of the high priest who wore, placed upon his forehead, the phrase "consecrated to Yahweh" and who on the Day of Atonement, alone and only on this one occasion, went into the holy of holies after having offered a bull and a goat in sacrifice, whose blood he sprinkled on the propitiatory. The closer one got to places sanctified by the presence of God, the stricter became the rules of prohibition.

The whole earth, given by God to his people, was holy (Zech 2:16; 2 Macc 1:7); no one should profane it by committing an impurity upon its soil. But above all, Jerusalem was holy—Yahweh set up his tent there (Ps 76:3; 84); it was the place of the temple. And the temple had always been set up in a sacred space. Its different parts were considered more or less sacred according to the degree that they approached the holy of holies. The court of the temple of Ezekiel had to "make a separation between the holy and the common" (Ezek 42:20). In the postexilic temple embellished by Herod, this courtyard was accessible to the Gentiles as well, a fact of immense importance, since it prefigured the day when

---

[9] There was a prohibition against eating blood, dead animals, and impure animals (Lev 11; Deut 14:3-9; and elsewhere). See the article "Prescriptions alimentaires," in *Dictionnaire encyclopédique de la Bible* (Turnhout–Paris: Desclée, 1960): col. 1482–1483. This prohibition still exists today among religious Jews in the dietary laws of kosher.

Where Does the "Sacred" Fit into a Christian Worldview?

the true temple would be called "a house of prayer for all the nations" (Mark 11:17; Isa 56:7).

However, a chancel, that no pagan could pass into under pain of death, separated the court of the Gentiles from the court of the women. This latter court was open to women even in a condition of impurity. Next came the court of Israel (or of the Jews), accessible only to men who were in a state of ritual purity. In the middle of this court could be found the place reserved for the priests, with its massive altar. After that came the temple properly speaking, with its vestibule, the "holy," where the priests of service burned incense and looked after the bread of offering, and finally, the holy of holies in which only the high priest entered once a year. Each of these successive courts represented a special degree of sacredness within the holy place, a variable sacredness which corresponded with stricter and stricter obligations of religious purity.

Feast days were sacred times, with religious services prescribed for each one. Each week, the Sabbath was a sort of "tithing of one's time."[10] The observances used to set the Sabbath apart from ordinary days and to mark its sacred character became more and more rigorous. They included the prohibition of carrying on business and of traveling (Isa 58:13), of carrying anything or of doing any work (Jer 17:21-22), and other limitations of many kinds, set out in detail within a subtle casuistry that Jesus condemned.

The Lord effectively had to completely change the structure of sacred norms canonized in Israel through the pedagogy of the law. "For he is our peace, who has made us both one, and has broken down the dividing wall of hostility, by abolishing in his flesh the law of commandments and ordinances, that he might create in himself one new man in place of the two, so making peace" (Eph 2:14-15).

Ezekiel (40f.; 43:12), and then Zechariah (14:20-21), had foretold a time that would become the messianic era, a time when the sacred character attached to the temple would extend to the whole of Israel. The Isaiah of the exile had predicted that all peoples would take part in the worship of the true God in a renewed temple (56:3-8). The prophets also preached a worship whose purity would be that of the heart. The Gospel is the realization of these prophetic predictions. Whether it was a matter of persons, places, or times, Jesus resolutely

---

[10] Roland De Vaux, *Les institutions de l'Ancien Testament* (Paris: Editions du Cerf, 1960): vol. II, 378.

At the Heart of Christian Worship

abolished the separation between a canonical sacred and an ordinary profane.

Beyond the Sacred and the Profane

The Samaritans had been excluded from the Israelite family (cf. Esd 4:1f.; John 4:9; 8:48). Nonetheless Jesus spent time with them (John 4:3-42), and he gave them the "Christian" role in his parables (Luke 10:33; 17:16). Jesus chose an apostle from among the publicans, and he ate with them and their kind (Matt 9:9-13). In his turn, Peter later learned that we can't call any person polluted or impure (see Acts 10:1-11, 18). In all of these cases, it is not so much the category of the sacred that Christianity abolishes, as that of the profane. The most important statement of the Lord with respect to this question is without doubt his remarks concerning an oath (Matt 5:33-37; cf. James 5:12).

An oath is a sacred word. Among so many other words that one utters, an oath has a privileged quality. It is a profoundly serious word, while other words may not be quite so serious. However, Jesus not only rejects a whole casuistry tied up with different types of oaths, he forbids all oath taking: "For my part, I tell you not to swear at all." He himself explains clearly the meaning of this prohibition. We shouldn't give special privilege to one word as sacred; all our words ought to be true and reflect simplicity of heart. "Let your language be Yes? Yes; No? No. Anything more that one says comes from the evil one" (cf. Matt 5:37).

The first Christian generations remained faithful to this absolute ideal: "We consider it an act of irreverence to fail to say the truth in all things."[11] There is no such thing as a profane word. That is precisely why one is considered to profane the word by lying. Later, however, people distinguished and justified the taking of oaths—even in the Scriptures, which furnished some support for oath taking. But there were always Christians, and not only those in the sects, who took the Gospel literally.[12]

[11] St. Justin, *Second Apology*, ch. 4.

[12] For further study of this question, see B. Guindon, *Le serment: son histoire, son caractère sacré* (Ottawa, 1957); Philippe Hofmeister, *Die christlichen Eidesforme: Eine Liturgie und Rechtsgeschichtliche Untersuchung* (1957); B. Bauer, *Der Eid: Eine Studie* (Heidelberg, 1884); J. Pedersen, *Der Eid bei den Semiten* (Leipzig, 1914); O Bauerfeind, *Eid und Friede: Fragen zum Wesen und zur Anwendung des Eides* (Stuttgart, 1956).

Where Does the "Sacred" Fit into a Christian Worldview?

The whole Sermon on the Mount announces a step beyond the ethical and religious perspectives of the Mosaic Law. This is a transcendence which is also a "fulfillment." In other words, there is never just one part of life or one certain kind of activity in which the faithful need to reflect the face of God; they should do so in the whole of their activities, and first of all with respect to the hidden region of the heart. They are called to a spirit of true fraternity (Matt 5:21-26); interior purity (5:27f.); forgiveness and unconditional love (5:38-48); almsgiving, prayer, and fasting "in secret" (6:1-18) . . . and finally, prayer is not linked to a place; it fits into the whole of life.

Nonetheless, Jesus genuinely loved the temple. He even urged people to observe the rules with regard to its sacred character (see Mark 11:16). In terms of the Gospel according to John, Jesus went up to the temple for the great Jewish feasts. But the interesting question is: what did he do there and what did he say there with respect to the temple? At the temple he exercised a kind of activity characteristic of the synagogue, that is, *teaching*, and of course he also prayed (even though this is not explicitly pointed out in the Gospels). He announced that the system of rules governing the temple had come to an end. Those rules and the temple itself were replaced by his own person.

He offered himself as the gift that is always living and life-giving, and that replaces the role of the temple.[13] He was condemned and given up to death precisely for this reason, and from his death has come forth our life: "We heard him say, 'I will destroy this temple that is made with hands, and in three days I will build another, not made with hand'" (Mark 14:58). He was speaking of the sanctuary of his body (John 2:21). He had already declared to the Samaritan woman: "The hour is coming when neither on this mountain nor in Jerusalem will you worship the Father . . . [but] true worshipers will worship the Father in spirit and in truth" (4:21, 23).

God's presence and our communion with his holiness are no longer linked to a place. Even the Old Testament had begun to perceive this truth in certain ways, but it lacked the capacity to give it its full realization. But now this truth is completely clear: Christ offers a new sacrifice by way of the new priesthood (according to the *heavenly* order of

---

[13] See my book, *Mystère du Temple—Lectio Divina*, 22, 2nd ed. (Paris: Editions du Cerf, 1963): 145–180. Also F. M. Braun, "L'eau et l'Esprit," *Revue Thomiste* 49 (1949): 5–30.

At the Heart of Christian Worship

Melchizedek), which is exercised outside the temple and even outside Jerusalem—indeed outside of any particular place specially set apart for it. This new worship is offered under the heavens, as though in the temple of the entire world.[14]

The veil which closed off the entrance to the sanctuary has been torn asunder; the holy place is now open to everyone. The barrier of separation which kept the Gentiles apart from the Jews has been destroyed. In place of the Mosaic Law with its consecrated sites and its ritual mediations, a new *place* has been given for us to encounter God, a place from which salvation and holiness will come forth. This *place* is the body of Christ, at once immolated and still living, from whose side has come forth a spring of living water for the whole world.

Everyone is able to enter inside the body of Christ through faith and baptism and so receive the Holy Spirit. There, the faithful become living stones of the new, spiritual temple. Like Christ and in him, by the Spirit's gift, they become the temple, the priest, and the sacrifice of the new dispensation.

And what is the sacrifice which they offer there? No longer "things" prescribed by a law of selection and consecration, but rather the whole of life, according its character of filial obedience to God, as thanksgiving, as mutual service in the community, and as ministry and witness.[15] We will come back to this idea very soon. The purity code for this temple (temple and purity are always linked) is that of the community as such: here it is *faith* that must be pure, and *charity*.[16]

---

[14] To the texts of St. John Chrysostom, St. Augustine, and St. Leo that I cited in *Mystère du Temple*, p. 157, let me add this text of St. Thomas Aquinas: "*Quia Ecclesia non erat concludenda sub finibus gentis judaicae, sed erat in universo mundo fundanda, ideo passio Christi non est celebrata intra civitatem Judaeorum, sed sub dio, ut sic totus mundus se haberet ad passionem Christi ut domus*—For the church was not going to be limited to the territory of the Jewish people, but was going to be extended to the whole world; therefore Christ's Passion did not take place within the city of the Jews, but out in the open countryside, in order that the whole world might serve as a domicile for Christ's Passion" (*Summa Theologiae*, IIIa, 83, 3, ad. 1).

[15] Cf. Rom 12:1; Eph 5:1-2; Heb 13:15-16; 10:22-25; 1 Pet 2:5.

[16] Cf. 1 Cor 3:10f. (also John 17; Acts 15:9); Matt 5:23; Eph 4:1-21. Circumcision no longer makes one pure, neither do dietary observances or ritual ablutions (Matt 15:10-20 and the parallel in Rom 14:14f.).

Where Does the "Sacred" Fit into a Christian Worldview?

As the new moment of grace moved beyond the consecrated places of the past, time itself took on a universal meaning. Jesus was insistent upon desacralizing the Sabbath as a privileged day—he made a point of it. This case is parallel to the case of the oath, which had been a privileged word; likewise, the temple precincts (*hieron*) or the sanctuary (*naos*) of the temple had also been a privileged place. But look at how many healings Jesus performed on the Sabbath day![17] When the Jews harassed Jesus because he did healings on the Sabbath, his reply was, "My Father is working still, and I am working" (John 5:17).

No other episode is more significant in this respect than the story of the disciples plucking heads of grain on the Sabbath day.[18] Jesus responded to the Pharisees, who accused the disciples of breaking the law, by pointing out three things. First, he referred them to the example of David (a layman) who ate and had others eat the bread of proposition from the temple at a time of need, foretelling in this way the limits of the law, which legitimately can be broken under certain circumstances. St. Mark explains this with the decisive statement, "The Sabbath was made for humankind, and not humankind for the Sabbath" (Mark 2:27). Life has primacy over law.

Second, Jesus uses the case of priests during their service in the temple and says, "But there is one greater than the temple here," meaning Jesus himself, who will replace the temple and the whole system of temple worship.

Third, he makes the decisive affirmation that "the Son of Man is Master of the Sabbath." He is also Master of the law (see Matt 5–7: "But I, I say to you . . .").[19] The sons and daughters of the kingdom

---

[17] For example, the man with the withered hand (Matt 12:9 and parallels), a demoniac and the mother-in-law of Peter at Capernaum (Luke 4:31f.), the crippled woman who was bent over (Luke 13:10-16), a man with dropsy (Luke 14:1-6), and the sick man at the pool of Bethesda (John 5:1-18).

[18] Matt 12:1-8; Mark 2:23-28; Luke 6:1-5 (cf. n. 112 of the *Synopse des Quatre Evangiles* by Pierre Benoît and M.–E. Boismard. The healing of the man with the withered hand follows in n. 113).

[19] Christ has mastery over all established norms; he regulates the religious relationship between man and God by a law that was mediated by creation and by the angels (Gal 3:19). Christ is from heaven, and he has full power on earth as in heaven. Cf. André Feuillet, "L'exousia du Fils de l'homme (d'après Mc 2, 10-28 et par.)," *Recherches de Science Religieuse* 42 (1954): 161–192. We know that the Codex D of Luke adds in this place the following verse: "That

of God are emancipated both from the law and from the Sabbath; in other words, they are emancipated from a consecration that sets them apart from ordinary life. We have to be careful and precise here, but this point should be taken seriously. It has immense importance.

The idea here is completely positive. The Gospel abolishes the sacred as a kind of withdrawal from the world only by abolishing the category of the profane.[20] In Jesus Christ everyone has complete access to God, whether they are Jews by birth or pagans.[21] All become members of one priestly body and, through their Head, they enter with him into the intimate court of the heavenly sanctuary.

The worship they are called to offer up is that of their very lives, insofar as they are given over to God and God's holy will. This was already evident in the deepest strata of the Old Testament.[22] The Greek translation of the Hebrew Bible, called the Septuagint, had already begun to avoid the term "priest" (*hieros*), loaded with pagan ritual meaning,[23] in translating the Hebrew *kadoš*, and so it chose the term "holy" (*hagios*).

---

same day, seeing someone working on the Sabbath, [Jesus] said to him: 'Man, if you understand what you are doing, blessed are you; but if you understand not, you are cursed and a transgressor of the Law.'"

[20] The word *bebèlos* (meaning that which can be crossed over or handled by anyone) is found in the N.T. only in Heb 12:16 and in the Pastoral Letters: 1 Tim 1:9; 4:7; 6:20; 2 Tim 2:16.

[21] Cf. Heb 4:16; 10:19f.; Eph 2:18f.; 3:12; 1 Pet 2:4f.; *Mystère du Temple*, 174 and 207.

[22] See the entry "Culte" by R. Martin-Achard, in J. J. von Allmen, ed., *Vocabulaire biblique* (Neuchâtel-Paris, 1960): 60: "For Holy Scripture, worship is a service that the chosen people owe to God, but this service is not just limited to certain religious ceremonies or ritual actions. It extends to every dimension of life. God asks to be honored in every aspect of human existence, as biblical legislation makes very clear (→Droit). It is significant that in Hebrew, one same word means work, service, and worship. In biblical thought, there is no watertight bulkhead between daily work and the adoration of God. Already in the opening pages of the Bible manual labor is linked to the service of the Creator . . ."

[23] Cf. Schrenk, the entry "Hieros," in Kittel, *Theologisches Wörterbuch zum Neuen Testament [TWNT]*, vol. 3, 221f. The only use of this term in the N.T. is 2 Tim 3:15, "the sacred scriptures." The Old Testament almost never calls the temple *to hieron* (but rather *oikos*). The N.T. does do so, because the temple has become out of date, surpassed, and its economy of worship with it.

Where Does the "Sacred" Fit into a Christian Worldview?

The New Testament became even clearer and more determined in this respect. For it, the central act of worship is constituted first of all by the holy life of Christians.[24] It is the whole of the Christian life which is sacred, with the sole exception of whatever becomes profaned by sin. Everything that is lived "in Christ" works toward building up the spiritual temple. This is the meaning of the Sermon on the Mount, which breaks down the separation between certain behaviors that are sacred from the totality of one's behavior. This is also the meaning of the "royal priesthood" of the New Testament and of the First Letter of Peter, which considers every Christian with respect to his or her whole life as spiritually a Levite [one given the duty of offering sacrifice].

The Fathers of the Church were not slow to emphasize the novelty of the New Testament. Naturally it makes sense to cite a number of their remarkable texts here. The age of the martyrs did not interpret Sunday as a sort of Jewish Sabbath: "The new law asks you to observe the Sabbath continuously."[25] Christians give a spiritual understanding to the precept of abstaining from servile labor, that is to say, an understanding according to the life of the Spirit. In this interpretation one should abstain from works unworthy of the children of God, and that counts not just for Sunday but for all days and for the whole of life.[26] The Sabbath was a kind of "tithing of one's time" (see n. 10 above), but Christians are expected to offer everything. This is a theme dear to St. Irenaeus:

> The ritual of offering sacrifices has not been suppressed. There were sacrificial offerings [in the Old Testament], and there are such today. There were sacrifices among the [Jewish] people, and there are sacrifices in the church; but the *type* of sacrifice has been changed. For now sacrifices are offered by those who are free, not those who are slaves. . . . The Lord is one and the same, but servile offerings had their proper nature, and the offerings of the free have their kind. . . .

[24] See meaning of the word in the entry "hagios" by O. Procksch, in *TWNT*, vol. 1, 87f. Worship = the holy life of Christians: 107, 109. Cf. Ph. Seidensticker, *Lebendiges Opfer (Röm. 12, 1)* . . . (Münster, 1954); Edward G. Selwyn, *The First Epistle of St. Peter* (London, 1958).

[25] St. Justin, *Dialogue XII*, 3. He adds elsewhere: "God never stops either working or governing the world on that day or on any other day."

[26] See Tertullian, *Against the Jews*, 4 (PL 2:644). There are a number of similar texts in the excellent article by H. Dumaine, "Dimanche," *Dictionnaire d'archéologie chrétienne et de liturgie*, vol. 4, col. 916f.

At the Heart of Christian Worship

Formerly they consecrated only one-tenth of their possessions, but we who have received true freedom, we set apart for the Lord's use every single thing which is ours. . . . Just like the poor widow, the church puts its whole life (*panta ton bion*—Luke 21:4) as an offering in the treasury of God.[27]

St. Ambrose commented on the episode of the heads of grain plucked by the disciples on the Sabbath, considering it to be a symbol of opening up the priesthood to all the sons and daughters of the church.[28] *All* are anointed, *all* are a royal priesthood, repeats St. Augustine.[29] We know his remarks about the small number and the simplicity of observances imposed upon Christians liberated from the slavery of the law—but we haven't paid sufficient attention.[30]

This process of moving beyond a religion of selective observances and acts of sacralization evidently has critical importance for our understanding of worship, for our style of morality, and for our sense of human solidarity. In addition, it shows us how to harmonize the ordinary with the liturgical and work in the world with the service of God.

Unfortunately, we have once again sacralized to excess, reestablished taboos, over-ritualized, and even preached separation. For example, although originally a new church structure was consecrated simply by offering the Eucharist on the altar, a long, complicated, and elaborate liturgy for the consecration of a church was later developed. It is a rite interesting enough perhaps for the clergy, who have sufficient culture to understand it, but confusing and uninteresting for the people who can't follow it. As another example, up to the fifth century, there was no particular costume for the clergy, but now special dress

[27] St. Irenaeus, *Adversus Haereses*, IV, 18, 2 (PG 7:1025). Cf. *Demonstrationes*, 96.

[28] St. Ambrose, *In Lucam*, bk. 5, n. 33 (PL 15:1645).

[29] *Quaestiones Evangelicae*, bk. 2, q. 40 (PL 35:1355); *Sermon 295*, 2 (PL 38:1349–50); *De civitate Dei*, XX, 10 (PL 41:676).

[30] *Letter to Januarius* 54, 1, 1 and 55, 19, 35 (PL 33:200 and 221), a text used by St. Thomas Aquinas in the *Summa Theologiae*, IaIIae, 107, 1; cf. *On Christian Doctrine* III, 9, 13 (PL 34:70–71). Here the idea of "sub signis" is linked to the condition of "servitude." Pierre Jounel has remarked in referring to these texts: "Such reflections make one wonder, when taking part in the consecration of a church, for example. . . . At least it is clear that for St. Augustine the sacred gains nothing in being smothered in smoke, and the rites are not improved by being transformed into ceremonials . . ." (*La Maison–Dieu* 40 [1957/1]: 173).

Where Does the "Sacred" Fit into a Christian Worldview?

is required. Also, anointings of the type found in the prescriptions for priestly ordinations in Leviticus have been introduced into the ordination of Christian presbyters.

The Eucharist, celebrated in the West with normal bread all the way up to the ninth century, now requires special hosts. Complicated, fussy ceremonies for the Eucharist gradually developed upon which, in the twelfth and thirteenth centuries, subtle symbolism was superimposed. While for the New Testament the sacred is clearly whatever is sanctified by human usage, later ecclesiastical practice re-created a category of sacred things.

The Greek word "holy" (*hagios*) that signified sanctification, became interpreted by the Latins, following a fantastic [and erroneous] etymology created by St. Isidore, to mean that which is outside the earthly: *a* (privative)-*gè* (earth)! Through the influence of monasticism, Platonic and Neoplatonic influences brought about the creation and the dissemination of a spirituality of detachment from sensible reality and of contempt for the world. This view of things is far removed from biblical spirituality or from the New Testament understanding of the meaning of the material world. Even though I cite these things here only to evoke some examples of a whole process of transformation, I could easily give documentation for each one of these points.

All of this has played its part in creating an unfortunate situation in the church under the banner of an opposition between the "sacred" and the "profane." In Péguy's view, this separation was a betrayal of the Gospel and the principal cause for what he called "dechristianization."[31] Others regret the damage done by this separation insofar as it is responsible for the formation of clergy exclusively interested in the "sacred."[32]

Even more significant, we should note the harm done to the laity. Olivier Rabut can claim, "The Christian is never completely interested

---

[31] Péguy's word is "*inchristianisation*": see his first "Clio," in *Œuvres complétes*, vol. 19 (Paris: NRF, 1955): 236f.

[32] See M.-J. Mossand and G. Quinet, *Profils de prêtres d'aujourd'hui* (Paris: Ed. Ouvrières, 1961): 136–158. See also J. M. Gonzalez Ruiz, who writes in the journal *Lumière et Vie* 73 (May–July 1965): 77: "The ministerial priesthood has moved in the direction of simply becoming more and more like the priesthood of the old covenant, abandoning its vision of a prophetic mission. This absorption of the prophetic mission by the liturgical has immediate consequences for the Church's role in the world."

At the Heart of Christian Worship

in this world."[33] "We can't get rid of the tendency to play the game of those who are pure and separated from the world. We tend to believe that Christians are more or less serious according to how far they have removed themselves from the profane. We get this all mixed up with a false hierarchy that involves making functional distinctions, leading us to conceive the church as a society made up of the *elite* (priests, who are separated from the profane) and the *common* (the laity, who are all mixed up with the profane) . . ."[34]

Nonetheless, someone said well: "God is not as ill at ease in the profane world as his clergy are." More profoundly, Carlos Santamaria wrote: "From my point of view, the big question is not how to belong to the Church as a layperson, but how to belong to the world as a Christian."[35]

The church is different from the world, and this fact alone transforms the question of the sacred. The Gospel teaches us clearly enough that nothing is profane for the Christian, because everything can be sanctified. Everything that God has made is good.[36] It is enough to use it with love and thanksgiving.[37] "Yet for us there is one God, the Father, from whom are all things and for whom we exist, and one Lord, Jesus Christ, to whom are all things and through whom we exist" (1 Cor 8:6). "All are yours; and you are Christ's; and Christ is God's" (1 Cor 3:23).[38]

What Is the Real Meaning of the Sacred?

Does the fact that nothing is any longer definitively profane imply that everything should be considered equally sacred or that nothing can be considered sacred in a particular way? Does it make any sense, for example, to speak of "sacred music" or "sacred art"? Is Sunday a day just like all the others? Is it a good thing to have special places set

[33] Olivier A. Rabut, *Valeur spirituelle du profane: Les énergies du monde et l'existence religieuse* (Paris: Editions du Cerf, 1963), 8. This is a book to be sure to read!

[34] R. de Montvallon in a report on the council in *Chronique sociale de France* (15 June 1962): 216.

[35] Reflection on a questionnaire about the laity in the life of the church in *Recherches et Débats* 42 (March 1963): 105.

[36] Cf. Gen 1:31; Eccl 3:11; 7:29; Sir 39:21-35; Ps 24:1; 1 Cor 10:26.

[37] 1 Cor 10:30; 1 Tim 4:4-6.

[38] Cf. F. M. Sagnard, *Ephemerides Theologicae Lovanienses* 26 (1950): 54–58.

Where Does the "Sacred" Fit into a Christian Worldview?

apart from others for the Lord's service, special times consecrated to the Lord, even special persons? A presbyter, a religious, a nun—are they not persons consecrated to God in a manner different from the baptismal consecration that is common to all the "saints"?[39] Could we really refuse to accept any ceremonial meant to mark the sacred character of things, to signify their divine orientation, to indicate that by their nature they have a character that goes beyond temporal earthly life and even beyond the ordinary character of life in this world?

Didn't Jesus himself admit, practice, and teach the existence of certain particular aspects of the sacred? He did not refuse this characteristic to the temple (see Matt 23:16-22). He even expressed in his Gospel word the precept, "Do not give dogs what is holy" (Matt 7:6). He accepted and even demanded certain signs of respect for the sacred with reference to his own person.[40]

The nature of the church, in any case, requires a new and more precise consideration of this question. Through the centuries we have unquestionably exaggerated the symbolism of the sacred, and we have reintroduced Jewish ritual tendencies; that much is historically certain and theologically regrettable. Nevertheless, with respect to essentials, the church has not gone astray from its fundamental orientation across twenty centuries of history. So there ought to be a satisfactory explanation for allowing a certain quality of the sacred into the messianic structure by which the church lives. What is it?

The Supernatural

Everything goes back to the fact that God initiated within human history an act which is totally original, new, and gratuitous by comparison with everything else in the created cosmos, a cosmos that is itself God's creation and which depends on God for its meaning. We call this initiative the supernatural order. Its apex, its center, its substantial

---

[39] "Saints" is the title given to Christians in the N.T.: Rom 15:25f.; 1 Cor 16:1; 2 Cor 8:4; 9:1, 12; Acts 9:13, 32, 41; 20:10. Note that the Dogmatic Constitution *Lumen Gentium* 44 and the Decree *Perfectae Caritatis* 5 say that religious life represents "a special consecration, which is deeply rooted in . . . baptismal consecration and is a fuller expression of it."

[40] Isn't this the meaning of the detail given by Mark 11:2 and repeated by Luke 19:30 describing the messianic procession of palms: "a colt . . . on which no one has ever sat"? Cf. also the article by A. G. Martimort, "Le sens du sacré," *La Maison-Dieu* 25 (1951/1): 51.

totality is Jesus Christ, and it leads us to affirm that only one sacred reality really exists, the body of Jesus Christ "full of grace and truth" (John 1:14). The Holy Spirit rests upon him (1:32); and he, the Christ, gives himself without limit (3:32). "For in him the whole fullness of deity dwells bodily, and you have come to fullness of life in him, who is the head of all rule and authority" (Col 2:9-10).

Christ's personal body, however, is not the only sacred reality; his body is *amplified* through what we call the Mystical Body, which is the church, something at once visible and yet surpassing what we are able to see. The body of Christ as a sacred reality exists in the world according to three senses that the New Testament applies to this term: the personal body of Jesus now glorified in heaven, the eucharistic body of Christ, and the ecclesial body which is both identifiable and, in part at least, unknown.

The complaints of the Reformation against medieval Catholic excesses in sacramentalization have to be taken seriously.[41] But the radicalism of the Reformation, at least in its Calvinist or neo-Calvinist form, seems to me to be inspired by doctrinal positions that are unacceptable to Catholics. The Reformation's position is dualistic, lacking a synthesis between Christianity and the natural world. It is suspicious of any ecclesiology that gives solidity to the church, because its idea of God's action is exclusively as "event."

From that perspective, formulas like "the church is only the world as it knows God and Jesus Christ," or "the church does not have its being in itself, but only in Jesus Christ," or even "the whole being of the church consists in its mission" emerge from this Protestant point of view. At the very least, these expressions are ambiguous. However, a similar functionalism or ecclesiological anti-substantialism can be found today in the views of certain Catholics, who no longer see the difference between the kingdom of God and the world, because the world seems to them to be the only reality which has any consistency in itself.[42]

[41] Some references for this: A. Dumas, "L'Eglise envahie par la distinction du profane et du sacré," *Foi et Vie* (May-June 1952): 188–214; Jacques Ellul, "Actualité de la Réforme," ibid., 39–64, esp. 41f.

[42] On this point, see the telling critique of Jacques Maritain in *Le Paysan de la Garonne* (Paris, 1966): 86f. and 94. His views are founded upon a positive reading of traditional doctrine.

Where Does the "Sacred" Fit into a Christian Worldview?

As a consequence, the church finds itself reduced to the role of revealing the meaning of the world. However intimately the church may be engaged with the world, the church always remains distinct with respect to its proper principles of existence and operation. Even if the energies of history have to be subsumed into the kingdom of God, the kingdom is not given to us through forces that belong to history or to the world.

Rather, the kingdom is given to us as a result of the series of divine initiatives that culminate in the twofold sending of the Word and Holy Spirit. But "given" under what conditions? Under the conditions of the real time of the economy of grace, in a sense that brings harmony and simultaneity between an *already* (the given) and a *not yet* (the *totally* given). St. Paul spoke of the "deposit" or the "first fruits" of the Spirit.[43] This vision of a situation between times is sufficiently common these days that I don't need to explain it too much. In this perspective we see that we already have a partial possession of the eschatological realities. In other words, the invisible realities of the other world (*"non huius creationis*—not of this creation" [Heb 9:11]) are communicated to us under conditions adapted to our earthly nature, conditions of a spirit in flesh.

The human person, as a consequence of being both metaphysical and religious, is destined to use symbols because the reality of the *beyond* transcends anything accessible to ordinary sense experience.[44] Further, humans only exist in history, and so symbols that speak of a *beyond* transcending sense experience cannot remain purely abstract for us, in a kind of metaphysical anthropology. They must be expressed concretely. So symbols must make reference to the historical consciousness of the human, drawing upon history, experience, and psychology to touch upon our most natural and deepest symbols.[45]

---

[43] 1 Cor 1:22; 5:5; Rom 5:5; 8:23; Eph 1:13-14. The most helpful and classic treatment of our situation of being in the "between-times" remains Oscar Cullman, *Christ et le temps*.

[44] See M.-D. Chenu, "Anthropologie et liturgie," *La Maison-Dieu* 12 (1947): 53–65, reprinted in his *La Parole de Dieu*, vol. 1: *La foi dans l'intelligence* (Paris: Editions du Cerf, 1964): 309–321. See also in this volume 159f. Also, E. Masure, *Le signe: Le passage du visible à l'invisible* (Paris: Bloud, 1953); Jacques Maritain, *Quatre essais sur l'esprit dans sa condition charnelle* (Paris: Alsatia, 1956); M. A. Kirchgässner, *Die mächtigen Zeichen* (Freiburg, 1959).

[45] See the brilliant study of this question by Louis Bouyer, *Le rite et l'homme: Sacralité naturelle et liturgie—Lex orandi* 32 (Paris: Editions du Cerf, 1962). I would not emphasize all the same things as Bouyer does, and I still have questions with respect to his understanding of sacrifice.

At the Heart of Christian Worship

The world of grace, the source of our communion with God, is a distinct, original domain, never completely homogeneous with the world itself. Grace is forced to appropriate suitable signs, whether it borrows natural symbols that touch the human heart and adapts them in fitting ways or creates a sacred world of its own, with both descending and ascending mediations in the form of actions, words of revelation, sacraments, institutions, even church law, liturgy, and the rest.

What is the economy of salvation? It is humanity's experience of God that unfolds between the biblical paradise, on the one hand, about which we know practically nothing except that it represented harmony between nature and communion with God, and the final heavenly kingdom, on the other hand, in which nature and the communion of grace will be rejoined within the final reign of God. That will be a communion even more perfect than in the first paradise because humans will see God and sin will be definitively destroyed.

Between these two times, however, we can only have parables of the kingdom that posit within the world signs that evoke something *other than itself.* We still need churches in this familiar world which is neither that former paradise nor the kingdom—not yet.[46] Here in this world we need a special day consecrated to the Lord inserted among all the other days.[47] Its purpose is to be a sign and a promise of what we are hoping for, namely, joy and peace in a new creation that flows out of Easter, for which Sunday is the weekly memorial.

There is even one sublime example of a portion of the world totally taken up and transformed as a sacrament of the Lord's Passover. It is the firstfruits of the transfiguration of the cosmos. In paradise, nature had been invested with the glory of God. Now as a result of our redemption in Christ, earthly elements once again receive the quality of being a means of salvation and signs of the presence of God. The Eucharist is this sublime example. In the Eucharist a bit of wheat made into bread and a bunch of grapes made into wine through the effort of human work are transformed not only functionally but substantially.[48]

[46] See "Théologie de l'église, maison du Peuple de Dieu," *L'Art Sacré* (August–September 1947): 205–211 and 213.

[47] See "La théologie du dimache," *Le Jour du Seigneur* (Paris: Laffont, 1948): 131–180, esp. 161f.

[48] See my "Eucharistie et achèvement du monde en Dieu," in *Voies du Dieu Vivant* (Paris: Editions du Cerf, 1962): 207–216. Compare with W. Dürig, "Die Eucharistie als Sinn-Bild der Consecratio Mundi," *Münchener Theologische*

Where Does the "Sacred" Fit into a Christian Worldview?

Let me clearly say this again: there is only *one* sacred reality, the body of Christ. It exists here below both in a sacramental form and in an ecclesial form, and in both cases it brings along with it a whole cluster of realities related to it which, because of that relationship, are also to some degree signs of our communion with God in Christ and thus become analogously sacred things.

Varieties of the Sacred in the Christian Order

Drawing from this explanation and remaining within its context, let me propose to distinguish four distinct levels within this vast arena of the sacred in a messianic context:

1. There is the substantial expression of the sacred in terms of the body of Christ that, according to the three uses of the New Testament for this expression, is at once temple, priest, and sacrifice.

2. There are signs of the sacred of a sacramental type, which includes the sacraments properly so called as well as human situations created by the sacraments, especially by the sacraments of baptism and confirmation, holy orders and matrimony.

3. There is the whole network of signs which express the religious relationship that we have with God in Christ or which prepare us to realize that relationship more fully. We might speak here, if the expression weren't a bit silly, of a "sacred pedagogy." This terrain is immense. In our earthly life Christians (or that *moral person* that is the church) have given and continue to give a particular character or form to certain words, gestures, customs, community rules, physical settings, moments of time, and even to silence—to dear, holy silence! This form is adapted to their function of enhancing our communion with God (a communion inseparable from our communion with our brothers and sisters in this world). They serve to signify God's presence among us. That's what I

Zeitschrift 10 (1959): 283–288; A. Auer, "Die Eucharistie als Weg der Welt in der Erfüllung," *Geist und Leben* 33 (1960): 192–206; A. W. Ziegler, "Das Brot von unseren Feldern," in *Pro Mundi Vita: Festschrift der Theologische Facultät München 1960* (Munich, 1960): 21–43; L. Scheffczyk, "Die materielle Welt im Lichte der Eucharistie," in M. Schmaus, ed., *Actuelle Fragen zur Eucharistie* (Munich, 1960): 156–179 and 190–194. On 177f., Scheffczyk places the Eucharist in the context of the progressive spiritualization of matter, a process that can be considered evolutionary.

At the Heart of Christian Worship

mean by sacred pedagogy. It is purely functional. It does not imply any depreciation of the "profane."

4. Then there is the whole gamut of things in ordinary life that we sanctify by our use of them, so orientating them toward God and according to God's plan. Nonetheless, they completely retain their intrinsically secular character.[49] Although the "profane" ceases to be profane when it is "consecrated" in the sense of being taken out of the ordinary, it does *not* cease to be profane when it is sanctified by Christian usage. Further, once we have moved beyond the specter of sacralization through separation and ritualization, then nothing impedes the creation of new expressions of our desire to be sanctified (in family life, in the city, at work) by way of prayers, blessings, monuments, etc. What is essential here is the ability to recognize the holiness that comes from humans using things in the world as part of their path toward holiness.

We know that this is the meaning of the word "holy" (*hagios*) in Scripture; it is also the foundation of the New Testament or Christian idea of worship, a worship for which each believer is the priest in his or her own life. The Gospel positioned itself at a great distance from the monastic movement of Qumran, which was contemporary with it. Throughout the Old Testament, God was proclaimed to be both very distant [transcendent] and very close [immanent], but the union of these two aspects of God was revealed only in a very imperfect way. That is why it was so easy to construe the idea of sanctity as a kind of separation from earthly life—a distancing from what is ordinary. The Fathers of the Church, of course, also provided us with a theory of only gradual, progressive learning about the things of God.

This otherworldly spirituality dominated the Essene community, known to us from the Damascus Document and, later, by way of the other manuscripts of Qumran. There, sanctity was sought under the

---

[49] On this point, see O. Rabut *Valeur spirituelle du profane*, op. cit.; and J. M. Gonzalez Ruiz, "L'Eglise, Peuple de Dieu dans le Monde," *Lumière et Vie* 73 (May-June 1965): 69–86; G. Martelet, "L'Eglise et le temporal," in G. Barauna, ed., *L'Eglise de Vatican II*, vol. 1—*Unam Sanctam* 51b (Paris: Editions du Cerf, 1966): 517–540; M.-D. Chenu, "Les laics et la 'Consecratio' du monde," ibid., vol. 2—*Unam Sanctam* 51c (Paris: Editions du Cerf, 1966): 1035–1052; and also his *Peuple de Dieu dans le monde—Foi vivante* 35 (Paris: Editions du Cerf, 1966).

Where Does the "Sacred" Fit into a Christian Worldview?

condition of flight from the world and of separation from the ordinary. At worship they aspired to imitate a purity imagined to be the result of separation from the world—as if living out the purity of angels.[50] They even developed a kind of speculative theory of spirituality with a gnostic flavor. St. Paul had already fought against the attachment of certain early Christian communities to this kind of thinking; he called it an enslavement to the elements of this world.[51]

But the truth has been given to us in Jesus Christ. He perfectly unites within himself the transcendent purity of God along with God's immanence in this world. Through him and with him, we as creatures are able to imitate the holiness of the Creator himself. Since there is no longer anything profane, sanctity can be the sanctity of our earthly life itself. Sanctity does not have to be expressed by flight from the sensible world, even though sanctity *can* be sought for under conditions or following means that involve a certain removal from the world. But Jesus Christ, to whom we become mystically incorporated and identified, is himself the fullness of sanctity, the Holy One of God. Every aspect of the question of the sacred needs to be seen in relation to Christ.

Concluding Remarks

What more can I say? Let me try, by way of conclusion, to make a few suggestions.

The status of holiness according to the Gospel is important first of all with respect to our understanding of Christian ethics. It gives us

---

[50] See Dominique Barthélemy, "Essenische und christliche Frömmigkeit im Lichte der Handschriften von Toten Meer," *Freiburger Zeitschrift für Theologie und Philosophie* 6 (1959): 249–263. I am not unaware that Qumran is the place of a particular "sect" in Judaism. André Neher (*Moïse et la vocation juive* [Paris: Editions du Seuil, 1956]: 86–138) interprets the actions of Moses and of the Exodus as a permanent reality of the history of the Jewish people—as a liberation taking place within earthly history in the "profane," human and earthly life of the Jewish people. For God had bound himself to them, and this people is, in its human reality, that portion of creation with which God had made a covenant, *pars pro toto*. However, because of the incarnation of his beloved Son, God becomes henceforth bound not to just a portion of humanity set apart by divine election and the Law but to the whole of humanity. At the same time, as a consequence of this universalization, God separates divine election from the faith and the national history of a single people as such. There is then not a separation but a distinction between the order of holiness and the order of civilization.

[51] Cf. Gal 4:3f., 9; 3:19; Col 2:8, 15, 18.

At the Heart of Christian Worship

the key to a morality without moralism. Of course, the positive always implies a negative contrary: if you love, you don't kill. But perfection ought not to be conceived in negative terms or in terms of abstaining from something—don't do this, don't eat this, don't touch this. The cross itself, a condition for every life that achieves sanctity, is inseparable from the resurrection.[52]

Our time and our culture are marked by a discovery of the world which sometimes takes on (in exaggerated fashion) the aspect of a conversion to the world. Sometimes we do not distinguish sufficiently the goodness of creation itself, on the one hand, from the yeast of sin that dwells in it, on the other hand. The tendency now is to renounce all sacralization. So the bodies of men and women are desacralized in the name of denouncing sexual taboos. There are even those who would like to get rid of church buildings as such, keeping only a simple functional gathering place which, apart from the Sunday Christian assembly, could serve for almost any other purpose.

This fails to recognize the necessity of what we have called a sacred pedagogy. Put another way, it fails to recognize our need for *signs* of something other than this earthly world. It is also forgetful of the fact that the world is not yet the kingdom of God, just as it is no longer paradise. In its midst, there exists a distinct order of holiness consisting in the presence of the body of Christ. For such persons, the reserved Eucharist, which is the sign of this special order of holiness as well as the promise of a complete sanctification of creation made new, has little meaning.

Further, there are those who would like to desacralize liturgy or at least liturgical language.[53] Their fundamental intuition is perhaps correct: they are looking for a worship that takes the earthly life of human

---

[52] Cf. my *Jalons pour une théologie du laïcat*, 624f.; Maurice Zundel, *Morale et Mystique* (Paris: Desclée de Brouwer, 1962): 100–101: "This path does not harbor a *No* capable of restraining the impulse of *Yes*; it is completely *Yes*. . . ." In this way we escape from the morbid confusion between prohibition and the sacred which has so seriously compromised a proper understanding of transcendence through associating what is holy and what is forbidden with a threat (Exod 19:21; 20:19; 2 Sam 6:6; cf. Exod 21:29, 22:17-23).

[53] There was a Missal, for example, in which the apostles were called "the militants." In response to all this, see the article of Gelineau cited in note 5 above. On this matter of the desacralization of the liturgy, *Questions liturgiques et paroissiales* (Louvain, 1966) points out two articles: H. Manders, "Désacralisation de la liturgie," *Paroisse et Liturgie* 62 (1966): 129–143 (trans. from the

beings seriously, a worship where the signs that are used make sense to them. But once again, they forget that Christianity fosters a new birth because it arises out of a series of irreplaceable divine initiatives that cannot be reduced merely to aspects of the natural creation.

Such people argue from the functional character that we have ourselves recognized here in a "sacred pedagogy." But here as elsewhere, for something to be functional, it must first of all *be*: there is no functional reality without an ontological foundation.[54] So the "sacred pedagogy" is functional, but it has certain requirements with respect to its being and its structures. Formally speaking, the sacred quality of a space, a building, a painting, or of music comes from its capacity to lead people to repose and to guide them into a state favorable for the act of prayer.

As Père Régamey has demonstrated, the secret of sacred art is found in its capacity to express the spirit of the Beatitudes.[55] However, this spirit inspires these forms and their sacred quality in such a way that they become *dispositive*, that is, that they somehow *lead us to the grace of the Holy Spirit.*[56] This same function, of course, can also be discerned in artistic forms that were not intended by the artist to be sacred.[57]

With respect to practical rules to observe, we can look for them elsewhere.[58] Here I only want to insist on two ideas—theoretical principles—which can serve as criteria:

Dutch: "Theologie en zielzorg"); and H. Schmidt, "Le renouveau liturgique," *Nouvelle Revue Théologique* 88 (1966): 807–829.

[54] As to the revelation of the saving mysteries, see "Le Christ dans l'économie salutaire et dans nos traités dogmatiques," *Concilium* 11 (January 1966): 11–16; or for a more developed statement, see my contribution to *Mélanges M.-D. Chenu* (Paris: Vrin, 1967).

[55] P. R. Régamey, *Art sacré au XXe siècle* (Paris: Editions du Cerf, 1952).

[56] This is the expression of St. Thomas in his *Summa Theologiae* IaIIae, 106, 1—an astonishingly bold and very profound text which provided me a powerful source for these reflections.

[57] This is how I understand the claim of Père A.-M. Couturier in *Art et liberté spirituelle* (Paris: Editions du Cerf, 1957): 66: "The religious or the profane character of a work resides *concretely* in the quality of its colors, its line and the materials used; in other words, it resides in the work of art itself."

[58] See, for example, A. G. Martimort, "Le sens du sacré," *La Maison-Dieu* 25 (1951/1): 47–74, and, of course, the whole series of issues of the journal *L'Art sacré* (Paris: Editions du Cerf).

At the Heart of Christian Worship

1. These material forms that dispose us to prayer are numerous and of great variety. Each historical period and each culture can and ought to contribute their own examples to the repertory of sacred forms, coherent with their spirit and their resources. These forms are limited, however, and we need to be careful in judging them. There are religious forms of some kind in all the religions. We can hardly avoid using them in Christianity. But Christianity is something other than just one religion among many others.

Christianity consists completely in the person of Jesus Christ, who is the center and the completion of the history of salvation. We can never allow Christian sacred expressions to be identified simply with those of a natural religious instinct. It is always necessary to verify the validity of sacred signs in terms of the history of the faith and the events by which God has disclosed himself in coming to us.

Christmas can deteriorate into a simple feast of childhood. However, in fact, Christmas is Jesus Christ. Easter is always something other than merely the celebration of springtime; it is the resurrection of the Lord who was crucified. And in our celebration of the saints, in our preaching and our pilgrimages, we must be vigilant to guide whatever there is of an instinctive religiosity or of a natural sense of the sacred back to the foundation of the faith, back to the facts of the history of salvation. This is the only way to avoid living a mere "myth," with the accoutrements of superstition and magic.

2. We will need to avoid as completely as possible an idea of the "sacred" that is identified with *things*, attached to things as such. We have to remain clear that the love and the prayer of the faithful is always the goal of our quest for sacred forms. The living experience of the faithful is the place where the value of these forms is verified. If we speak of building up the church ("edifying" in the biblical sense, not in the pious sense of the word), what we're talking about is lifting the faithful up into the authenticity of a life of communion with God through Jesus Christ and in the Spirit.

The critical discernment of forms of worship, begun by the liturgical movement and pursued by the council, has to go much further still. The purely ceremonial use of sacred elements, sometimes derived from a purely secular origin, is still excessive. It's not a question of reducing sacred liturgical signs to nothing, as we have shown; but it is important to make them less burdensome, to simplify, and to critique liturgical forms according to criteria of truly Christian meanings, assuring them a real intelligibility for the faithful.

Where Does the "Sacred" Fit into a Christian Worldview?

We will never stop *becoming* Christians, free citizens of a messianic people on pilgrimage through this earth toward the holy of holies. Already, in mystery, we have access to that fulfilling end.

⅌

Agenda for Personal and Group Reflection

Questions for the Individual Reader

1.What are some examples of Jesus transcending the Old Testament categories of pure and impure? Do the Gospels' accounts of Jesus in conflict with the Pharisees take on new meaning in the light of this shift in the idea of the sacred?

2. Congar says that the Sabbath was a sort of "tithing of one's time." How does this phrase help you to appreciate the meaning of Sunday as a day of rest? Do you think it is important to retrieve the idea?

3. "The Gospel abolishes the sacred as a kind of withdrawal from the world only by abolishing the category of the profane." What does this mean? Why is there no longer anything profane for the Christian living in a world touched by the incarnation?

4. In saying that the sacred body of Christ is the *only* sacred reality in the new covenant, Congar *extends* rather than *diminishes* human access to the holy. Explain how that is the case.

Questions for Group Discussion

1.What implications for the uses of sacred art in the church flow from an understanding of the sacred as "the whole gamut of things in ordinary life that we sanctify by orienting them toward God"? What is the difference between sacred art as *decoration* and sacred art as the *disposition of environment* conducive to the experience of God?

2. Congar cites St. Justin, saying, "The new law asks you to observe the Sabbath continuously." What might be some expressions of sacred art or environment, positioned in the context of your everyday work and life, that might give a Sabbath dimension to your thoughts and actions?

3. Congar seems to reject an otherworldly spirituality (using the Essene community as an example) because it suggests a *separation* from the world rather than an *engagement* with the world. On the other hand, he also says that "sanctity can be sought for under conditions that involve a

At the Heart of Christian Worship

certain removal from the world." Discuss these two tendencies, and see if you can understand them not as total contraries but as poles that hold us in a dynamic tension and that energize our quest for the truly sacred.

4. The author says that each historical period and each culture ought to contribute their own examples to sacred forms. In your experience, where is the North American church (and more specifically, where is your parish) positively contributing to signs of the sacred in this way?

Chapter 5

What Is the Meaning of Sunday?

> Translator's observations: *This very brief exposition on the meaning of Sunday is the earliest of these essays to be published. Congar must have just returned to France after his captivity in Germany. His tone is entirely pastoral, simple and down to earth. It appears as just a few pages in the relatively new journal of pastoral liturgy that had recently been launched by his Dominican colleagues in Paris. The French title that he gave to it, literally translated, is "a simple presentation of the essential idea of Sunday."* It is just that—a few lines sketched to suggest how to develop a catechesis for the day of the Lord.*

Sunday is different from other days. It calls for a different rhythm of life. We even wear different clothes. We ring the church bells and we enter into an atmosphere of rest and celebration. This is all because we are celebrating the anniversary of Christ's resurrection.

The Jews had their day of rest and worship on Saturday. Formerly, in cities where there was a Jewish community, we used to see the synagogue opened and lighted on Friday night and Saturday morning.

At first the apostles observed the Sabbath for a while, and then they abandoned it entirely. They took as their day of worship the day following the Sabbath because that was the day of Christ's resurrection. They did this with the understanding that with the resurrection of Christ, a new world came into being—the world of eternal life. Christ, crucified and buried, arose from the tomb and thereafter lived a new life, the life of an immortal soul, a life "for God" (Rom 6:10).

The meaning of Sunday, then, is to affirm and to celebrate our own call to a new life, the life of an immortal soul, a new life "for God," with Christ and in Christ. Further, Sunday is meant to celebrate the beginning of this life in the present, here below.

---

* "Présentation simple de l'idée essentielle du dimanche," *La Maison-Dieu* 13 (1945): 133–135.

Why church bells, why good clothes, why go out to church? we might ask. The answer is because we know, because we believe that we have a soul, an immortal soul, and that we are called not only to live the mortal life of our bodies here below but to live eternally—even now—an immortal spiritual life. So observing Sunday means that we are in tune not only with the ways of the earth and with living on earth but that our lives are also in tune with God and are meant for God in the manner of an immortal soul.

This explains why on Sunday we put aside the tools of our earthly life and we come to church to take up the work of eternal life. During six days we have done the tasks of the earthly city, working to construct the city here below. We have been busy with the tools that build the city of our earthly life: our machines, our hammers, our saws, our spades, our threshers, our calculators, and our trucks . . .

All that is important and necessary. How could we go on living without all that? But on Sunday we put them behind us in order to make clear that we are not merely the citizens of this world but—with Jesus Christ, through him, and in him—citizens of heaven, already living an eternal life.

There is more. A Sunday that was nothing but a day off from work would become the day of humanity, not the day of the Lord. And even for humanity, it would only be the day of the body, of passing life, not the day of the soul, not the day of the soul's life.

A Sunday given up exclusively to leisure or to recreation, to hiking or to camping, to taking a break, to dancing or to going to the movies—not only would such a day *not* be the day of the Lord, even for humankind it would be nothing but the day of the body—perhaps, dare we say it?—the celebration of the animal part of ourselves. It would not be the day of citizens of the city of souls who are called to live an eternal life.

While all these earthly things are good, they are not meant to take precedence over everything else. Let's not break out from under the tyranny of work simply to fall under the tyranny of the body, the tyranny of an exclusive interest in the body, in pleasure and even perhaps in things that are sinful.

Our special task on Sunday is to get to work building the eternal city, the city that belongs to the heavens, where we are called to live forever. When Sunday comes around, we have to take up in a special way—with Christ, through Christ, and in Christ—the tools for building the city of immortal souls, the tools of prayer and adoration. That is why we come to church with others to join ourselves together to

At the Heart of Christian Worship

the One who, resurrected and living for God, Master of that heavenly city, is able to introduce us into its midst. He is the bread of life, not for earthly life, but for the life of our souls.

He is the bread of life in two ways, by word and by sacrament (cf. John 6). First, because he has the words of eternal life and because he is himself the living bread come down from heaven, he is the source of life for us. In order to live in tune with the earth, we have to be nourished by the things of the earth. In order to live in tune with God, in tune with the life of an immortal soul, we have to be nourished by the bread of heaven. We receive the bread of heaven by the word of God—by faith. But we also receive God's word in the Lord's flesh, in communion, which should develop within us a genuine love.

That is why we go to Mass on Sunday. The Mass in its two parts gives us instruction for our faith by the Word of God and communion in the body of Jesus Christ offered up for us.

To complete the perspective evoked here, we should draw practical conclusions and make applications of these ideas to life in the parish, according to the special needs and circumstances of each particular place. We should draw out of these ideas reasons for making Sunday a day of rest, for emphasizing participation in the Mass, for taking an active part in liturgical song, and for stressing the importance of the nourishment that comes from God's word—in the sermon, the catechism, the Bible, etc.

Note, however, that I have presented here only one of the themes touching the meaning of Sunday. We could develop equally well parallel ideas touching upon the honor and worship due to God, or touching upon the idea of the people of God. This is a vast topic, and I have only scratched the surface.

৵৹

Agenda for Personal and Group Reflection

Questions for the Individual Reader

1. Congar describes a different world from our own—an older, more traditional world. Do people still dress up in their best clothes for Sunday Mass where you go to church? Do you have church bells ringing? If not, is something missing?

2. Congar says that we celebrate Sunday because we have an immortal soul—an immortal spiritual life. How does this argument strike you? Have you thought about it before? Does it make sense to you?

3. Congar talks about being fed at the two tables: the table of the word of life and a table of the bread of life. Is the "table of the word" a genuine feast where you go to church? Is the one table poorer without the other?

Questions for Group Discussion

1. Congar describes leaving aside the tools of our earthly life and our weekday work and taking up the tools of the work of eternal life. Does this metaphor ring a bell for you? In terms of celebrating Sunday, what do you think are the tools for the work of eternal life?

2. Congar describes coming to church on Sunday to join ourselves, together with others, to the One who is able to introduce us into the heavenly city. In the light of the previous four chapters, how would you expand on the importance of the *corporate* character of Sunday worship? Does something need to be added to Congar's essay here in that respect?

3. In the light of this chapter, assess your own parish experience. Do you think that your parish community needs a catechesis for Sunday? What elements here seem appropriate for your community? What additional points might need to be added to be convincing for those with whom you live and worship?

A World Sanctified by Grace

The five chapters presented here in translation are an excellent sample of Yves Congar's theological and literary gifts. He is at once both attentive reader of the Sacred Scriptures and careful theologian, both historian and social critic, both committed devotee of tradition and sensitive to the need for institutional renewal. As careful and erudite as these essays on Roman Catholic liturgy are (especially chapters 2, 3, and 4), they are nonetheless practical and engaged. Congar's focus in all these cases is to assist the church and its leaders to understand the church's Tradition and to judge wisely, according to a pastoral wisdom that represents solid grounding in the best of sources and in continuity with the deepest streams of constant Catholic teaching.

In this brief conclusion, my goal is to point out some of the pastoral implications of the ground that Congar has covered here. In my view, these essays touch upon questions that are very actual, that is, very relevant to the dilemmas with which contemporary Christians find themselves confronted. From that point of view, the essays gathered here, although written decades ago, are still quite timely.

Without ever framing his subject matter in so precise a way, Congar is nonetheless effectively dealing in each case with the broader potential for each baptized disciple of Christ to live the Christian life as a dynamic agent of the Body of Christ. Beyond being gifted with faith and grace through the sacraments, the faithful are called to actively transform the world in which they find themselves. Beyond receiving healing and spiritual comfort from their life in Christ, they become, each in his or her own context, participants in Christ's mission to proclaim the kingdom of God in the whole world. This perspective will allow me, I believe, to highlight the practical importance of Congar's theological contributions as enlarging our vision of the Christian life within our present pastoral contexts.

The Faithful as the Acting Subject of the Liturgy

The Catechism of the Catholic Church, referencing the Dogmatic Constitution on the Church (LG 10), summarizes succinctly the key point that Congar explores in chapter 2. The Catechism states:

> The celebrating assembly is the community of the baptized who, "by regeneration and the anointing of the Holy Spirit, are consecrated to be a spiritual house and a holy priesthood, that . . . they may offer spiritual sacrifices." This "common priesthood" is that of Christ the sole priest, in which all his members participate. (CCC 1141)

The same theological insight had already become a liturgical norm in number 14 of the Constitution on the Sacred Liturgy, where it says: "In the restoration and development of the sacred liturgy the full and active participation by all the people is the paramount concern . . ."[1] It is clear therefore that the fundamental claim of Congar's second chapter has been solemnly reaffirmed by the church's teaching authority. However, what he succeeds in doing is to trace the destiny of this idea across millennia of cultural and social changes.

On the one hand, he demonstrates how changes in society and in society's understanding of authority have consequences for the way the faithful have seen themselves at worship. In the distant past, centuries of largely illiterate lay faithful, assisting at Mass celebrated in a Latin language that they scarcely grasped, conceived of themselves as passive consumers or observers of sacred rites performed *for* them but *without* them. Yet, on the other hand, Congar takes pains to show us how, despite such ritual exclusions that came to be commonplace, the rites themselves never ceased to express the corporate language that proclaimed the liturgy to be the celebration of the whole church. The "we" of the prayers never changed.

Further, Congar explains for us why many of the faithful end up feeling disconnected from liturgy, with nothing to invite their personal investment or spark their imagination. How can they transcend the limitations and frustrations of their actual experience of parish life? He illustrates the variety of historical and cultural forces through the centuries that set up this continuing challenge for Catholic pastoral life: how to be an actively participating member of the common

---

[1] *Vatican Council II: Constitutions, Decrees, Declarations*, Austin Flannery, O.P., gen. ed. (Dublin: Dominican Publications, 1996), 124.

At the Heart of Christian Worship

baptismal priesthood of Christ and, in so doing, become an agent of transformation of the world.

Simply reaffirming the unchanging tradition of the church with respect to the active role of the faithful in the liturgy will not in itself transform our Catholic pastoral world; but a clear and cogent reaffirmation helps nonetheless. What helps even more, however, is to observe (as Congar allows us to do) how celebration in the vernacular, the oral proclamation of the Eucharistic Prayer (clearly and in the name of the faithful), and the extension of liturgical ministries to the baptized faithful have the potential, if properly understood, to reengage the assembly in the liturgical action by undoing some of the very obstacles that fostered their passivity.

With the promulgation in coming months of a revised typical edition of the Roman Missal, the church will have an occasion to undertake a fundamental and radical catechesis about the most basic structures of the rite of the Eucharist. At that time, perhaps, the most important catechetical lesson of all should be the reaffirmation and profound explanation of the integral role of the faithful in the church's liturgical prayer. For the Mass, in addition to being the church's self-offering to its Father and Lord, is also a mission-sending rite. The faithful are told to go forth, are sent out to return to their life and action in the world. From experience, we have learned that active participation in the liturgical rites will likewise enable the laity to be more engaged in their apostolic mission as they are sent forth from the Eucharist. The grace-filled challenge—now as never before—is to link their active participation in the common baptismal priestly role of liturgical worship to an apostolic activity that can and will change the world.

A Transformed World

It seems to me that the fundamental insight of Yves Congar in these writings, as in all of his other theological work, is that Christians—baptized and anointed in the spirit of Christ—live in a transformed world. In the introduction to this book I mentioned the importance of the word "economy" for Congar. I am sure that this theological term, borrowed from Greek theology, had a profound and special meaning for him. I think that for him "economy" meant how God's reality is visible to us. Put another way, to affirm that we are living in the "economy" of Christ's incarnation is to insist that we are living in a world personally touched by God and transformed by grace.

Conclusion: A World Sanctified by Grace

141

Congar had a passion to communicate to all the baptized their vocation to take their part in the dignity, the responsibilities, and the privileges that belong to Christ. To be grafted onto the Body of Christ is an unimaginable favor, but likewise an indefectible duty: this is a privilege that bears consequences, a dignity for which we shall be held accountable. We receive spiritual gifts that implant our lives into a divine context, but these very gifts imply a vocation to an apostolic resonance. In Congar's view, the church's evangelical power made perfect sense, *if only* the faithful could understand and accept the mission that is theirs.

The option, as Congar saw it, was to go beyond seeing ecclesiastical rites as preoccupied with awe-inspiring ceremonies and to arrive at understanding the apostolic life of all the faithful as preoccupied with proclaiming the kingdom of God. In terms of the categories developed in chapter 1, Congar feared that a theological vision of the Eucharist utterly absorbed by a fascination with the *sacramentum et res*, the species of bread and wine consecrated into the body and blood of Christ, would fail to migrate outside the ritual context of the Mass to inspire an apostolic presence in the world. That is why he insisted so strongly upon the *res* of the Eucharist—the realized mystery verified in the piety, lives, and actions of the faithful. In Congar's view, sacramental sanctification in the sanctuary must be directed beyond itself to the transformation and consecration of the world at the hands of all the people of God, clergy and laity alike, fed with the body and blood of Christ as nourishment for their own mission.

As we noted in the introduction, this vision of Congar's in no way diminishes or demeans respect for the *sacramentum et res*, the eucharistic species. But for Congar, limiting the notion of "real presence" to the *sacramentum et res* does not go far enough. The Great Commission of Christ in classic biblical terms is not "Do this in remembrance of me" (Luke 22:19), but rather "Go into all the world and proclaim the good news to the whole creation" (Mark 16:15). It is in this way that the real and ordinary world in which we live and move becomes progressively the transformed world proclaimed by Christ—the kingdom of God that is coming still.

Congar's desire was to awaken a priestly people to their true identity. Although never expressed in these terms, Congar's theology fought against an ecclesiastical complacency that could be satisfied with the administration of the sacraments as the maintenance of the piety of the already saved but that lacked missionary passion and pastoral creativity. As in his important work on the theology of the laity, here too Congar felt obliged to articulate the commission of a gifted people of the baptized to conjoin themselves to the apostolic mission of the whole Body of Christ. He knew that in the modern world the church had to learn to invite initiative, promote personal investment, and enrich pastoral imagination on the part of those who have the widest outreach into the circles of society and culture—the laity themselves. From this wide resonance of the realized mystery of the Eucharist will emerge, in God's good time, the transformed world of the ever-growing kingdom of God.

Living Priesthood in the Ordinary

In these essays, as in Congar's other writings, we find a reaffirmation of the New Testament teaching of a priestly people of the baptized. He is careful to insist upon the context of this teaching. Congar is concerned that the church understand that it is as a *people* that the faithful are priestly, not first as individuals. While there are surely liturgical implications of this doctrine, namely, the conjunction of the spiritual sacrifices of the baptized to the one true priestly sacrifice of Christ offered in the Eucharist, this priesthood is not fundamentally and essentially liturgical.

Proceeding from the teaching of the Letter to the Hebrews that Christ's priesthood inaugurates a "new covenant," that is, an entirely new way of seeing our relationship to God in the light of Christ's incarnation, Congar draws out two points of great importance. First, it is the whole life—the entire incarnation—of the divine Son that is offered in sacrifice to the Father, following his passion, death, and resurrection. His paschal journey opened the pathway that leads from human self-offering, in a sacrifice of love, to the court of heaven. But, second, by his incarnation, Christ, by "being born in human likeness and found in human form" (Phil 2:7), transforms the valences of meaning of our human condition. By assuming (taking upon himself) the predicament of mortal and changeable human beings in all things save sin, he sanctifies our circumstances and makes of them occasions for imitating God.

In a fashion that parallels Christ's own progressive human incarnation, our lives become a priestly self-offering. This self-offering arises from our spontaneous intention to make of our lives acts of praise and thanksgiving to our creating and redeeming God. The priestly quality of this offering derives from our solidarity with Christ, into whose mystical body we are baptized and by whose Spirit we are anointed. It is the whole of our lives, lived and invested in all the ordinary ways

Conclusion: A World Sanctified by Grace

143

of human duties and freely chosen options, that expresses the material reality of our sacrifice—of our participation in Christ's priesthood.

An important and much-celebrated text of the Dogmatic Constitution on the Church spells out in some detail two important aspects of this idea. First, speaking of the baptized and their share in the priestly office of Christ, it states: "For all their works, if accomplished in the Spirit, become spiritual sacrifices acceptable to God through Jesus Christ: their prayers and apostolic undertakings, family and married life, daily work, relaxation of mind and body, even the hardships of life if patiently borne . . ." It is the whole of life, as I put it just above, that becomes potentially the material reality of our spiritual sacrifices. This same section reiterates that: "In the celebration of the Eucharist, these are offered to the Father in all piety along with the body of the Lord. And so, worshiping everywhere by their holy actions, the laity consecrate the world itself to God" (LG 34).

In this instance, the consecration of the world to God is the reorientation of the familiar and habitual dynamics of human life and of our human world toward God's glory. In his Letter to the Romans (8:22f.) Paul speaks of the whole creation groaning in labor pains awaiting the adoption and redemption of the children of God. Whether or not this theological point was what Paul had in mind in writing this passage, it illuminates nonetheless the impact (what I called above the "resonance") of Christian faith and discipleship upon the structures of this world. To revisit the theme of "both/and," we are offered the option both to invest our lives with the grace of Christ's priesthood as well as to offer ourselves and our human contexts to God as a sacrifice of love and thanksgiving. We are called to appreciate the priestly sacrifice into which we are integrated, thus rendering our human environment transformed into a sacramental sign of God's presence and action among us. The laity are positioned at a critical point, described in *Lumen Gentium* as follows: "to make the church present and fruitful in those places and circumstances where it is only through them that it can become the salt of the earth" (LG 33).

Here again, this theological reflection requires a mighty exercise of conscience and imagination. The Christian life does not mean occasional and periodic visits to a special, sanctified world made accessible through liturgical rites, but rather the immersion in this actual, ordinary world in such a way as to bring about a radical transformation of its structures, what we called a moment ago "consecration." The agents of this consecration of the entire world are not the ordained alone, but the ordained and all the faithful called to discipleship. "For

At the Heart of Christian Worship

144

those whom he foreknew he also predestined to be conformed to the image of his Son, in order that he might be the firstborn within a large family" (Rom 8:29). Put another way, the newborn disciples of the "Firstborn" have been given the vocation to live their baptismal priestly self-offering always and everywhere in such a way as to be agents of Christ's sanctifying presence in this world.

The Sacred as Seen by Redeemed Eyes

In his essay on the sacred within a Christian worldview, Congar is eager to draw the implications that flow from the characteristics of the new covenant of grace. In the new covenant the priestly actions of the People of God take place in the ordinary, not in a temple alone. Congar draws a striking contrast between the immense multitude of the formal prescriptions that developed in the old covenant, creating temple precincts and liturgical paraphernalia weighted with highly complex differentiations of relative sacredness, and the unique source of the sacred that is the Body of Christ in the new covenant.

Congar's preoccupation, following the theological arguments of the Letter to the Hebrews, was to liberate the Christian imagination from the burdens of formalism and legalism that rose up in the Levitical tradition and that made religious life so difficult and complicated. In such a world, only experts could hope to know how to please God. Jesus, condemning the Pharisees as hypocrites, said of them: "They tie up heavy burdens, hard to bear, and lay them on the shoulders of others; but they themselves are unwilling to lift a finger to move them. They do all their deeds to be seen by others . . . [But as for you] the greatest among you will be your servant" (Matt 23:4, 11).

In chapter 25 of Matthew's Gospel, Jesus goes further in showing the ways in which the holiness of God is extended into our human contexts so as to transform them into concrete acts of divine pity, sacramentalized by gestures of fraternal love performed by his disciples. As to ministering to the Son of Man when he was hungry or thirsty, when he was a stranger and welcomed, naked and clothed, sick and cared for, in prison and visited, Jesus explains: "Just as you did it to one of the least of these who are members of my family, you did it to me" (Matt 25:40).

The option gradually becomes clearer: one chooses not to live in a now-artificial world of Levitical complexity, measuring out canonical sanctifications by the spoonful, but rather one accepts the radical premise of the incarnation, namely, that living members of the Mystical Body of Christ, acting in his name and in the power of his Spirit,

Conclusion: A World Sanctified by Grace

share the gifts of holiness with which they have been anointed. In the legalistic world, one's preoccupation is obviously self-absorbed, hoping to be able to point to precise and prescribed acts declared holy by canonical lists and regulations. But in Christ's story in Matthew 25, the disciple is never completely certain just what's going on: "Lord, when was it that we saw you hungry and gave you food, or thirsty and gave you something to drink?" (25:37). However, Christ's story presupposes that genuine disciples habitually extend themselves to the poor and the needy in the spirit of Christ himself.

Just as we have explained that the *res* of the Eucharist is always an effect that takes place within the Mystical Body of Christ, so here the sacred in a Christian worldview always has reference to the Body of Christ, either as a preparation for its sacramental celebration or as an enhancement of its consciousness of the risen Christ's presence in its midst. To the eyes of the redeemed, wherever they may find themselves, Christ is always present; his Spirit is always active. And there, where Christ is, is holy ground.

The Day of the Lord

In his brief catechesis on the meaning of Sunday in chapter 5, Congar shifts our attention away from Sunday Mass as the essential and perhaps exclusive meaning of the Day of the Lord and reminds us that this day is a form of temporal tithing. Just as the law in ancient Israel required the sacrifice of one-tenth of one's goods as a thanksgiving gift to the Lord, so the Sabbath was a form of tithing of one's time. We have so thoroughly lost this perspective that this brief essay of Congar's is the more telling for the way in which it contrasts the building of the earthly city on our workdays with the building of the city of God in our Sunday worship.

Moreover, this brief essay is richer in this present collection for coming at the end of the fertile reflections in the first four chapters. We are therefore able to understand and interpolate into this brief reflection about the meaning of Sunday the doctrine of the offering of the spiritual sacrifices of the faithful which belong to their day-to-day ordinary world of family life and work. We are able to understand as well the conjoining of their intentional self-offering to Christ's priestly offering to his Father in the Eucharist. Likewise, we are able to understand how Sunday represents both the gathering together of the faithful into a visible sign of Christ's Mystical Body in this time and place, and the harvesting of all their spiritual sacrifices as a celebration of their priestly solidarity with their Lord and head.

At the Heart of Christian Worship

146

It is critically important to recapture the real meaning of Sunday. As Pope John Paul II put it, in his apostolic letter on the Day of the Lord, reflecting on the third commandment:

> Before decreeing that something be done, the commandment urges that something be remembered. It is a call to awaken remembrance of the grand and fundamental work of God which is creation, a remembrance which must inspire the entire religious life of [the faithful] and then fill the day on which [the faithful are] called to rest. Rest therefore acquires a sacred value: the faithful are called to rest not only as God rested, but to rest in the Lord, bringing the entire creation to him in praise and thanksgiving, intimate as a child and friendly as a spouse.[2]

The pope then goes on to draw the connection between Sunday and the day of the Lord's resurrection, as well as between Sunday and the day of the gift of the Holy Spirit to the church.

We might summarize the challenge of this perspective by saying that the option before us is not only to choose to celebrate Sunday as a moment of personal spiritual comfort that, on a given day, may or may not match our moods and interests, but also to celebrate it as a supreme act of love and obedience that allows us to express our true identity as living members of Christ. We express in faith and rite both the ways in which the Spirit of Christ has graced and transformed our lives in the week just past (our spiritual sacrifices) as well as our availability to be agents of the Spirit's action in the week ahead (our apostolic mission). We offer our lives; we likewise acknowledge God's great gifts and God's ruling power.

A Certain Kind of Theologian

Finally, let me return to a point made in the introduction. Yves Congar was a scientifically trained and immensely gifted theologian whose work was unfailingly inspired by his evangelical perspective. He used the word "evangelical" in a special sense (it is used in this way more commonly in French than English). For him, it means both *teaching* drawn from the Gospels (the *evangelia*, in Latin) as well as *inspiration* for a broad popular investment of the faithful in a Christian apostolic mission (more common in our American usage).

In Congar's view, too often in the history of the church the faithful have been relegated to a non-evangelical role as clients of the church's

---

[2] John Paul II, "Dies Domini–Observing and Celebrating the Day of the Lord," *Origins* 28:9 (July 30, 1998), 138.

Conclusion: A World Sanctified by Grace

ministry, rather than agents of the church's apostolic mission. As a theologian, Congar's interest in this point was not ideological but historical and pastoral. His lifelong searching of the Scriptures, the Fathers of the Church, and the church's theological writings was with a view to establishing with clarity and certainty the dynamic character of the Christian life of every baptized believer.

In a way different from the majority of theologians whom Congar had met in his youth, he immersed himself in the primary sources of the church's tradition, learning their original languages, reading extensively in ancient documents, and he was always concerned to review the writings of others who, like him, studied the ancient authors. Although a scientific theologian in the most demanding sense, Congar also had a literary charism and was sensitive to subtle and evocative passages of ancient and medieval theologians. Although deeply versed in historical and contemporary theology, Congar remained unflaggingly attentive to the documents of the papal magisterium, eager to compare and show their coherence with the rich Tradition that he never ceased studying. His hope was always to uncover the ferment of the evangelical yeast residing in the church's witness to divine truth, a witness richer than any one epoch of culture or theology.

As I noted in the introduction, it was because of this breadth of learning and depth of understanding that Congar was so widely solicited and so sincerely trusted as an expert at the Second Vatican Council. In my view, one of the most valuable contributions of this present collection of essays is to disseminate more widely some important and fundamental ideas that Congar shared with the bishops and with his fellow experts during those years of the council. It is my contention that the failure to appreciate this point of view, so representative of the church's long continuous theological tradition, accounts for the difficulty in the reception of certain parts of the council's documents during the past forty-five years.

Perhaps it is fitting that the last word might be these lines written by Cardinal Avery Dulles in his preface to a collection of critical articles on the work of Yves Congar:

> Congar emphasized the dialectic between structure and life in the Church. He held that laypersons, even without holding any office, could enjoy the gifts of the Holy Spirit and participate in the prophetic, priestly, and regal ministries of Christ. Reacting against the centralism of the previous few centuries, he resuscitated the concept of the local church and envisaged the universal Church as a communion of

At the Heart of Christian Worship

particular churches—themes with which Protestant, Anglican, and Orthodox could resonate. Together with several colleagues in France and Belgium, he retrieved the ancient idea of collegiality among the bishops. In his great work on *True and False Reform* he laid down principles for authentic Catholic reform, carefully distinguishing it from revolutionary proposals that are sometimes marketed under the banner of reform. Open though he was to new research, he firmly adhered to the dogmas and divinely given structures of the Church.[3]

Another way of saying the same thing, perhaps, is that Cardinal Yves Congar represents one of the most solid witnesses to the pastoral and theological teaching of the Roman Catholic Church. Even though early in his life his pastoral passion and his ecumenical sensitivity were judged "premature" in the expressions he gave to them in some of his writings, his intuitions and judgments were vindicated by the council. Passing on into the mystery of eternal life, he has left behind for us a testimony both profound and interesting, both rigorous and practical, a testimony whose utility and fruitfulness are well exemplified in this book.

[3] Avery Cardinal Dulles, "Preface," in Gabriel Flynn, ed., *Yves Congar: Theologian of the Church* (Louvain: Peeters Press, and Grand Rapids, MI: Eerdmans, 2005), 28.

Conclusion: A World Sanctified by Grace

Acknowledgments

For decades I referred to and discussed Congar's critically important essay, translated here as chapter 2, with my colleague Rev. Gerard Austin, O.P., who first made me aware of it shortly after its publication. Recently, I encountered the director of the Institute Supérieur de Liturgie in Paris, Brother Patrick Prétot, O.S.B., who spoke so enthusiastically about Congar's essay on real liturgy and real preaching (chapter 1 here) that I hunted it down and translated it immediately. I am happy to acknowledge that the editor of *Worship*, Father R. Kevin Seasoltz, O.S.B., has published this essay in the July 2008 issue.

Subsequently, my confrere Gerard Austin requested that I translate what is here chapter 2, and that led to my expanding the project to the present selection of texts. I am also extremely grateful to Rev. Kenneth Martin for encouraging this project and offering helpful suggestions for the revision of the text.

Having had the privilege of knowing Cardinal Yves Congar personally, I consider it a great joy to be able to render his work accessible in English in this present edition. I am grateful to Rev. Nicolas-Jean Sed, O.P., and Les Editions du Cerf for making the rights to these texts available for translation and publication.

Finally, I wish to thank Liturgical Press, especially Hans Christoffersen, Editorial Director, for his encouragement in bringing this work to press and Mary Stommes, Managing Editor, for her careful and invaluable assistance in preparing the manuscript.

Index of Names

Index of Subjects

Index of Subjects